ADRENALINE

(2001)

THE YEAR'S BEST STORIES OF ADVENTURE AND SURVIVAL

ADRENALINE

2001

THE YEAR'S BEST STORIES OF ADVENTURE AND SURVIVAL

EDITED BY CLINT WILLIS

Thunder's Mouth Press
New York

ADRENALINE 2001: THE YEAR'S BEST STORIES OF ADVENTURE AND SURVIVAL

Compilation copyright © 2001 by Clint Willis
Introductions copyright © 2001 by Clint Willis

Adrenaline ® and the Adrenaline® logo are trademarks of
Avalon Publishing Group Incorporated, New York, NY.

An Adrenaline Book®

Published by
Thunder's Mouth Press
An Imprint of Avalon Publishing Group Incorporated
161 William Street, 16th floor
New York, NY 10038

A Balliett & Fitzgerald book

Book design: Sue Canavan

frontispiece photo: © Stephen Venables

Library of Congress Cataloging-in-Publication Data is available.

ISBN: 1-56025-334-7

9 8 7 6 5 4 3 2 1

Printed in the United States of America
Distributed by Publishers Group West

For Ellen Brodkey
with thanks and love

c o n t e n t s

p h o t o g r a p h s

introduction

A dventure is nothing but bona fide experience—the kind that changes you. Such experience generally has an unexpected quality that brings with it the sense that you are fully alive, maybe in ways that you haven't felt before. As our culture of commerce and entertainment closes in on us and our children, we must go further out of our way for that kind of experience—for adventure—but it's out there.

Where do we go to find it? And how do we get there? Many of us might think to start a search for adventure with an activity that may seem reckless: Mountaineering comes to mind. But it's not clear that extreme risk is essential to adventure. This book includes several climbing stories, but while the danger the climbers encounter is part of their experience, it isn't the point—at least not for them. The same goes for the explorers, doctors, sailors, boxers and other adventurers whose stories you'll read here.

What is the point, then? That's a question to carry with you as you read the selections in Adrenaline Books' second annual collection of the year's best adventure and survival stories. The most convincing answers to the question are personal and, as you'd expect, complicated. The adventurers in these stories are coming to grips with issues that matter to them.

The issues may be political or ethical in the deepest sense: Polish journalist Ryszard Kapuściński has spent four decades reporting on the Third World, bearing witness to and trying to understand the suffering he sees there. In so doing, he makes himself vulnerable to the terrain and the people he encounters—a good way (the only way?) to have an adventure. "I knew nothing about the man who held my life in his hands," he writes, ". . . I thought, if Salim chases me away from the truck and the water . . . I won't last even until nightfall."

The doctors and scientists who study the Ebola virus and treat its victims in Tom Clyne's story are adventurers in a similar sense. They risk and sometimes lose their lives to learn something and to be of use to strangers. Tim Cahill is looking for something he values that seems to be lost—the Caspian tiger—and finds himself in the custody of Turkish soldiers (they turn out to be friendly but that's just luck.) Stanley Williams wants to know more about how the volcano Galeras works—information that might save lives and property in the town of Pasto in Colombia—and almost dies when Galeras erupts under him.

Adventures often are like that: unexpected or even brutal. The adventures we seek aren't always the most interesting or important ones—but they may lead us to the ones that are. The three young climbers in Greg Child's piece are looking for a first ascent on difficult rock in a remote setting; an adventure in the conventional sense. They wind up facing a question most of us manage to avoid: When, if ever, should a person kill another person?

Likewise, Lynn Snowden Picket goes looking for "the pure pleasure of violence" in her boxing memoir, only to find something more interesting, more frightening and more profound—information to go along with her battered face and body. "I wanted to feel powerful, to take up space in the world, to stop apologizing," she writes in her book *Looking for a Fight*. "That I thought I could do this by learning to box now strikes me as ludicrous and deranged."

Real adventure—real experience—sometimes inflicts the worst kind of damage. Donald Crowhurst began a sailboat race around the world with one set of intentions that evolved into another; he found himself alone and in the deepest waters there are. Likewise, the soldiers who appear in these stories encounter adventure's most serious aspects, as experience that marks or even destroys a person through madness, pain or death.

And what can you take away from an adventure that ends in a person's death, as adventures sometimes do? You might take a sense that adventure is as deep and wide as all experience. Here are parts of two adventures you'll encounter in this book:

"I couldn't get the artery. I was trying so hard. And all the while, he just looked at me, he looked directly into my face."

"It wasn't just adrenaline, it was happiness. It was as if I'd got my childhood back in the way childhood is supposed to be—without the tantrums and confusion."

Adventure claims its victims, and marks its survivors in ways that are painful or glorious or illuminating. The best adventure stories have a similar power to change us, providing that we're open to the news they bring—which isn't always good but is somehow always good to hear: They hurt us and they help us and they light our way.

—*Clint Willis*

Peccary Hunting in the Amazon
by Mike Tidwell

Mike Tidwell has written books about working for the Peace Corps in central Africa and about Amazon natives' struggles against oil company encroachment. Tidwell is not content to observe and report on the world's far-flung places: he meets his surroundings on their terms, as in this essay from his collection In the Mountains of Heaven.

C arrying a dead, eighty-pound, piglike animal on my back through a jungle swamp with only one shoe on my feet and thorns in my hand and mosquitoes blanketing my face and my eyeglasses fogged to uselessness—this had never been part of my plan for visiting the Amazon rain forest.

But when the outboard motor of Bolivar's dugout canoe broke for the second and final time that afternoon, our agenda changed dramatically. The original goal had been to travel fifteen miles up the Zabalo River—a distant tributary of the Amazon in the eastern jungles of Ecuador—to visit an oil well these Cofan Indians had recently burned to the ground. Twenty-six-year-old Bolivar, who wore a friendly smile on his face and a menacing bat tattoo on his upper arm, was part of a clan of seventy Cofan who were defying the illegal and highly destructive entry of oil companies onto their tribal forest land. I had come down to South America to write about the Indians' vigilante campaign and to photograph the destroyed well platform.

But it was the dry season in this part of the Amazon and the water level of the Zabalo River was extremely low, exposing all manner of fallen tree trunks and other hazards. We'd been laboriously chopping logs and portaging the canoe for most of the day when, in rapid succession, the boat motor's spark plugs grew fouled and the rip cord broke, snapping right in half.

It was too late in the day to continue on foot to the oil site, so we reluctantly scuttled the expedition. We would now have to turn around without a motor and head back to the village where we'd arrive deep in the night. Thoroughly crestfallen, my Cofan companions decided to temporarily brighten their moods by doing what they do best: hunt wild animals.

After a restorative round of banana beer along the riverbank, Bolivar's father, Elias, a soft-spoken man dressed in a traditional Indian cotton tunic, began signaling for silence. He detected some sort of noise in the forest.

"Monkeys," he said to me in Spanish, cocking his head to one side, letting his straight, black hair hang toward the ground. He was sure he heard monkeys.

He and Bolivar grabbed their single-barrel shotguns, and I followed them unarmed into the jungle. Behind me was Norma, Bolivar's beautiful wife with ruddy cheeks and midnight-black eyes. She brought our hunting party to four.

Elias led the way, shotgun on one side, machete on the other, single-handedly cutting a trail through the undergrowth as fast as he could walk, slicing and slicing, never breaking his stride. He was almost too mechanical to be real.

For a moment the sudden excitement of the quest, combined with the sun-dappled grandeur of the verdant forest, restored my flagging spirit. Fragile beams of light fell all around us, streaking through the luxuriant canopy overhead to illuminate a poetic riot of lianas and creepers and the massive trunks of kapok trees streaked with epiphytic mosses that looked like water colors—red and orange and yellow and violet.

But we soon lost the sound of the monkeys and came to a halt. The river was no longer in sight, and I wasn't sure in which direction it lay. As we stood at the end of this blind alley, wondering what went wrong, Bolivar detected the grunt of a tapir (that strange, hoofed, long-snouted animal common to the Amazon) somewhere in the distance—and suddenly we had another mammal to pursue. He and Elias put keen ears and eyes to work, probing in all directions, casting about for more clues.

Standing apart from these bronze-skinned men, watching as now they gestured and discussed in spirited Cofan which way to go, I realized that with the physical switch to the forest interior the Indians had made a shift in states of mind as well. At warp speed their senses processed hundreds of bits of data altogether hidden from me, the visiting gringo, the man doing all he could just to keep up. The Indians' presence here was as natural and as graceful as the spread of monstrous trees in every direction. These were not visitors, after all, not in a forest hosting Amerindian inhabitants for more than fifty thousand years, a stay which had nearly the aspect of geologic time. It would have been as easy to contemplate the absence of kapok trees and macaws and river dolphins here as that of Bolivar and Elias in their *ondiccuje* tunics, cupping their ears to hear their prey better, wrinkling their noses to smell the forest's clues. The men were part of the scenery. They *belonged*. It wouldn't be a proper rain forest without them.

Bolivar chose a direction and off we went in pursuit of the tapir. It was a good sign that we passed half-devoured mauritia fruit along the ground, a favorite food of both tapirs and peccaries. And now the hoof-prints were so clear even I could see them. For a long time we followed the prints, pushing farther and farther into the forest, which became denser the deeper we traveled into it—and concomitantly darker. It became so dark at one point that usually nocturnal mosquitoes, thinking it their witching hour, began attacking us in swarms each time we paused.

The tapir was now taking us in and out of steep-banked muddy streams and standing pools of swampy water. Up front, Elias continued his brisk machete work, leading us to all manner of naturally fallen trees which we crawled over or under according to size. My eyeglasses kept fogging up badly, meanwhile, like a mirror after a shower—a condition brought on by my own heavy perspiration and the almost soupy forest humidity all around.

Then the tapir tracks petered out. We lost the animal. There were no more sounds to follow, either. Another dead end. Given how far we had strayed from the river, I was almost glad of this second dose of failure. Just how we would have gotten a two-hundred-pound tapir from this distant spot to the canoe was beyond me.

Yet no sooner had we made an about-face, retracing a few of our steps, then Bolivar and Elias stopped and began taking deep breaths through their noses. "Smell that?" Bolivar asked me in Spanish, still inhaling deeply. "Smell that? Peccaries. Lots of them."

I employed my nose to its fullest capacity, but failed to detect anything in the air indicating a bevy of large-tusked, wire-haired, piglike creatures was near. Not that anyone was seeking my confirmation, mind you. The next thing I knew, Bolivar, Elias, and Norma—without any notice—were disappearing in a virtual sprint to my right, fading into the jungle. Here we go again, I thought, as I commanded my legs to do everything they could to keep up.

Our quarry was very close this time, the pursuit red hot. There was no time for clearing any semblance of a trail with the machete. The rules changed to every person for himself. Leafy branches whipped across my face. Hanging vines nicked my shoulders and arms. Unseen divots in the soil caused missteps. I was aware of vague human figures bounding and darting up ahead of me, and, for fear of being abandoned more than anything, I stumbled and bumbled my way forward, staying more or less within sight of the figures.

Then, abruptly, the Cofan stopped and I reached them. Bolivar and Elias cocked their ears and whispered to each other while I tried catching my breath. But too soon, they were off again, bolting away. We splashed through a swampy area, then plunged into some very thick foliage that left an odd scratchy feeling in my throat as if, in the act of plowing face-first through the branches and leaves, I had swallowed some delicate, feathery forest thing.

We came to another steep-banked stream across which a fallen tree acted as a convenient bridge—for the Cofan. For me it was impossibly narrow. The Indians scurried across with mystifying dexterity while I threw myself into a crashing slide down one bank, sloshed through the current, then flung myself up the muddy far slope before redoubling my running pace to catch the others.

Then we stopped again. We really stopped. We stopped because we were almost on top of our prey. Bolivar and Elias stood stock-still, fingers to their lips to indicate silence as they surveyed the surroundings with their ears. This was clearly the point at which absolute stealth and quiet were at a premium, but the vexing hair ball or whatever it was lodged in my throat was threatening to jeopardize our cover. The urge to clear my windpipe with a huge, satisfying cough was almost overwhelming, and repressing it literally brought tears to my eyes. I held out as long as I could for the sake of the group, but then a short, muffled cough escaped.

Everyone turned to me with fingers pressed to their lips, eyebrows arched in anger, silently shouting at me that the peccaries were oh-so-close. I shrugged apologetically just as three very loud, full-bodied coughs burst forth which were no doubt at that moment scaring away every peccary with functioning ears for miles around. Bolivar gave me a disgusted look just before leading us on another short sprint. We stopped again, and again I coughed idiotically, but by this point it didn't seem to matter because we were so close that even *I* could smell the peccaries. It was a thick, mildly unpleasant scent that filled my nose, a murkiness mingled with what vaguely resembled the pungent bite of human body odor.

We were moving again, this time through thick mud. Bolivar and Elias, shotguns drawn, were running in a crouch, so I did the same. I could hear animal grunts up ahead now, and when I looked I saw pig figures flashing and scrambling, running away. Bolivar turned sharply to the left and disappeared at the same moment Elias stopped, stood, aimed, and fired. The explosion reverberated through the forest, drawing shrieks from a group of parrots overhead. I followed Elias forward to a downed peccary weighing at least eighty pounds. It lay on its side, rear legs twitching violently from a bleeding, mortal wound to the head. Its cylindrical black snout was stained red with blood just above its long, curving yellow tusks.

Panting from the run, my chest heaving, I took in the sight while Elias grabbed a long, thin branch from a nearby palm. He jammed the branch into his shotgun muzzle, ejecting the spent shell from the breach end of the barrel—a necessity with this simple model. He reloaded, but by now the rest of the peccaries were gone—as was Bolivar, who was in hot pursuit.

Elias and Norma busied themselves gathering vines of varying widths and lengths to tie the now motionless pig into a crescent shape, a hind leg threaded through the tied-shut jaws. A thicker vine rose from either end of this arrangement and formed a U that served as a sort of carrying handle or sling. This allowed the peccary to be carried on Elias' back, anchored by the vine sling which would be looped over his head to come to rest across the front of his front shoulders.

As the peccary was being so prepared, another shotgun blast sounded a short distance away. Bolivar had finally drawn a bead on others in the pack. We set off in that direction as a second shot boomed, then a third—and by the time we arrived, three peccaries lay dead at Bolivar's feet, victims of flawless marksmanship. While they collected more vines for transport, all three Indians burst into their native Cofan, reliving the hunt several times over with descriptive hand gestures and theatrical speech—the benedictory habit of successful hunters everywhere.

It was probably just as well I couldn't understand the particulars of what was being said. My brain was elsewhere, already focused on the disturbing arithmetic and geography of our situation. With his deadly aim, Bolivar had dropped two adult peccaries indistinguishable in size from Elias's—about eighty pounds—plus an offspring caught in the melee weighing roughly fifteen pounds, a poodle-sized runt. So there we were with our game more than a mile, it turned out, from the river. In all, there were four of us human beings, three men and a woman. And there were four peccaries, three adults and a poodle-size pip-squeak baby.

In one respect, the Cofan were different from most of the traditional peoples I had visited in my life. Women were not exploited as de facto mules, routinely given the hardest physical labor as in, say, most of Africa. Cofan men tended to share in the heaviest lifting, the toughest grunt work. More than this, though, it was my own vanity, my own old-fashioned or New Age (take your pick) sense that a man was a man with certain responsibilities no matter what the culture or situation, that led me to reject two possibilities. I would not watch Norma moan under the heft of a brawny adult peccary while I skipped to the river with the lithe poodle dangling around my neck. Nor would I abide the sight of Bolivar or Elias making two trips in order to transport all three adult peccaries between the two of them.

That left one option.

"I'll carry a big one," I told Bolivar. "Give it to me."

The same question had been on his mind, I could tell, as he finished tying up the last peccary. Both he and Elias had been casting specula-tive glances my way in an apparent effort to assess my mettle. Was the gringo going to resolve this awkward situation with honor? their eyes seemed to ask.

"It's very heavy, Mike," Bolivar said, skepticism in his voice. "Are you sure you want it?"

"Give it to me," I repeated.

Bolivar lifted one of the peccaries and I slipped my head through the vine loop, the vine itself coming to rest across my chest and around my shoulders. When he let go completely, I grew very confused. It was an eerie shock to feel the warmth of the peccary's body heat, not yet diminished, spreading across my back. But it was the weight, the aston-ishing leaden load suddenly resting on my spine, that made me think for a moment that Bolivar, too, was piggybacking atop my frame as a prank. When I swung slowly around, however, and saw Bolivar standing five paces off, staring back at me with a look of deep concern, I knew I was in a fix of Mayday proportions.

The problem wasn't the weight alone—though the weight *was* like carrying a small person on my back. The problem was just as much the technique. I could already feel the anchoring front vine of this mini-malist Indian backpack digging sharply into my shoulders. The vine had a discomfiting straightjacket effect, lashing my upper arms like cement to my torso, leaving the limbs all but useless for maintaining balance. I found that in order to walk at all I had to lace my thumbs through the front of the vine and lean significantly forward. But then the awkward shape of the peccary itself came into play, the contours of whose skull I could feel in painful profile against my upper back.

Carrying so much weight in such a fashion for more than a mile might have been a survivable ordeal had the land before us been flat, dry, and unobstructed. But of course it was none of these. All I had to do was walk one hundred feet with the peccary—struggling in a wad-dling fashion through thick mud and around a fallen tree—and I knew I'd never make it even halfway to the river. I knew it.

But I tried. I put one foot in front of the other and followed Bolivar, Elias, and Norma to the last stream we had crossed. There, despite their own charges, the Indians tightroped along the same narrow log as before. Then I crossed my way. Without the use of my arms, I somehow slid down the bank to the stream and entered the water. Wading through, though, the mud was so thick that my left foot, with a pro-tracted sucking sound, came sliding completely out of my boot. The boot itself remained mired in the gook. Bolivar had to retrieve it and put it back on my foot for me when—by some miracle—I made it to the top of the far bank on my own.

Everything became a blur after these ugly opening moves. It was a strange slow-motion torture of forward movement full of blood, sweat, and mosquitoes, of long waddles through stagnant swamps, of tricky footing on strained knees, of almost, almost, almost falling with every tenth step. I slipped badly coming out of the next stream and only at the last second freed my thumb from under the straightjacket vine in time to grab the closest tree to steady myself. But the narrow trunk I reached for was a peculiar species of palm with needlelike thorns protruding thick as hair from its bark. Bolivar turned around just in time to see me pulling three of the thorns from my palm with my teeth— and I realized I was embarrassing myself more with this mammoth adult on my back than if I'd carried the poodle.

Bolivar couldn't have agreed more, I'm sure, though he was trying to be delicate.

"Just put it down," he kept saying, only a soupçon of scorn in his voice. "It's heavy. Let my wife carry it for a while. It's okay."

But idiotically, the weaker I became from the beating and the fatigue of the march, the more obsessed I grew with making it to the river. I've long since given up trying to explain it, for the drive far outstripped any western sense of finish-what-you-start Puritanism. Some schmo in a lab coat might have honed in on an inordinate fear of failure—and be close to the mark. But whatever the case, my thinking grew as piggish as the meat on my back: I *had* to reach the canoe with this lashed-on cargo or I'd never be able to face myself in the mirror reflection of the Zabalo River again.

"I'll make it," I kept telling Bolivar after each of his appeals. "I'll make it."

But to continue trying I had to resort to an even slower pace, a walking crawl, really. Elias and Norma broke off for the river, leaving Bolivar behind to tend to me. Every time I looked up he was standing still, waiting for me. He was barely stooped under the weight of his own pig, his taut body a work of steel that silently mocked the wreck of my own arms and legs. I began resting every fifty yards now, discovering that if I stopped and bent far forward I could table the peccary on my back, relieving the pressure on my shoulders and neck. As for the carrying vine across my front shoulders that was now digging and scraping into my skin to the point of drawing blood, I tried padding it by stuffing copious amounts of leaves between it and my flesh. That this didn't help wasn't important after a while when the entire area became utterly numb. I lost all sensation across my shoulders.

I'm not sure how I made the last quarter mile. We entered the dense, dark stretch of trees where mosquitoes attacked us mercilessly. With my arms immobilized by the vine, I could do little to swat the insects away. Nor could I reach up and remove my glasses when they again fogged to uselessness. Bolivar removed the glasses for me, an act which dramatically reduced my ability to see the approach of face-level branches and other nuisances. My head became a punching bag.

In the deep mud of the next creek bed I lost my boot a second time. I pulled myself out of the creek with enormous effort, one foot exposed, and called up to Bolivar. He turned and stared—and despite obvious effort he couldn't stifle a laugh at the humpbacked, mud-spattered, half-blind gringo covered with mosquitoes limping toward him with just one boot on, cursing a wild streak of English bad words. It was my rock-bottom bottom. I didn't try to hide it. Bolivar went back to fetch the boot, still chuckling to himself, while I paused to table the peccary on my back for a breather.

And that's when I quit. I tossed in the towel—finally. This was preposterous, I realized. I was faint with exhaustion, close to collapse. What exactly was the point?

I was just about to sling the lead-weight peccary onto the ground when, still hunched over, I saw two muddy feet step into my frame of vision. They were Elias's feet. He had reached the river, deposited his peccary in the canoe, and come back.

"How far is it?" I asked him, still staring at his feet, unable to stand just yet.

"Close," he said. "Give me your animal."

Somehow I straightened my spine. Still carrying the pig, I stepped back into the boot Bolivar was now holding for me like Cinderella's royal suitor.

"I'll make it," I said. "I want to make it."

Bolivar grimaced. "But Mike, you can't . . ."

I started walking.

Cruelly, just as victory seemed nearest, the pain was greatest, cracking out all over my body during those last few stubborn steps. Up ahead, I could see a clearing. It was getting closer, bigger. There was more sunlight. Then the river was before me, down one last sloping bank which I negotiated in one last rump slide, reaching the beached canoe. I maneuvered my fanny to a gunwale, wobbled slightly, and then unloaded my charge in a loud thunk to the canoe floor. I then made my own thunk on the sandy shore, lying on my back, limp with relief, smiling despite the lingering hurt. I was too spent to whoop or otherwise vocalize the fact that, inwardly, my soul was doing a pirouette of utter joy against a backdrop of happy, booming fireworks.

I looked up and saw Bolivar and Elias bending over me, silhouetted against the sky, grinning down at me.

"*Gracias,*" Bolivar said. "*Muchas gracias,* Mike. Muchas gracias for carrying the pig."

"*De nada,*" I managed.

"Rest now," he said. "Rest a long time. It's okay"

"I'm not a Cofan," I whispered back.

The men were still peering down, straining to hear. "What?" they said.

"I'm not a Cofan," I repeated.

They heard me clearly this time, but were no less baffled.

"What I mean," I said, still breathing hard, "is I don't know how you do these things. I'm not a Cofan. I almost died carrying that pig."

My comments struck them as absolutely hilarious for some reason and the men laughed uncontrollably, and for the rest of the day they kept asking me, "Mike, are you a Cofan?" and I'd say "no" and they'd laugh some more.

We all rested there on the riverbank for a while, reposing long enough to face up to the implacable fact: We were still a long way from the village without a motor and now with 250 pounds of added peccary meat to contend with.

It was well past sunset when we finally pulled up to the huts, tired and hungry. We'd been caught in a heavy rainstorm along the way and our hair and clothes were miserably wet. I was shivering uncontrollably.

Bolivar's oldest son came to greet us on the riverbank to help carry gear.

"Come take the backpack of this Cofan man," Bolivar said to his son while gesturing toward me. His son was confused. "Carry this Cofan man's *bag*," Bolivar repeated with some sharpness. I managed to produce an exhausted smile—as did Bolivar and Elias and Norma, as his son finally reached for my gear.

from Looking for a Fight

by Lynn Snowden Picket

Journalist Lynn Snowden Picket (born 1958) has spent time in a boxing ring, so her opinions about the sport count. After ten months of training—accompanied by panic attacks and bruises—she fought her first public bout.

Carol and I are introduced by Bruce to loud cheers as "the big event of the evening." To my surprise, it sounds as if he means it. We're beckoned into the center of the ring by Dominick, who sternly summarizes the rules of boxing. I'm far too preoccupied by the stunning and unfamiliar presence of a crowd to listen to him: their noises and rumblings, the smell of 150 people exhaling in a place where I'm going to need to suck in as much air as possible, the odd and distracting scraps of conversation. "Yo, Tina!" a man calls out, and it's all I can do to resist the urge to help him scan the crowd for her. The assemblage takes up a surprisingly large chunk of mental space, with its pressure to perform, my fear of failure in their eyes, the self-consciousness of being on display in a skintight leotard. Who can concentrate on boxing, with all this going on? My friends are smiling.

Carol and I touch gloves, hop backward to our corners, and Bruce sounds the bell. Our first jabs meet headlong before we both exchange a flurry of blows; I resort to a barrage of jabs to keep her away, to wait until the hysteria of the opening seconds subsides. She throws two punches simultaneously, both arms flying up—a silly blunder due to nerves. *I'm sure she didn't mean to do that,* I think in a momentary flash of empathy, but I nevertheless duck down to catch her in her unprotected ribs, then tap her on the side of her head. Her eyes roll wildly away from my fist like those of a spooked horse. It's a moment that starts to hang up, taking longer to complete than usual.

Until this evening, I thought boxers were so focused in the ring that the crowd receded from their consciousness. I imagined they experienced the crowd in much the same way as a rock star: just one big blur of noise. But tonight I can hear everyone and everything they say. I'm in the center of a giant game of charades, where every move provokes another opinion.

"Take her! Knock her down!"

"Move in, all right!"

"Pop it!"

Carol's fist blocks most of my jabs halfway, but one slips past and lands on her nose. Her eyes glitter crazily.

"Jab, Leen!" Hector's voice rises above the din. "Tha's it! Good!"

She hits my face hard, twice, and nausea, like seasickness, washes over me. Still, we continue our slow clockwise tango to the left. Recovering my equilibrium, I successfully evade several of her jabs by ducking my head. Then I lash out at her ribs. The round ends just after she smashes a right into my cheekbone.

"You doin' *very* good out there, *very* good," Hector says gently, squirting water into my open mouth. His encouragement is such a relief, I nearly start crying. "Make sure you arm comes back fast!" He demonstrates, quickly pulling his fist close to his chest. It dawns on me that my arms must be hanging out there in the air after each punch, which is why she's able to hit me in the head. "You look good, doin' good." He rinses my mouthpiece and puts it back in. "You okay, doin' great." Biting down, I turn to face her and to wait for the bell. Angel is still talking to her, making big animated gestures, as if he's narrating a children's story. The round bell sounds.

Carol runs at me with a fury that literally stops me in my tracks. Four punches land on me within the space of two seconds, three to my head, the last one snapping my head to the side and up; the sight of the ceiling is terrifying. Am I going down? Barely recovering, I dart to the right.

Coming back hard to her ribs, I throw a right to her jaw, but it's deflected by her glove. Another right to her face, and her lips pull back to reveal a white mouthpiece, clear back to its edges. I hear Hector's chant of "Jab! Jab! Jab! Jab!" The audience is roaring louder now, the surges in their enthusiasm corresponding exactly to the landing of each punch, an obvious fact that suddenly appalls me. *This is like getting into a car accident for sport* is what goes through my mind, the sudden absurdity of boxing and my place in it.

Carol smashes me hard in the nose, the tip folding down on itself in a way I wouldn't have believed possible, mashing into my upper lip. The force of her fist grinds my mouthguard into every possible surface of my gums, tearing and ripping the soft tissue as if it were a razor. A numbing, tingling sensation spreads from my nose along the sides of my face, and heat pours into my sinuses, spreading backward into my throat. My upper torso rockets to the side with the momentum, and somehow my legs catch up and move under me. I'm spared any further punishment for the moment, but only because she's as exhausted as I am.

Both of us throw jabs as we follow each other in a clockwise circle around the ring. She's staring at me as if I'm planning to kill her whole family and burn down her home; as if her one chance at survival is to find the kitchen knife and plunge it deep into my heart. Her face is contorting, her eyes wide, mouth shifting from snarling to pleading to determination. I've never fought anyone who looked at me this way; maybe this is how I'm looking at her, how I've looked at all my sparring partners.

I land a right to her face, and the force of it expels spit and mucus from her mouth and nose. A fine spray now rests on the part of her headgear just near her cheek. My eyes move to her nostrils, waiting for the appearance of blood. We're poised like this for what seems like minutes, hours. Suddenly I wonder if I'll be standing in this ring until time rolls to a complete stop. How sad never again to swim in the ocean, never to lie down in sweet-smelling grass, or see my family again. I have no idea how much real time is passing; within this little bit of eternity, Carol hits me twice, and I jab back weakly. Eli is chanting "Strong! Strong!" when the bell finally rings.

Hector offers water, soothing advice. My gums are raw from the mouthpiece, I swish the cool liquid around as a balm. He reassures me that my nose isn't bleeding, my big concern at this moment. "You doin' good!" he says. "You doin' jus' fine. She running! She scared of you!"

"Really?"

"Yes!" Hector rinses the mouthguard and gently slides it in. I bite down, wincing. No matter what, it's just two more minutes: I don't have to pace myself, I can give it my all. After that, it's over.

The bell sounds, and again Carol flies out of her corner, her head reared back, her expression somewhere between hysteria and determination as she throws four desperate blows. Both of her hands swing wildly around my head and neck, so I tuck my chin to my chest and pound at her ribs. She leaps back, then runs forward, grabbing me in a clinch. "Don' stop, baby!" Hector yells. "Don' stop!" I plant a left into her ribs, and she eases back enough for me to swing at her face. We revolve again, both throwing jabs, batting them away. I can see she's wiped out, but I only wish I had the strength to capitalize on it.

Angel's voice soars over the crowd. "Pop it!" he says. "Pop it!" She throws a left hook that lands neatly, by the book, right on my left temple. Staggering to the side, I recover to throw a few more jabs and land a right to her head as the bell rings. Dominick flings himself between us, but we drop our arms and push him aside so we can quickly embrace. I don't feel warmth from her, and I'm sure she doesn't feel it from me. We're standing still for a time, just resting before we have to make the long walk to our corners. The fight is over.

Hector is leaping up and down, arms raised triumphantly, smiling, bursting with pride. He gives me a big hug and rushes around to hug Carol. Dominick walks over and claps me on the shoulder. "You did it!" he says. There's an incredible uproar. The crowd is yelling and I think it's for me. I get another hug from Hector, and a kiss on the neck. He removes my headgear as Bruce enters the ring again.

"Presenting the trophies for this bout," he says, "is the contender for the world title, Merqui Sosa." A tall light heavyweight in a nylon jacket with matching pants doffs his baseball cap as an acknowledgment of the applause. He hands Carol and me identical trophies, and the three of us pose for a photo.

Climbing down out of the ring, I see my friends coming over to me. Another fight is just starting, so the crowd's attention has moved on to new business. "I never thought I'd see you again," I say to Eli. He's pointing the video camera at me.

"What?" he says, peering at me through the viewfinder. "I was screaming for you!"

Anne and Mark are busy snapping photos of me clutching my trophy. Cameras are passed around, clusters of friends form and re-form around me.

"You were awesome," says Kristin. "Awesome!" I'm smiling like crazy, but it's because I'm finally out of purgatory. Eli ushers me over to Hector, who removes my gloves and wraps.

"She scared of you! Four year she boxes! You beat her!"

Another boxer darts over and bumps his fist into my glove. "Good fight, man! You killed her!"

I nod and smile, grateful it's all over. "She didn't touch me here," I say, running my hands down my sides. Hector hands me my gear, and I quickly walk into the locker room, pausing for a moment before opening the door. Is she in here? No; it's empty. Opening my locker, I grab the roll of paper towels and liquid soap and head for the sink.

Tipping my head back, I see a triangle of red under my nose. Dabbing with a wet paper towel, there's a tiny smear of blood from one nostril. Lifting up my lip, there's purple bruising, and tiny cuts along my gumline. My eyes are a little puffy, as if I've been crying. Splashing cold water on my face, I wash up quickly and carefully blot dry. Hurrying back over to my locker, I unlace my sneakers, rip down my unitard, and yank off my socks.

Pulling Anne and Kristin's coats and purses out of my locker, I throw my headgear and gloves back in, slam it shut, and stagger out. The effort of carrying everything makes my face, particularly my nose, throb in protest. Is it possible to get a nosebleed this way? Practically tossing them their belongings, I fish a quarter out of my pocket, and that scrap of paper.

"Bruce," I hiss at him, as he gathers up his papers from the table next to the ring, "did I win?"

He looks down at a piece of paper and takes a moment before saying softly, "I have you taking rounds one and three, with Carol taking round two."

"So I won."

He shrugs. I take that as a yes.

The morning after the fight, I'm supposed to spend most of the day on the corner of First Avenue and Sixty-eighth Street, to cheer on my friends as they pass by in the Marathon. At the end of the race, there's going to be a party at my gym for the Marathoners, as it's perfectly located half a block from the finish line. I'm one of the two dozen members who've volunteered to wait at checkpoints along the route with bananas, orange slices, Gatorade, and water bottles. But right now I'm scared to leave my bathroom. I can't shake the feeling that someone's out there, waiting to beat me up.

My paranoia began the night before. For weeks I'd been looking forward to my postfight victory celebration at the opening of a friend's new restaurant, and so I shook my head adamantly when Eli suggested that it might be better to stay in. "I want to eat a steak, I want some wine, I want to relax," I said peevishly. "I'll just hop in the shower, get dressed, put some ice on my face for a little while, take some Advil, and we can go. I'll be ready in twenty minutes."

The restaurant, located on a small side street in SoHo, was a madhouse by the time we arrived at eleven. People were crowding the bar and spilling into the eating area, surrounding the seated guests. Holding my hand, Eli hauled me through the mob.

A blonde with bright red lipstick muscled her way toward us, shoving me aside with enough force to knock me off my balance. Pulling Eli's hand to try and right myself, I fell into a man in a leather jacket standing at the bar, stepping indelicately on his foot. "I'm so sorry," I told him, grateful that my aching nose didn't smash into his chest.

Eli and I pushed on again. Suddenly, there wasn't nearly enough air in the room. All the smoke, all these people. A small wave of panic began to rise, but it subsided once I saw a woman holding menus. "Miss!" I yelled over the din. "Is it possible to get a table for two, please?"

She waved at us to follow her, and we clawed our way deeper into the restaurant, to a smaller, much less crowded back room. She cheerfully gestured at a small table in a corner and put down two menus.

"Thanks! So much!" I said, plopping into a chair, absurdly thrilled at this magically free table. Eli sat down. "Does my face look okay?" I said. "You know, normal?"

"Uhhhmmmm . . ." he said, squinting, his head tilted.

"Never mind. I just got my answer." I turned my attention to the menu, gingerly touching the bridge of my nose. That was when I sensed it coming: something big hurtling toward me. My right forearm flew up to protect my face, and I ducked. My left hand curled tightly around the laminated menu, and my legs tensed under the table, one lashing out and kicking Eli.

"Can I tell you about our specials?" The big, scary thing rushing toward my skull was our waiter solicitously bending over the table to tell us about the food.

"You okay over there?" said Eli. I nodded slowly, trying to look calm. When the waiter's lips stopped moving, I smiled and asked for a glass of red wine.

"I keep seeing her," I told Eli when our waiter left.

"Seeing who?"

Seeing who. "My opponent," I said, enunciating. "I see that look in her eyes. She wanted to kill me before I killed her."

"You're just having a delayed reaction," he said. "Are you getting an appetizer?"

I woke up the next morning, on the day of the Marathon, with a start, as if from a nightmare. Eli didn't stay over, having mentioned something about attending a funeral early today, although he was vague about whose. I actually was relieved to say good-bye after our late dinner last night, impatient to go home, to bolt and chain the door, to pack ice around my face, and to finally be alone. But now in the morning, shaking in my bed, near tears, unsure of what scared me and why, I wish he were here, even though the relationship is unraveling. I wish my mother were here too, if she would promise not to tell me I brought all of this on myself. I wish anyone were here.

While inspecting my ruined face in the bathroom mirror, I turn on the all-news radio station. The forecast is for bitterly cold temperatures, which is bad news for the runners but good news for me, as my face will feel iced anytime I'm outdoors. Bundled up and ready to leave, I try on my sunglasses to see if they cover any of the more dramatic bruises, but they don't, and the weight of them is painful on my nose, so I wrap a scarf around the bottom of my face and set off for the subway. Half a block later, I pull it down: the chafing of the material is unbearable against my raw, sensitive skin.

On the uptown train, I realize that two women and a man on the opposite side of the car are regarding me with some concern. Quickly dropping my gaze, I pretend to root around inside my purse for something, trying to keep the underside of my nose out of view. A woman with a banged-up face is always a victim. A man could still come off as a tough guy. Should I tell them I'm a boxer? The train stops, and they get off: a moot point.

Happy to think about anything other than boxing or last night, a couple hours of standing in the cold makes everyone's face look purpled and bruised; my injuries are eventually forgotten and pass unremarked upon. As I watched my friends run past, it seems incredible that I was in their shoes only a year ago. This time last year, I thought boxing sounded interesting, that it would put me in the best shape of my life, that I was tired of taking crap from guys, and that I wanted to know the pure pleasure of violence. This time last year, running in this race, I'd never been beaten up.

Back in the gym, when the party is in full swing, people are asking about the fight, my injuries, if I want to sit down. The Broadway actress Betty Buckley walks over at one point to ask me, gently, "Should you be doing this to your face?"

I shrug off her concern, chugging more wine. "Hey, I could fall down in the shower and get hurt much worse," I tell her, reflexively giving the standard response usually reserved for my parents. "I'm a writer," I tell her. "We don't have to be attractive."

"Don't be so eager to get rid of your looks," she tells me. "They'll go away soon enough."

Four days pass before I can bring myself to watch the videotape of the fight. The first time I see it, I'm alone, curled up on the couch, my stomach in a knot, every muscle poised and tense. My hand rests on the remote, ready to turn it off if it gets too much. The images flicker on my television, and even though I know exactly what happens, I'm terrified. Flinching with every blow thrown, I will my video image to throw more jabs, to protect my face.

After the fight ends, the tape jumps to a shot of me sitting on this same couch, a bag of ice at my face. It takes me a moment to figure out that this occurred before we went out to dinner. I have absolutely no memory of it happening. Eli asks me questions about the fight, and as I watch the tape, I'm surprised to hear my answers. In between questions, I look over at Eli behind the camera and regard him warily.

I tell my friend Anne that I don't even like to think about the fight, much less talk about it.

"You probably have post-traumatic stress syndrome," she says.

"No, it's just an unpleasant experience that I don't particularly want to relive." But it's not just the fight: anything that recalls boxing gives me the shakes. The bell that announces the closing of subway doors, a poster for an upcoming bout on Pay-Per-View, even a black leather club chair in a furniture showroom makes me walk away, disturbed by how much it recalls headgear and gloves. Am I still so angry, and so terrified of being thought of as cowardly that I have to box for the rest of my life? I have my proof, I went the distance, and now it's time to stop.

The sensation I carry everywhere is the shock of waking up from a horrible nightmare: I dreamed I was a boxer for a year. The crap was beaten out of me three times a week, my trainer was a bully. Then I had a big fight where a whole crowd of people screamed for my blood and my opponent's blood. Then I woke up.

In the four years that have passed since I've boxed, I've moved from enthusiastic and knowledgeable fight fan to queasy, reluctant spectator. It would be simplistic to say that the reason I don't enjoy watching people box anymore is because it makes me relive my own experiences, but it's more than that. It reminds me of how close I came to damaging myself permanently, all to prove how fearless I was, to settle a score that was started back in the sixth grade when I was pushed off the swings by a bully, and that sensation of helplessness was dramatically revived during my divorce. I wanted to feel powerful, to take up space in the world, to stop apologizing. That I thought I could do this by learning how to fight now strikes me as ludicrous and deranged. I don't even have the luxury of wondering why no one tried to talk me out of such a stupid idea. "There was just no talking to you," says my brother, an apt assessment of my determination.

I start realizing all of this during the week immediately following my fight, when my friends ask me over and over: "When's your next bout?"

There would be no next bout. I'd had it.

Megatransect Part II
by David Quammen

Michael Fay in 1999 and 2000 spent 15 months walking 1,200 miles through some of the world's most punishing terrain—an almost superhuman venture. He hoped to gather data and earn publicity that would aid conservation efforts in the region. Nature writer David Quammen (born 1948) joined him for several legs of the journey; this piece ran in National Geographic *as Quammen's second report on the trip.*

It takes a hardheaded person to walk 1,200 miles across west-central Africa, transecting all the wildest forests remaining between a northeastern corner of the Republic of the Congo and the Atlantic. It takes a harder head still to conceive of covering that terrain in a single, sustained, expeditionary trudge. There are rivers to be ferried or bridged, swamps to be waded, ravines to be crossed, vast thickets to be carved through by machete, and one tense national border, as well as some lesser impediments—thorny vines, biting flies, stinging ants, ticks, vipers, tent-eating termites, foot worms, not a few nervous elephants, and the occasional armed poacher. As though that weren't enough, there's a beautifully spooky forest about midway on the route that's believed to harbor the Ebola virus, cause of lethal epidemics in nearby villages within recent years. The logistical costs of an enterprise on this scale, counting high-tech data-gathering gizmos and aerial support, can run to hundreds of thousands of dollars. The human costs include fatigue, hunger, loneliness, tedium, some diseases less mysterious than Ebola, and the inescapable nuisance of infected feet. It takes an obdurate self-confidence to begin such a journey, let alone finish it. It takes an unquenchable curiosity and a monomaniacal sense of purpose.

J. Michael Fay, an American ecologist employed (on a long tether) by the Wildlife Conservation Society in New York, is as obdurate and purposeful as they come. But even for him there arrived a moment, after eight months of walking, when it looked as if the whole adventure would end sadly. One of his forest crew, a young Bambendjellé Pygmy named Mouko, lay fevering on the verge of death. Hepatitis was taking him down fast.

Mouko's illness was only the latest travail. Within recent days Fay had been forced to backtrack around an impassable swamp. His 12 Bambendjellé crewmen, even the healthy ones, were exhausted and ready to quit. That border crossing, which loomed just ahead, had begun to appear politically problematic—no Gabonese visas for a gang of Congolese Pygmies. And then a Muslim trader went missing between villages along one of the few human footpaths with which Fay's route converged; as authorities reacted to the disappearance, Fay began dreading the prospect that he and his feral band might come under suspicion and be sidetracked for questioning. Suspending the march to nurse Mouko, he found himself stuck in a village with bad water. He was running short of food, with not even enough pocket money to buy local bananas. The Megatransect was in megatrouble.

If Mouko dies, Fay thought, it's probably time to roll up the tents and capitulate. He would abandon his dream of amassing a great multidimensional filament of forest-survey data, continuous both in space and in time. He would stop recording all those little particulars—the relative freshness of every pile of elephant dung, the location of every chimp nest and aardvark burrow, the species and girth of every big tree—in the latest of his many yellow notebooks. He would stop walking. Human exigencies would preempt methodological imperatives and vaulting aspirations. If Mouko dies, he figured, I'll drop everything and take the body home.

Even from the start, in late September of 1999, it looked like a daunting endeavor—far too arduous and demented to tempt an ordinary tropical ecologist, let alone a normal human being. But Fay isn't ordinary. By his standards, the first three months of walking were a lark. Then the going got sticky.

Having crossed Nouabalé-Ndoki National Park and a stunning wedge of pristine forest known as the Goualougo Triangle, having hiked south through the trail-gridded timber concessions and boomtown logging camps of the lower Ndoki watershed, Fay and his team angled west, toward a zone of wilderness between the Sangha and the Lengoué Rivers, both of which drain south to the main stem of the Congo. What was out there? No villages, no roads. On the national map it was just a smear of green. Fay traveled along elephant trails when possible, and when there were none, he bushwhacked, directing his point man to cut a compass-line path by machete.

A strong-armed and equable Pygmy named Mambeleme had laid permanent claim to the point-man job. Behind him walked Fay with his yellow notebook and video camera, followed closely by Yves Constant Madzou, the young Congolese biologist serving as his scientific apprentice. Farther back, beyond earshot so as not to spook animals, came the noisier and more heavily burdened entourage—12 Pygmy porters and a Bakwele Bantu named Jean Gouomoth, nicknamed Fafa, Fay's all-purpose expedition sergeant and camp cook. They had proceeded that way for many weeks, in a good rhythm, making reasonable distance for reasonable exertion, when gradually they found themselves submerged in a swale of vegetation unlike anything Fay had ever seen.

Trained as a botanist long before he did his doctoral dissertation on gorillas, Fay describes it as "a solid sea of Marantaceae"—the family Marantaceae constituting a group of herbaceous tropical plants that includes gangly species such as *Haumania liebrechtsiana*, which can grow into stultifying thickets, denser than sugar cane, denser than grass, dense as the fur on a duck dog. The Marantaceae brake that Fay and his team had now entered, just east of the Sangha, stretched westward for God-knew-how-far. Fay himself, with a GPS unit and a half-decent map but no godlike perspective, knew not. All he could do was point Mambeleme into the stuff, like a human Weedwacker, and fall in behind.

Sometimes they moved only 60 steps an hour. During one ten-hour day they made less than a mile. The green stems stood 15 feet high, with multiple branches groping crosswise and upward, big leaves turned greedily toward the sun. "It's an environment which is completely claustrophobic," Fay says later, from the comfort of retrospect. "It's like digging a tunnel except there is sunlight." The cut stems scratched at their bare arms and legs. Sizable trees, offering shade, harboring monkeys, were few. Flowing water was rare, and each afternoon they searched urgently for some drinkable sump beside which to camp. When they did stop, it took an hour of further cutting just to clear space for the tents.

On the march Fay spent much of his time bent at the waist, crouching through Mambeleme's tunnel. He learned to summon a Zen-like state of self-control, patience, humility. The alternative was to start hating every stem of this Marantaceae hell, regretting he ever blundered into it—and along that route a person might go completely nuts. Mambeleme and the other Pygmies had their own form of Zen-like accommodation. "*Eyali djamba,*" they would say. "*Njamba, eyaliboyé.*" That's the forest. That's the way it is.

But this wasn't the real forest, woody and canopied and diverse, that Mike Fay had set out to explore. It was something else, an awesome expanse of reedy sameness. Later he named it the Green Abyss.

They reached the Sangha River, crossed in borrowed pirogues, then plunged westward into more of the same stuff. Fay had flown this whole route in his Cessna, scouting it carefully, but even at low elevation he hadn't grasped the difficulty of getting through on foot. Villagers on the Sangha, whose own hunting and fishing explorations had taught them to steer clear of that trackless mess, warned him: "It's impossible; you cannot do it. You will fail. You will be back here soon." Fay's response was: "We have maps. We have a compass, and we have strong white-man medicine. We will make it." He was right. But it took ten miserable weeks. Having spent New Year's Eve in the Green Abyss, he wouldn't emerge until early March.

"We drank swamp water for three weeks in a row. We did not see any flowing water for almost a month," Fay recalls. "Miraculously, we only had one night where we had to drink water out of a mudhole." It was an old termite mound, excavated by an aardvark or some other insectivore and lately filled with rain water. The water was thick with suspended clay, grayish brown like latte but tasting more like milk of magnesia.

Food was another problem, since their most recent rendezvous with Fay's logistic-support man, an ever reliable Japanese ecologist named Tomo Nishihara, had been back at the Sangha; they were now days behind schedule and would be on starveling rations long before they reached the next resupply point. So by satellite phone Fay and Tomo arranged an airdrop: 20-kilogram bags of manioc and 50-can cases of sardines dumped without parachutes from a low-flying plane. The drop was a success, despite one parcel's ripping open on a tree limb, leaving a plume of powdered manioc to sift down like snow and 50 sardine cans mooshed together like a crashed Corvair. They binged on the open sardines, then resumed walking.

Other problems were less easily solved. There were tensions and deep glooms. There were days that passed into weeks not just without flowing water but without civil conversation. Not everyone on the team found his own variant of *Njamba, eyaliboyé*. By the time they reached the Lengoué River, Yves Madzou had had enough, and Fay had had enough of his enoughness. By mutual agreement Yves left the Megatransect to pursue, as the saying goes, other interests. He was human, after all.

Fay was Fay. He marched on.

After six months Fay and his crew paused for rest and resupply at a field camp called Ekania, on the upper Mambili River, within another spectacular area of Congolese landscape, Odzala National Park. Odzala is noted for its big populations of forest elephants and gorillas, which show themselves in small meadowy clearings known as *bais*, sparsely polka-dotting the forest. Mineral salts, edible sedges, and other tooth-some vegetation at the bais attract not just elephants and gorillas but also forest buffalo, sitatungas, bongo, and red river hogs, sometimes in large groups. Of course Fay wanted to visit the bais, which he had scouted by plane but never explored on foot; he also wanted to take the measure of the forest around them.

Odzala's elephants suffered heavily from poaching during the late 1980s and early 1990s, until a conservation program known as ECOFAC, funded by the European Commission, assumed responsibility for managing the park, with a stringent campaign of guard patrols and a guard post on the lower Mambili to choke off the ivory traffic coming downriver. Access deep into Odzala along the Mambili, a chocolaty stream whose upper reaches are narrow and strained by many fallen trees, is still allowed for innocent travelers not carrying tusks. That's how Tomo brought the resupply crates up to Ekania. It was a ten-hour trip by motorized dugout from the nearest grass airstrip, and on this occasion I traveled with him.

Fay, bare-chested and walnut brown, with a wilder mane of graying hair than I remembered, stood on a thatched veranda taking video of us as we docked. Without pulling the camera from his eye, he waved. I can't remember if I waved back; more likely I saluted. He had begun to remind me of a half-mad, half-brilliant military commander gone AWOL into wars of his own choosing, with an army of tattered acolytes attending him slavishly—rather like Brando's version of Conrad's Kurtz in *Apocalypse Now*, only much skinnier.

It was the first time I'd seen Fay since Day 13 of the Megatransect, back in October, when I split off from his forest trek and walked out to a road. Now his shoulder bones stood up like the knobbed back of a wooden chair, suggesting he'd lost 20 or 30 pounds. But his legs were the legs of a marathoner. The quiet, clinical smile still lurked behind his wire glasses. Greeting him again here on Day 182, many hundreds of miles deep in the equatorial outback, I felt like Stanley addressing Dr. Livingstone.

"Every day that I walk," Fay volunteered, "I'm just happier that I did the Megatransect." He said *did* rather than *am doing*, I noticed, though in fact he was only halfway along. Why? Because the advance planning and selling phase had been the most onerous part, I suspected, and the actual walk felt like raking in a poker-game pot. Aside from a chest cold and a few foot-worm infections, and notwithstanding the weight loss, he had stayed healthy. His body seemed to have reached some sort of equilibrium with the rigors of the forest, he said; his feet, I saw, were marked with pinkish scar tissue and pale sandal-strap bands against the weathered brown. No malaria flare-ups, no yellow fever. Just as important, he was having fun—most of the time anyway. He described his ten weeks in the Green Abyss, making clear that *that* passage, far from fun, had been "the most trying thing I've ever done in my life." But now he was in Odzala, lovely Odzala, where the bongo and the buffalo roam. He had a new field companion to help with the botany, a jovial Congolese man named Gregoire Kossa-Kossa, forest hardy and consummately knowledgeable, on loan from the Ministry of Forestry and Fishing. Fafa, his crew boss and cook, had grown into a larger role, which included data-gathering chores earlier handled by Yves. And his point man, Mambeleme, now with a buffed-out right arm and a machete so often sharpened it was almost used up, had proved himself a champion among trail cutters. The rest of Fay's crew, including the brothers Kati and Mouko, had suffered badly from that chest cold they all caught during a village stop but now seemed fine.

Meanwhile his own data gathering had continued, providing some new and significant impressions of Odzala National Park. For instance, one day in a remote floodplain forest Fay, along with Mambeleme and Kossa-Kossa, had sighted a black colobus monkey, the first record of that rare species within the park. In the famed bais of Odzala he saw plenty of elephants, as he'd expected, but during his long cross-country traverses between one bai and another he found a notable absence of elephant trails and dung, suggesting that a person shouldn't extrapolate from those bais to an assumption of overall elephant abundance. His elephant-sign tallies, recorded methodically in the current yellow notebook, would complement observations of elephant distribution made by ECOFAC researchers themselves.

Maybe those notebooks would yield other insights too. Maybe the Megatransect wasn't just an athletic publicity stunt, as his critics had claimed. It occurred to me as an intriguing possibility, not for the first time, that maybe Mike Fay wasn't as crazy as he looked.

After a few days at Ekania we set off toward the Mambili headwaters and a large bai called Maya North, near which was another ECOFAC field camp used by elephant researchers and visiting film crews. The usual route to the Maya North camp was upriver along the Mambili, traveling some hours by motorized dugout to a point where ECOFAC workers had cut a good trail. We came the back way, bushwhacking on an overland diagonal. That evening, as we sat by the campfire trading chitchat with several Congolese camp workers, the talk turned to boat travel on the upper Mambili. Well, we didn't use a boat, Fay mentioned. *You didn't?* they wondered. *Then how did you get here?* We walked, Fay said. *Walked? All the way from Ekania? There's no trail.* True but irrelevant, Fay said.

At daybreak on Day 188 we were at the bai, watching 18 elephants in the fresh light of dawn as they drank and groped for minerals in the stream. Some distance from the others stood an ancient female, emaciated, failing, her skull and pelvic bones draped starkly with slack gray skin. Amid the herd was a massive bull, who swept his raised trunk back and forth like a periscope, tasting the air vigilantly for unwelcome scents. He caught ours. There was a subtle shift in mood, then the bull initiated a deliberate, wary leave-taking. One elephant after another waded off toward the far side of the bai, disappearing there into the trees. By sun-up they were gone.

By midday so were we, walking on.

From then upper Mambili, Fay planned to ascend toward an escarpment that forms the divide between the Congo River basin and a lesser system, the Ogooué which drains to the Atlantic through Gabon. I would peel off again on Day 195, using another resupply rendezvous with Tomo as my chance to exit. As it happened, Tomo needed three boatmen and a chain saw to get his load of supplies that far up the snag-choked Mambili, but going back downriver would be easier, and we figured to reach the airstrip in two days.

On the morning before my departure, Fafa was laid flat by a malarial fever, so Fay himself oversaw the sorting and packing of new supplies: sacks of manioc and rice and sugar, cans of peanut butter and sardines, bundles of salted fish, big plastic canisters of pepper and dried onions, cooking oil, granola bars, freeze-dried meats, cigarettes for the crew, many double-A batteries, a fresh stack of colorful plastic bowls, and one package of seaweed, recommended by Tomo as a complement to the salted fish. Finally the packs were ready, the tents struck; Fafa rallied from his fever, and I walked along behind Fay and Mambeleme for an hour that afternoon.

Fay and I had agreed where I'd rejoin him next: at an extraordinary set of granite domes, known as inselbergs (or "island mountains"), that rise up like stony gumdrops from a forest in northeastern Gabon. The forest, called Minkébé, is ecologically rich but microbially menacing; many months earlier, as we knelt over my map on the floor of an office at the National Geographic Society in Washington, D.C., this was where Fay had written "Ebola region" in red ink. "We'll meet you on the other side of the continental divide," he told me cheerily now. "On our way to the Atlantic Ocean."

Backtracking on the trail to catch Tomo's boat, I shook hands with Kossa-Kossa, Fafa, and each of the Pygmy crew, thanking them for their good company and support. I was fascinated by these rough-and-ready Pygmies, whom Fay had somehow cajoled and bullied across hundreds of miles, leading them so far from their home forest into an alien landscape, an alien realm of experiences. They had been challenged beyond imagining, stressed fearfully, but so far they hadn't broken; they put me in mind of the sort of Portuguese seamen, uneducated, trusting, adaptable, who must have sailed with Ferdinand Magellan. By way of farewell, I told them in bad Lingala: "*Na kotala yo, na sanza mibalé.*" I'll see you in two months.

I was wrong. It would be three months before Fay reached the insel-bergs, an interval encompassing some of his most hellish times since the Green Abyss. And when I did rejoin him there, Mambeleme and all the others would be gone.

Fay and his team followed the escarpment northward along its crest, a great uplifted rim that may have once marked the bank of an ancient body of water. Kossa-Kossa left the troop, as planned, to return to his real-life duties. The others shifted direction again, heading into a thumb of territory where the Republic of the Congo obtrudes westward against Gabon. They struck toward the Ouaga River and found it defended by a huge swamp, which at first seemed passable but grew uglier as they committed themselves deeper. By insidious degrees, it became a nightmare of raffia palms and giant pandanus standing in four feet of black water and mud, the long pandanus leaves armed with rows of what Fay recalls as "horrid, cat-claw spines." He and the crew spent two nights there in a small cluster of trees, among which they built elevated log platforms to hold their tents above the muck. Pushing forward, Fay saw the route get worse: deeper water, no trees, only more raffia and cat-claw pandanus, five days' distance of such slogging still ahead, with a chance that any rainstorm would raise the water and trap them. Finally he ordered retreat, a rare thing for Fay, and resigned himself to a long detour through a zone for which he had no map.

After circumventing the Ouaga swamp, they converged with a human trail, a simple forest footpath that serves as an important highway linking villages in that northwestern Congo thumb. The foot-path brought them to a village called Poumba, where they picked up two pieces of bad news: The Gabonese border crossing would be diffi-cult at best, due to festering discord between local authorities on the two sides, and a Muslim trader who dealt in gold and ivory had van-ished along the footpath under circumstances suggesting foul play. From a certain perspective (one that the local gendarmerie might well embrace) the trader's disappearance coincided suggestively with another bit of odd news—a white man with an entourage of Pygmies had materialized from the forest on a transcontinental stroll to count aardvark burrows and elephant dung (so he claimed) and making fast tracks for the Gabonese border. It could look very suspicious, Fay knew. He felt both eager to move and reluctant to seem panicky. Added to those concerns was another, seemingly minor. For the third time in two weeks one of the Pygmies, Mouko this time, was suffering malaria. But a dose of Quinimax would fix that, Fay thought.

Over the next few days Mouko got weaker. He couldn't lug his pack. At times he couldn't even walk and had to be carried. Evidently it was hepatitis, not malaria, since his urine was dark, the Quinimax brought no improvement, and his eyes were going yellow. Fay slowed the pace and took a turn carrying Mouko's pack. Hiding his uncertainty, he wondered what to do. *All the Pygmies think Mouko is going to die now*, he wrote in his notebook on Day 241. Mouko seemed languid as well as sick, with little will to live, while the others had already turned fatalistic about his death. Fay himself became Mouko's chief nurse. He scolded the crew against sharing Mouko's manioc, using his plate, making cuts on his back to bleed him, and various other careless or well-meant practices that could spread the infection. To the notebook, Fay confided: *I am so sick and tired of being the parent of 13 children, it is too much. Thank god I never had children—way too much of a burden. Solo is the way to go—depend on yourself only. The trouble in a group like this is it's like you're an organism. If one part of you is sick or lost the whole organism suffers.* For another ten days after that entry, Mouko's survival remained in doubt.

They pushed toward Garabinzam, a village near the west end of the footpath, on a navigable tributary of the Ivindo River, which drains into Gabon. On the last day of walking to Garabinzam, the team covered nine miles, Kati carrying Mouko piggyback for most of the way. That evening, Fay wrote: *I need to ship these boys home. You can just tell they are haggard, totally worn out. No matter how good they were they are just going to go down one by one. I would love to keep my friends but I would be betraying them if I made them stay on any longer—it would be unjust.*

Several days later, he departed from his line of march—and from all his resolutions about continuity—to evacuate Mouko downriver by boat. They'd try for a village at the Ivindo confluence, on the Gabonese side; from there, if Mouko survived, he could be moved to a hospital in the town of Makokou. Fafa would meanwhile escort the others back to their home forest, hundreds of miles east, sparing them from the onward trudge and the unwelcoming border. Fay himself would pick up the hike in Gabon. One stretch of the planned route would remain unwalked—roughly 25 miles, from Garabinzam overland to the border—a rankling gap in the data set, a blemish on the grand enterprise, and a token (this is my view, not his) of Fay's humanity.

Left Garabinzam, all is well, he wrote briskly on May 24, 2000, which in Megatransect numeration was Day 248. But also: *Pygmies didn't say goodbye.*

Mouko survived and went home. Starting from scratch, Fay gathered a new crew from the villages and gold-mining camps of the upper Ivindo region. He found an able young Baka Pygmy named Bebe, with good ears for wildlife and a strong machete arm, who emerged before long as his new point man; he found a new cook and eight other forest-tough Pygmy and Bantu men; he found energy, even enthusiasm, to continue. They set off on a long arc through the Minkébé forest, targeting various points of interest, most dramatic of which were the inselbergs. That's where I next see Fay, on Day 292, when I step out of a chartered helicopter that has landed precariously on one of the smaller mounds.

Skin browner, hair longer and whiter, he looks otherwise unchanged. Same pair of river shorts, same sandals, same dry little smile. I have brought him three pounds of freshly ground dark-roast coffee and a copy of Michael Herr's *Dispatches,* another of the Vietnam War memoirs that he finds fascinating. If he's pleased to see me, for the company, for the coffee, he gives no sign.

At once he begins talking about data. He's been seeing some interesting trends. For instance, the gorillas. It's true, he says—picking up a discussion from months earlier—that there's a notable absence of gorillas in the Minkébé forest. Since crossing the border, he hasn't heard a single chest-beat display and has seen only one pile of gorilla dung. Back in Odzala National Park, over a similar stretch, he'd have counted three or four *hundred* dung piles. Elephants are abundant; duikers and monkeys and pigs, abundant. But the gorillas are missing. He suspects they were wiped out by Ebola.

The Minkébé forest block, encompassing more than 12,500 square miles of northeastern Gabon, represents one of the great zones of wilderness remaining in central Africa. Much of it stands threatened by logging operations (in the near or midterm future), bush meat extraction such as inevitably accompanies logging, and elephant poaching for ivory. But the Gabonese government has recently taken the admirable step of designating a sizable fraction (2,169 square miles) of that block as Minkébé Reserve, a protected area; and now, in addition, three large adjacent parcels are being considered for possible inclusion. The Gabonese Ministry of Water and Forests, with technical help and gentle coaxing from the World Wildlife Fund, has been studying the farsighted idea that an enlarged Minkébé Reserve might be valuable not just in ecological terms but also in economic ones for its role in the sequestration of carbon. With greenhouse gases and climate change becoming ever more conspicuous as a global concern, maybe other nations and interested parties might soon be willing to compensate Gabon—so goes the logic—for maintaining vast, uncombusted carbon storehouses such as Minkébé.

But before the reserve extension can be approved, on-the-ground assessments must be made. So in the past several years a small group of scientists and forest workers made reconnaissance expeditions into Minkébé—both the original reserve and the proposed extension. They found spectacular zones of forest and swamp, stunning inselbergs, networks of streams, all rich with species and virtually untouched by human presence. They also found—as Mike Fay has been finding—a near-total absence of gorillas and chimpanzees.

It wasn't always so. In 1984 two scientists named Caroline Tutin and Michel Fernandez published a paper in the *American Journal of Prima-*

tology describing their census of gorilla and chimpanzee populations throughout Gabon. Using a combination of field transects, habitat analysis, and cautious extrapolation, Tutin and Fernandez estimated that at least 4,171 gorillas lived within the Minkébé sector, representing a modest but significant population density. Something seems to have happened between 1984 and now.

It may have happened abruptly in the mid-1990s, when three Ebola epidemics burned through villages and gold camps at the Minkébé periphery, killing dozens of humans. One of those outbreaks occurred in early 1996 at a village called Mayibout II, on the upper Ivindo River. It began with a chimpanzee carcass, found dead in the forest and brought to the village as food. Eighteen people who helped with the skinning, the butchering, the handling of the chimp flesh became sick. Suffering variously from fever, headache, and bloody diarrhea, they were evacuated downriver to the Makokou hospital. Four of them died quickly. A fifth escaped from the hospital, went back to Mayibout II, and died there.

These numbers and facts come from a report published three years later, by Dr. Alain-Jean Georges and a long list of co-authors, in *The Journal of Infectious Diseases.* Although the raw chimp flesh had been infectious, the cooked meat evidently had not; no one got sick, the Georges paper asserted, simply from eating it. But once the disease broke out, there were some secondary cases, one human victim infecting another. By early March, according to the World Health Organization, 37 people had fallen ill, of whom 21 died, for a fatality rate of 57 percent. Then it was over, as abruptly as it started. Around the same time, according to later accounts, dead gorillas were seen in the forest too.

Mike Fay isn't the only knowledgeable person inclined to connect Minkébé's apparent gorilla depauperation with Ebola. Down in the Gabonese capital, Libreville, I heard the same idea from a lanky Dutchman named Bas Huijbregts, associated with the World Wildlife Fund's Minkébé Project, who made some of those reconnaissance hikes through the Minkébé forest, gathering both quantified field data and anecdotal testimony. Gorilla nests, he reported, were drastically less abundant than they had been a decade earlier. About the gorillas themselves, he said: "If you talk to all the fishermen, hunters, gold miners, they all have a similar story. Before there were many—and then they started dying off." The apparent population collapse, not just of gorillas but of chimps too, seemed to coincide with the human epidemics. In a hunting camp just north of the Gabonese border someone showed Huijbregts the grave of a man who, so it was said, had died after eating flesh from a gorilla he'd found dead in the forest.

I spoke also with Sally Lahm, an American ecologist who has worked in the region for almost 20 years, studying wildlife and wildlife-human interactions. Lahm has focused especially on the mining camps of the upper Ivindo, where gold comes as precious flecks from buried stream sediments and protein comes as bush meat from the forest. Her study, plus the epidemic events of the mid-1990s, have led her toward Ebola. When the third outbreak occurred, at a logging camp southwest of Minkébé, she went there with several medical people from the Makokou hospital and played a double role, as both nurse and researcher.

"I'm scared to death of Ebola, because I've seen what it can do," Lahm told me. "I've seen it kill people—up close." Fearful or not, she's engrossed by the scientific questions. Where does Ebola lurk between outbreaks? What species in the forest—a small mammal? an insect?—serves as its reservoir host? How does its ecology intersect the ecology of hunters, villagers, and miners? So far, nobody knows.

"It's not a purely human disease," Lahm said. "Humans are the last in the chain of events. I think we should be looking at it as a *wildlife-human* disease." Besides doing systematic field research, she has gathered testimony from hunters, gold miners, survivors of Mayibout II. She has also made field collections of tissue from a whole range of reservoir-candidate species, shipping her specimens off to a virology institute in South Africa for analysis. And she has grown suspicious of one particular species that may be the main transfer agent between the reservoir host and humans—but she declined to tell me what species that is. She needs to do further work, she explained, before further talk.

On the evening of Day 299, at Fay's campfire, I hear more on this subject from one of his crewmen, an affable French-speaking Bantu named Thony M'Both. *Mayibout deux?* Yes, he was there; he recalls the epidemic well. Yes, it began with the chimpanzee. Some boys had gone hunting with their dogs; they were after porcupine, and they found the chimp, already dead. No, they didn't claim they had killed it. The body was rotting, belly swollen, anyone could tell. Many people helped butcher and cook it. Cook it how? In a normal African sauce. All who ate the meat or touched it got sick, according to Thony. Vomiting and diarrhea. Eleven victims were taken downriver to the hospital—only that many, since there wasn't enough fuel to carry everyone. Eighteen stayed in the village, died there, were buried there. Doctors came up from Franceville (in southern Gabon, site of a medical research institute) wearing their white suits and helmets, but so far as Thony could see, they didn't save anyone. His friend Sophiano Etouck lost six family members, including his sister-in-law and three nieces. Sophiano (another of Fay's crew, also here at the campfire) held one niece in his arms as she died, yet he didn't get sick. Nor did Thony himself. He hadn't partaken of the chimp stew. He doesn't eat chimpanzee or gorilla, Thony avers, implying that's by scruple. Nowadays in Mayibout II, however, *nobody* eats chimpanzee. All the boys who went porcupine hunting that day, they all died, yes. The dogs? No, the dogs didn't die.

The campfire chatter around us has stilled. Sophiano himself, a severe-looking Bantu gold miner with a bodybuilder's physique, a black goatee, a sweet disposition, and an anguished stutter, sits quietly while Thony tells the tale.

I ask one final question: Had he ever before seen such a disease? I'm remembering what I've read about horrible, chain-reaction Ebola episodes, with victims bleeding profusely, organ shutdown, chaos and desperate efforts to nurse or mop up, leading only to further infection. "No," Thony answers blandly. "This was the first time."

Thony's body count differs from the careful report in *The Journal of*

Infectious Diseases, so do some other particulars, yet his eyewitness testimony seems utterly real. He's as scared of Ebola as anybody. If he were inventing, he wouldn't invent the chimpanzee's swollen belly. Added to it all, though, is one fact or factoid that he let drop on the first evening I met him—a detail so garish, so perfectly dramatic, that even having heard it from his lips I'm unsure whether to take it literally. Around the same time as the Mayibout epidemic, Thony told me, he and Sophiano saw a whole pile of gorillas, 13 of them, lying dead in the forest.

Anecdotal testimony, even from eyewitnesses, tends to be shimmery, inexact, unreliable. To say *13 dead gorillas* might actually mean a dozen, or lots, too many for a startled brain to count. To say *I saw them* might mean exactly that or possibly less. *My friend saw them, he's unimpeachable.* Or maybe: *I heard about it on pretty good authority.*

Scientific data are something else. They don't shimmer with poetic hyperbole and ambivalence. They are particulate, quantifiable, firm. Fastidiously gathered, rigorously sorted, they can reveal emergent meanings. This is why Mike Fay is walking across central Africa with a little yellow notebook.

After two weeks of bushwhacking through Ebola's backyard, we emerge from the forest onto a red laterite road. Blinking against the sunlight, we find ourselves in a village called Minkouala, at which the dependable Tomo soon arrives with more supplies. Day 307 ends with us camped in a banana grove behind the house of a local official, flanked by a garbage dump and a gas-engine generator. The crew has been given an evening's furlough, and half of them have caught rides into Makokou to chase women and get drunk. By morning one of the Pygmies will be in jail, having expensively busted up a bar, and Fay will be facing a new round of political hassles, personnel crises, and minor ransom demands, a category of inescapable chores he finds far less agreeable than walking through swamp. But somehow he will get the crew moving again. He'll plunge away from the red road, diving back into the universe of green. Meanwhile he spends hours in his tent, collating the latest harvest of data on a laptop.

Within the past 14 days, he informs me, we have stepped across 997 piles of elephant dung and not a single dung pile from a gorilla. We have heard zero gorilla chest-beat displays. We have seen zero sprigs of Marantaceae chewed by gorilla teeth and discarded. These are numbers representing as good a measure as now exists of the mystery of Minkébé.

Measuring the mystery is a crucial first step; solving it is another matter.

I make my departure along the laterite road and then by Cessna from the Makokou airstrip. The pilot who has come to chauffeur me is a young Frenchman named Nicolas Kozon, the same fellow who circled the Green Abyss at low altitude while Tomo tossed bombs of manioc and sardines to Fay and the others below. As we point ourselves toward Libreville now, the road and the villages disappear quickly, leaving Nicolas and me with a limitless vista of green. Below us, around us in all directions to the horizon, there's only canopy and more canopy, magisterial and abstract.

Nicolas is both puzzled and amused by the epic daffiness of the Megatransect, and through our crackly headsets we discuss it. I describe the daily routine, the distances made, the swamps crossed, and what Fay faces from here onward. He'll visit the big waterfalls of the Ivindo River, I say, then turn westward. He'll cross the railroad line and two more roads, but otherwise he'll keep to the forest, following his plotted route, staying as far as possible from human settlements. He can do that all the way to the ocean. He'll cross the Lopé Reserve, yes, and then a big block of little-known terrain around the Massif du Chaillu. Another four months of walking, if all goes well. He's skinny but looks strong. He'll cross the Gamba complex of defunct hunting areas and faunal reserves along the coast, south of Port-Gentil, and break out onto the beach. He expects to get there in late November, I say.

With a flicker of smile, Nicolas asks: "And then will he swim to America?"

Dangerous Medicine

by Tom Clynes

Most people try to stay as far away from the Ebola virus as they can. But each outbreak attracts doctors and researchers who risk their lives to learn more about the mysterious virus. Tom Clynes (born 1961) joined a team of them in November 2000 and brought back this report.

After the sun sets, a distant clanging begins. It starts faintly, a rhythmic din that gets closer and louder. Soon it's joined by deeper drumbeats. At the beginning of the outbreak, the drumming—on pots and pans as well as drums—became a nightly ritual to chase away the Ebola demon. After a few weeks it diminished as the local population began to feel more secure. Now the drumming is back.

Dr. Anthony Sanchez got the news on a Sunday afternoon in mid-October when he stopped by his lab at the Centers for Disease Control and Prevention (CDC), in Atlanta. Sanchez was surprised to find his boss, Pierre Rollin, in the office.

Rollin began by telling Sanchez that he could decline the assignment. After all, Sanchez had a four-month-old daughter at home.

"Feel free to say no, Tony," Rollin said. "But I'm putting together a team to go over and set up a lab; we could use you." This was the first

Sanchez had heard that Ebola, after a four-year respite, had resurfaced, this time in northern Uganda.

Sanchez, 47, had spent much of his career researching the Ebola virus, often in the CDC's maximum-containment lab, protected by a space suit. But he had never seen it operate in a human epidemic. Once, a few years ago, he wondered if he had missed his chance, if it would ever come again.

Now the agency was spread thin, with a team in Saudi Arabia trying to contain an epidemic of Rift Valley fever. And an on-site laboratory could give the Ebola containment operation a tremendous advantage. Sanchez walked to his office and picked up the phone. He dialed his home number and told his wife that there was something he needed to talk about when he got home, something important. The line was silent for several long seconds, and then:

"I'm not going to be happy about this, am I?"

The old Czech prop plane lurches to a halt at the side of the military airstrip; the doctors unfurl their stiff legs, disembark, and begin unloading. They shift 47 boxes—a metric ton of laboratory gear—onto a truck and drive toward town, trailing a spiral of orange dust as they pass army checkpoints and outsize churches, roadside vendors, and crowds of people listening to radios, talking, and singing.

The most surprising thing is how ordinary it all looks, at first. Set in the middle of a fertile, if unrelieved, savanna, the town of Gulu, Uganda, could be any other East African provincial center. Everywhere, people are on the move, some pedaling bikes, others riding on the fringed rear seats of bicycle taxis, most just walking. They walk upright, with stone-straight posture, some carrying babies on their backs, some balancing loads on their heads, some barefoot, others in sandals. They walk—and the doctors drive—past the field where the pope once spoke; past the turnoff that leads to the witch doctor's house; past another road that leads to a small village near the forest, where, maybe, it all started.

It takes a few minutes, as if their eyes were getting used to a new light, before hints begin to emerge that life here is far from normal: There are none of the usual swarms of schoolchildren in uniform. White trucks drive through town, emblazoned with the red crosses and acronyms—UN, WHO, MSF—that portend crisis. The hospital building, where the doctors pull up, is wrapped in white plastic sheeting; a hand-lettered sign warns "No entrance without permission." The sign is illustrated with a crude human figure with an X drawn over it.

Five weeks into the crisis, a crowd of foreigners occupies a government office room in a yellow concrete-block building on the north side of Gulu. Doctors and scientists hunch over notebook computers and speak into walkie-talkies. Amid the babble of languages and accents, an American woman's voice talks into a satellite telephone: "We've got more Ebola-positives in Pabo now—we've got to get on top of this."

Whenever a serious epidemic is confirmed anywhere in the world, an alert goes out to members of the Global Outbreak Alert and Response Network, and scores of doctors, scientists, and humanitarian workers start packing bags and booking flights. The international disease-fighting team assembled to combat the Ebola outbreak in Uganda ultimately numbers more than a hundred professionals from a dozen countries, plus more than a thousand Ugandans. Among them are epidemiologists and virologists, physicians and nurses, laboratory workers, logistics specialists, and educators. Later, they'll be joined by researchers eager to take advantage of a rare opportunity to learn more about a virus that has baffled scientists for 25 years.

The Ebola virus is named after the river in Zaire (now called the Democratic Republic of the Congo) where it was first identified in 1976, during an outbreak that killed 280. Since that epidemic, and a concurrent outbreak in Sudan, the disease has struck in Côte d'Ivoire, again in Sudan and Congo, and three times in Gabon. Ebola is one of the deadliest, most infectious pathogens known to man; once in the bloodstream, it wipes out the immune system within a matter of days, causing high fever, vomiting, diarrhea, and, in a small but well-publicized number of cases, uncontrolled bleeding. There is no cure and no effective treatment. No one knows its natural host—the organism it usually infects—and no one knows why or how it sometimes leaps into the human realm.

Right now, though, the focus is not on solving Ebola's mysteries. Right now, everyone in this room has only one goal: to stop the epidemic.

The woman on the satellite phone, Cathy Roth, a 47-year-old physician with the World Health Organization (WHO), is currently coordinating the containment operation. She hangs up, and I walk over to introduce myself. When I extend my hand, she throws both of hers over her head in a "Don't shoot!" gesture.

"Uh, we're not actually doing that anymore," Roth says, smiling down at my retreating hand. Ebola is spread through contact with bodily fluids, including sweat. And although it's unlikely that either of us is carrying the virus, people are avoiding handshakes like . . . well, like the plague.

A dozen or so exhausted-looking professionals trudge in for Roth's afternoon update meeting. "Everyone's getting really tired now," she tells me. "We were thinking we had it under control, and I was thinking about giving the mobile teams a Sunday off. After five weeks of 24-7, they're at risk of making mistakes and they need rest." But now Roth is worried that the illness is flaring up again, threatening to break through the containment operation.

In the past, Ebola has struck only in rural areas, and the disease's rapid death sequence has actually worked in favor of containment, since infected people couldn't travel far before they succumbed. But the Gulu area is densely populated, with transport links to East Africa's major cities—and, from there, to anywhere in the world. No one in this room is interested in finding out what might happen if they were to give the virus a chance to take advantage of these more favorable conditions.

CDC medical epidemiologist Scott Harper begins the meeting with bad news from Pabo, a refugee camp north of Gulu. "A woman came into the clinic last Sunday and miscarried, and there was a lot of hemorrhaging," he says. "No one knew she was Ebola-positive, and she spent at least two days in the maternity ward, bleeding."

His colleague Marta Guerra picks up the story: "She had five women in the maternity ward with her, plus at least 15 visitors. Eleven nurses and other workers were exposed before they got her isolated. So far, we've taken blood from all but one."

Roth tucks her hair behind her ears. "This thing has the potential to blow up into a huge problem," she says.

A few blocks from the international team's headquarters, a teenage boy motions for me to follow him. "Miracle," he says, and he leads me into a crowd gathered at a gate, peering into a brown-dirt courtyard. In the shade of a sprawling tree, a woman sits in a plastic chair, her head arched backward. Eyes wide and teary, she stares into the branches while another woman cuts her hair, felling the thin braids with slow, deliberate snips of the scissors.

A preacher stands in front of her, aiming a video camera with his outstretched left hand, rocking back and forth as he calls out a surreal narration: "She was mentally deranged for 12 years," he says. "She was possessed by evil powers. The family took her to many witch doctors, but the demon inside would not relent."

He turns toward the crowd. "We prayed and we urged her to surrender her witch doctor gadgets. And now, look at her!" The woman smiles and sobs silently as her braids fall. "Look at her!" the preacher says, his voice rising. "The Lord has rescued her from demonic oppression!"

Watching the faces in the crowd, I have no doubt that everyone wants to believe that a miracle—be it religion, witchcraft, or science—could defeat a demon. But the woman's gaze remains unsettled, and her eyes dart tentatively, searching among the branches.

Dr. Simon Mardel enters the dressing room outside the isolation ward at St. Mary's Lacor Hospital and pulls a full-length surgical smock over his head. He stretches a first layer of gloves over the top of the smock's tight elastic cuffs, then he pulls knee-high gum boots over his feet and tucks in his pants. He puts on a paper shower cap and a thick plastic surgical apron, then a second pair of gloves and a mask. Just before he walks through the first of two disinfectant boot baths, he places the final protective barrier—goggles—over his eyes.

An expert in emergency and refugee health care, Marcel had taken a leave of absence from his duties as an emergency room physician in England's Lake District to assist at a recent epidemic of another highly contagious hemorrhagic fever—Marburg—in Congo. He was on his way home in October when he was diverted to Gulu. A few years earlier, during the war in Bosnia, Mardel hiked into Srebrenica to treat wounded civilians while the city was under siege—a heroic action that earned him the Order of the British Empire for humanitarianism.

Mardel arrived in Gulu with the first WHO team and took charge of the isolation wards, calmly demonstrating barrier-nursing techniques to terrified hospital workers. "Remember," the clear-eyed 43-year-old told a group of nurses and nuns, "the system is only as strong as its weakest moment."

Mardel enters the suspect ward, set aside for people who are symptomatic but unconfirmed as Ebola-positive. In one corner of the room, a male patient lies sideways on a bed, coughing and moaning. He holds a wad of tissues to his nose, which streams with black blood. He seems utterly indifferent to the doctor's presence.

"We'll get some blood from him," Mardel says, and the patient offers his arm weakly to the needle.

The Lacor hospital is well endowed and well equipped by African standards, and its wood-trimmed wards and array of diagnostic equipment stand in contrast to the bare concrete of the government-run Gulu Hospital, across town, where doctors scrounge for basic supplies. In the mission-hospital tradition, Lacor's care is intensive and hands-on. Because of the vomiting, diarrhea, and hemorrhaging, Ebola patients need massive care; at Lacor, nurses and nuns are responsible for everything from mopping up to helping patients die with as much dignity as possible.

Inside the isolation ward, health workers are fully enveloped in protective gear; their goggled eyes are their only semirecognizable features. To aid identification, many have scrawled their names with markers on the fronts of their white plastic surgical aprons.

Mardel spots an apron across the room labeled "Dr. Matthew" and heads over to a corner where Matthew Lukwiya is treating an Ebola-stricken nurse. Lukwiya, 42, Lacor's medical superintendent, had been on leave in Kampala, 200 miles south of Gulu, where he received word of "a strange new illness" making its way through the hospital's wards. He immediately left his wife and five children in the capital and drove up to Gulu. Within two days of his arrival, 17 people—including three nurses—were dead or dying with the same dire symptoms.

"At first it looked like some sort of super-malaria," he says. "But the patients did not respond to quinine treatment, and it was killing people very quickly." He began flirting with the possibility that one of the rare diseases of the filovirus family, Ebola or the somewhat less deadly Marbug, might have come in from Sudan or Congo. However unlikely this diagnosis—Ebola had never been seen in Uganda—he sent samples off to a laboratory in Johannesburg. Three days before the results were due, Lukwiya concluded that all signs were pointing to the worst possible scenario—Ebola—and that he needed to act immediately. He stayed up all night reading a manual titled "Infection Control for Viral Hemorrhagic Fevers in the African Health Care Setting," downloaded from the Internet. In the morning, he and his staff started setting up a barrier-nursing environment, using whatever resources were on hand. They built hands-free boot removers from scrap wood and constructed an incinerator out of a 55-gallon drum. They fashioned aprons from duct tape and plastic sheeting and converted a hospital pavilion into an isolation ward. Then, from behind these crude protective layers, they began nursing Ebola patients.

Through the goggles, Mardel's eyes meet Lukwiya's, which are heavy with concern. The nurse he is treating is in critical condition.

"If she dies," Lukwiya says, "she will be our seventh."

• • •

In the morning, volunteer James Kidega reports to the Red Cross office, where a map hangs on one wall, dotted with pushpins: green for refugee camps, red for land mine sites, pink for recent ambushes. Since the mid-1980s, a nebulous guerrilla force known as the Lord's Resistance Army (LRA), whose stated objective is to carve a Christian state out of Uganda, has terrorized the region's civilian population. To protect their children at night, when the rebels usually operate, most of the rural population has moved into refugee camps near Ugandan army barracks. Every day since the containment operation began, scores of Red Cross volunteers have fanned out to these "protected villages" to follow up on Ebola rumors, call for ambulances, educate the populace, and relay information about hospitalized relatives and neighbors.

Before the epidemic hit, the 25-year-old Kidega had worked at a charitable agency that helps children who have escaped from the rebels. Because of his extensive contacts in the villages and his polished demeanor—he is rarely seen without a clean shirt and necktie—Kidega was recruited as a volunteer leader.

Today, he will lead a team that will visit two villages north of Gulu. With red-and-white flags flying, two trucks set out. As Kidega guides the trucks north, he recalls the first few days of the epidemic. At Gulu's two hospitals, he says, many nurses and orderlies stopped coming to work, fearing that they might be assigned to the isolation wards, and some international agencies based in Gulu left town. In the villages surrounding Gulu, rumors of sorcery circulated as entire families were wiped out. In Rwot Obilo village, the virus moved through one family so quickly that a dying woman told her young grandson, moments after his mother's death, "Suck your mother's last milk so you, too, can die—there is no one here to look after you now."

"It felt like being on a sinking ship," Kidega says. "You can't believe the fear." Some victims swarmed the hospitals; others ran away in panic as nurses fell ill all around them. Even the rebels were spooked; the LRA released 40 prisoners, fearing that they might be carrying the virus.

When the trucks pull into Akwayugi, villagers look up from their work of sifting maize and wheat. This isn't as bad as sub-Saharan Africa gets, but there's serious squalor here. About a fifth of the children have the bulging bellies that indicate severe malnutrition.

The Red Cross volunteers divide into four-person teams and move through the village, asking questions of the small crowds that gather wherever they go: Has anyone had a fever? Has anyone had bloody diarrhea or vomit? Was there a sudden death?

The team has a "reintegration kit" for two girls who survived Ebola after they lost their mother to the disease. They find them with their father, Charles Odongo, outside the family's round, mud-brick hut. Two weeks earlier, Odongo returned from the fields to find his wife in the hut with a headache and a high fever. "It took six hours for the ambulance to get here," he says. "By the time they arrived, she had died." When he sees the kit—cooking pots, blankets, soap, salt, and clothing—he smiles gratefully. "Immediately after we left for the hospital with my wife's body, our things were burned by the neighbors," he says.

Although the Ebola-Zaire strain can kill nearly 90 percent of its victims, the Gulu virus is similar to the less lethal Sudan strain, which has a mortality rate of about 50 percent. Odongo's three-year-old daughter, Skovia, survived the disease that killed her mother. "You should not fear her," a volunteer says to a circle of onlookers. "This is not a contagious little girl." The motherless girl seems to brighten when she sees the dress the team has brought for her, but her nine-month-old sister, Geoffrey, clings to her father listlessly. She's severely malnourished, weakened by the disease, and silent except for an occasional phlegmy cough. It's hard to imagine her making it to her first birthday.

On the way back to town, Kidega stops by his mother's house for a cup of tea. "James," his mother asks him, putting the kettle on the stove, "why so many coffins passing by here today?"

"It's going up again," Kidega says. "We were beginning to think it was nearly over, that they would reopen the schools, but I think now they will wait. People are hiding the facts. They think they will be shunned."

"Why don't they put the coffins inside when they transport them?" she asks. "This is making people very nervous." As she pours the tea, her 20-year-old niece, Sarah, walks in.

"This Ebola, I wish we could see it," Sarah says, clucking her tongue. "If we could see it, then we could beat it to death, with a stick."

Later, Kidega's radio crackles. A teenage girl has run into the clinic in Pabo, terrified of bleeding that would turn out to be nothing more than her first menstrual period. There's gunfire on the road near the Lacor hospital. And north of Gulu, a soldier in an armored personnel carrier has broken out in a fever and is vomiting red inside the vehicle. The other soldiers have run away.

"Can you send an isolation ambulance?" the military commander pleads.

Saturday morning at the hospital guest house, Tony Sanchez and Pierre Rollin are finishing breakfast in the dining room, getting ready to suit up for the lab. Since arriving in Gulu, they've been occupied controlling the outbreak; they're hoping to soon shift their focus to research.

"You can't do productive field research on Ebola when it vanishes," says Rollin. "So you need to get the information when you can."

Researchers at the National Institutes of Health recently announced progress in developing an Ebola vaccine that works in monkeys, but the virus's underlying logic is still beyond the reach of science. Since coming to the world's attention in 1976, the disease has baffled a generation of researchers, who have collected hundreds of thousands of specimens from plants, animals, and insects. Humans are what research virologists like Sanchez and Rollin call "accidental hosts" for the Ebola virus. "We don't know where it hides," Rollin says. "It may turn out to be something right under our noses. There are different schools of thought. Some say it is carried by rodents, or insects, or bats. . . ."

At that moment, as if summoned, Bob Swanepoel strides into the dining room, decked out in a khaki bush-hunter outfit. Swanepoel is a bat man. The director of the Special Pathogens Unit of the South

African Institute for Virology in Johannesburg, the goateed, 64-year-old veterinarian has made a career out of tramping into Africa's remote jungles, looking for the natural reservoirs of Ebola and other hemorrhagic fevers.

"He's at every outbreak," says Rollin. Over the past 20 years, the 47-year-old Rollin and Swanepoel have developed a bond that's fed by a shared fascination for viral diseases. When they're not working together at an outbreak, they communicate over the phone, from Atlanta to Johannesburg, at least once a week.

Swanepoel was in Saudi Arabia at the Rift Valley—fever epidemic when the first samples of Ebola-infected blood, sent by Lukwiya, arrived at his Johannesburg lab. Now he has finally made it to Gulu, along with two assistants and several bundles of nets and poles. "Pierre told me not to come," he says, settling in at Rollin's table. "He said there is nothing here, that we're too far downstream in the epidemic. But what do you do when you hear that? Do you stay home? No, you have to see for yourself."

Swanepoel is eager to do some reservoir hunting, but his bat-nabbing nets remain bundled outside his room. "Right now," he says, "there are several hurdles. First, I need to know the focal point before I start trapping. Did one person get it first, or were there a lot of people who separately picked up this thing from nature? It's the Sudan strain of Ebola, but was it brought in by a rebel from Sudan, or did it start near here? Northern Uganda and southern Sudan have roughly the same terrain and ecology, and the entire region is like a Bermuda Triangle of filoviruses. We're close to the Ebola River, to Durba, Mount Elgon, Kitum Cave—all the hotbeds of Marburg and Ebola.

"The second hurdle is, I need approval. You go out in a place like this without approval, and the next thing you know you're into ten kinds of sh—. We got arrested in Congo, and it took half a day before they tracked down the colonel to vouch for us. He was at a brothel.

"Third, there are security issues. It's best to work at night, but . . ."

Rollin finishes Swanepoel's sentence: "But if you put a net up at night, you're more likely to catch a rebel than a reservoir."

Rollin often raises an eyebrow when he talks, which gives him a wryly comical look. "What I would like to know," Rollin says, "is did somebody do something in the bush that people don't normally do? Something seemed to be happening in September, before Matthew arrived. There was a lot of diarrhea, and rumors about some unusual malaria in a certain village. What you want to find is, was there a village where it started? But because of stigma, and because so much time has passed and so many people are dead, you don't get the straight story."

As Rollin talks, a dark spot forms above his left eyebrow. No one says anything, but in a minute Rollin feels the liquid as it starts to run down his forehead. He wipes it with his index finger.

"Hmm. It's blood. Very strange. I don't think I cut myself here. And I haven't shaved my forehead lately."

He wipes it away. When it keeps coming, he gets up and grabs a tissue. He succeeds in stanching the flow and sits back down. All conversation has stopped.

"Maybe I have started to bleed with Ebola a new way," he says, smiling as he raises an eyebrow. And everyone laughs.

Nervously.

After breakfast, Tony Sanchez walks out of the Lacor guest house, toward the lab. An ambulance pulls around the corner, and Sanchez averts his eyes as an Ebola suspect is led into the ward.

"What we don't experience up in Atlanta is the wards, the bleeding," he says. "I talked to Pierre about what to expect, but to tell you the truth, I've never seen large numbers of people dead and dying before— and the way they suffer. . . . During the day, you're doing your job, and you don't think about it. But at night, you see their faces. Your subconscious comes up with questions you can't answer."

Brother Elio Croce calls Sanchez's name and trots over. A Verona missionary who runs Lacor's technical and transportation services, Brother Elio, 54, is a plump Sean Connery look-alike with a compassionate demeanor that's balanced by a cranky sanctimoniousness.

"Tony, I need to take you out to Bardege Village," Elio says, "to get blood and a skin sample for a biopsy from a little girl who just died. We need to get there before they bury her."

I introduce myself to Elio and extend my hand—it's amazing just how reflexive the custom is. Before I realize my mistake, Elio reaches out, grabs my hand, and looks me straight in the eye. "We're not shaking hands here anymore," he says, shaking my hand. "There's an Ebola epidemic going on here you know."

Actually, the Gulu epidemic was initially spread more by contact with the dead than with the living. According to local ritual, a dead body stays in the house for a day or two while extended family and friends wash the corpse, eat and drink, and wash hands in a communal basin. Then they bury the body next to the house. ("For you, the dead take care of themselves," James Kidega says. "For us, we take care of the dead.")

The viral count is at its peak in a just expired body, but despite the risk and despite an aggressive education campaign, it's been extremely difficult to get people to stop customs that have been entrenched for generations. For that reason, health workers have encouraged residents to report deaths in neighboring families.

Sanchez grabs his gear, and we jump into a truck with Elio. As the clergyman drives, he talks nonstop in a singsongy Italian accent that seems incongruous with the content of his monologue: "The nurse, Grace Akulu, died. She was conscious until the very end—it's not true that everyone is demented in the final stages. She died singing; she never feared to encounter our Lord. We buried her behind the hospital in a beautiful ceremony. I have tape-recorded the singing. I will play it for you later."

"I thought it was supposed to be slowing down," Sanchez says.

"I do not think it is slowing down now," Elio says. "Tomorrow, we have to dig more graves."

With the isolation ambulance trailing, Elio turns off the road and drives through the elephant grass, following a single-track trail that terminates in a tidy dirt courtyard surrounded by a half dozen round mud-brick huts with thatched roofs.

The deceased girl's name is Sunday Onen; she was two years old. Her mother sits next to two other women, who are nursing young children; her grandfather, Peter Ola, talks to Sanchez and Elio.

"The child was healthy," Ola says incredulously. "She ate breakfast around nine, then she had a fever and began vomiting. When her diarrhea became bloody, my daughter began to carry her to the hospital. But midway, she did not cry out any longer, so she brought her back here."

Ebola doesn't usually work that quickly, but there are enough Ebola symptoms that it must be treated as a suspect case. The villagers watch in silence as Sanchez suits up; the three ambulance crew members stand in the sun, sweating inside their protective clothing.

As Sanchez bends down and leans into the hut, Brother Elio pulls out his tape recorder and begins a peculiar commentary.

"He's down on one knee, entering the hut. Yes, that's it, careful."

Encumbered by the hut's darkness and his layers of protective gear, Sanchez draws blood and cuts a skin sample from the tiny corpse. It takes longer than it should, because the lab has run out of biopsy punches, devices that work like high-tech cookie cutters to neatly remove a small patch of skin. He has to tug the girl's skin up, then make the cut with surgical scissors, working slowly, with full awareness of the consequences of even the smallest nick to his hands.

"He's down on both knees now," Elio continues. "Respect. Respect."

Sanchez backs out of the hut and straightens up, breathing hard through his surgical mask. He walks to the center of the clearing and lays out a sheet of white cloth, then he kneels down to pack the specimens. An ambulance crew member comes over with a garden-pump dispenser of disinfectant and sprays the bottoms of Sanchez's feet. Then the sprayer follows the other two crew members into the hut. Sanchez stands up just as the crew emerges, carrying a small white bundle.

"My God," Sanchez says. "I thought this was going to be an easy day." His right hand is twitching.

As the body is brought to the ambulance, the villagers suddenly become agitated. They gather around Brother Elio, talking to him in the Acholi language. Elio approaches Sanchez.

"See the problem now, Tony," he says, "there's been a misunderstanding. They thought that we would come out and test the girl, and if it wasn't Ebola, we would leave her here for them to bury her according to tradition."

Sanchez does his best to explain that he needs to bring the blood back to the lab to test for the Ebola antibody. The test takes several hours, and it may not be conclusive. They need to send the skin samples away for testing in Atlanta. In the meantime, the whole village may be vulnerable to infection until the body is taken away and buried at the isolation graveyard.

After a few minutes, the villagers stop talking; they just stare at Sanchez, the white man in the white suit insisting that their loved one be sent off to the afterlife unprepared, buried as if she had never lived at all. There is no actual threat—apart from the threat of having to remember these faces for the rest of a lifetime.

Sanchez takes Elio aside, and the two men's roles flip-flop. Sanchez, the scientist, wants to compromise, to humanize the rules. The body was in good condition, he says. It may not have been Ebola. Maybe it was a snakebite. . . .

"But the grandfather said she did not cry out," Elio says sharply. Sanchez's hand twitches again.

"What are we going to do?" he asks.

"We're not going to do anything," Elio snaps. His face is pinched, and the words come out that way, in a clipped staccato. "We can't let them bury her here. They will not do it the way we want."

Sanchez and Elio move toward the truck, and the villagers follow, forming a crescent around the front of the vehicle, continuing to stare as the two men get in.

It feels as if the air had been sucked out of the sky.

Elio starts the truck and shifts it into reverse. He begins to let out the clutch—then he stops.

"Hey," he says, looking at Sanchez. "What do you think? We let them bury her here. We stay, we supervise, they dig the grave very fast. It's more human, no?"

In an instant, they're out of the truck. Elio makes the announcement, and the dirt starts flying, with Sunday's father, who can't be more than 17 years old, leading the dig. A half hour later, the hole is completed, six feet deep. The ambulance crew lowers Sunday Onen's body gently into the ground.

Saturday evening, the team gathers in the courtyard at the Acholi Inn, tucked behind the roofless carcass of a burned-out building on the northern edge of town. Under a canopy of trees thick enough to block a light rain, a waitress runs back and forth with food and rounds of the local beer, Nile Special, politely requesting that the foreigners not lean back on the rear legs of the fragile plastic chairs. As the shadows lengthen, monkeys and an occasional rat scurry around the garden's perimeter; after sunset, bats swoop among the overhead branches.

Even the Nobel Peace Prize—winning Doctors Without Borders (Médecins Sans Frontières) is perennially short of recruits who are willing to turn their backs on comfortable, lucrative careers to come to needy places like Gulu, where the patient-to-doctor ratio approaches 18,000 to 1. (In the United States, it's around 400 to 1.) Yet despite the high stress and low comfort, despite the sound of machine gun fire in the night, everyone seems to feel privileged to be here.

"I had been wanting to do something like this since I was a teenager," says Patricia Campbell, an American physician with Doctors Without Borders. "I saw medicine as a passport to the world. But then I got married and had children, so I had to put it off until my kids were older." Now in her mid-60s, Campbell says she's "addicted."

"I go home to Scarsdale [New York], and I wonder how anyone can stand it, treating rich kids for tonsillitis. After a few weeks, I'm saying, 'Get me out of here!'"

The obvious question: Are you afraid?

"No," Campbell says flatly. "You follow protocol. Unless you're in direct contact with body fluids, you won't get Ebola."

Murmurs of agreement wash over the table. "If there was that high of a risk," says Simon Mardel, "I wouldn't be here."

Of course, playing down the risks is a coping mechanism, a way of keeping panic at bay. Like cigarette smoking or gallows humor, denial keeps you functioning effectively in the presence of danger and death—whether you're a doctor in a plague zone or a soldier in a battle zone.

For all the talk about managing risk, though, the odds don't look very good for medical people in their ongoing battle with the Ebola virus. In the 1995 Ebola outbreak in Congo, 80 medical workers became infected; 63 died. Hospitals—especially deprived African hospitals—provide an ideal environment for the virus to prosper, and health workers are vulnerable targets because of their close contact with bodily fluids. Ebola does not forgive even the smallest mistake.

On Sunday morning, grief takes a holiday. James Kidega walks through the double doors of Christ Church and joins the congregation in the throes of a full-blown dance party. At the front of the low altar, a band of musicians strum on stringed gourd instruments; they're nearly drowned out by a platoon of drummers, whacking away in a polyrhythmic fury. Around the musicians and into the back pews, people of all ages pogo up and down, driven in a raucous call-and-response by a young woman croaking through a distorted sound system.

"The love of Jesus has taken away the sins of the people," she sings.

"Evil can't touch us!" the dancers cry.

Outside his guest room in a wooded corner of the Lacor hospital compound, Bob Swanepoel slouches in a chair, flinging pebbles into the trees with a wrist-rocket slingshot. Nearby Pierre Rollin sits on the concrete floor of the patio, his back against the door, his legs stretched in front of him. Someone brings over a straw-colored fruit bat killed by a local boy, and Swanepoel perks up.

"These things are vicious," Swanepoel says, spreading the bat's wings. "Look at these teeth, and these claws—they're like razors. They'll go after you like a dog." He asks one of his researchers to put it in the refrigerator, along with a cobra that was killed on the Lacor grounds yesterday after menacing some nurses.

Swanepoel's bat-trapping expedition has been approved, but he's pessimistic about what the fieldwork might turn up. If you don't know where the epidemic started, he says, "it's a shot in the dark."

"Also," he says, "we've learned that the caves in the Kalak Hills aren't what we thought they were. Apparently, there are lots of very narrow caves that are difficult and dangerous to navigate. Maybe we can go up to the top and drop the nets—I don't know."

Elio rides up on his bike. He wants Rollin to test him for Ebola.

"That will be the third time you've been tested," says Rollin. "You keep thinking you're infected."

"We lost another nurse today," Elio says. "That makes eight, plus a nurse's boyfriend. We can't figure out how the boyfriend was exposed, since the nurse did not get Ebola. He was a young man, and strong. At the end, he told me he wanted to get married before he died, so I got the priest and sent for the girl. But as she was on her way here, we realized that we had time only to give him his last sacraments. When she arrived, the father went out to meet her." Elio pauses.

"He told her that he had already left for the long safari."

At headquarters, Cathy Roth comes outside and announces that she's "canceled the cancellation of this afternoon's meeting." Everyone troops inside.

There have been five deaths today so far. The CDC's Scott Harper reports that six people were admitted yesterday, and they aren't on any contact lists. "People seem to be hiding family members," he says. "The system seems to be breaking down. In Atiak, a suspect was buried, and no one got a specimen."

In Pabo, some recovering patients have been lost. At Gulu Hospital, an Ebola-positive patient "escaped" last night. (He later turned up at Lacor.) As for the infected woman who miscarried, there are now 32 contacts, including 11 health-care workers. After her procedure, two deliveries were performed on the same table.

Dr. Paul Onek, the district health director, gives voice to everyone's frustration. "If we have escaped patients, if we are not even able to take specimens from deceased people, then we are back to square one." He is silent for half a minute, then he speaks. "Yesterday, we breathed a sigh of relief. But now . . ." He purses his lips and sighs. There's no relief in it.

After the church service, James Kidega travels past the field where the pope spoke. He approaches a cluster of huts. The witch doctor, Abodtu, is in, although the authorities ordered him to remove his "traditional African healing" banner after a witch doctor in Rwot Obilo treated—and possibly infected—up to 30 people before dying of Ebola.

But Abodtu doesn't claim to cure Ebola—at least, not yet.

"Right now, I have no medicine for this," he says, lighting a candle inside his hut. "I cure people who are lame or berserk. I make the leg stop swelling and the brain start working. Or I send death to someone who has done wrong to your family.

"As for the white man's medicine and the white man's religion, I do not cross there. *This* is what I know." He sweeps his eyes over his altar—a clutter of beads and bones, snake skins and rattles, jugs and strings of shells.

Where does Ebola come from?

"I have asked my bad-thing where it came from. The spirit tells me to wait for instructions, then to go to the forest and look up to a special big tree. This tree has the answer; it will tell me where it comes from." He inhales deeply. "I will look up to the tree, and I will learn from the tree how to stop it."

Dr. Mike Ryan arrives from London, and three-quarters of the international team and seemingly half the town converge in the headquarters' parking lot within minutes to welcome him. A WHO medical officer, Ryan, 36, led the first team to hit the ground in Gulu, and he spent the next four weeks coordinating the operation before being summoned to London to represent the WHO at an infectious-disease conference. Now he's back, and with his long red sideburns bursting out from under his baseball cap he jumps from a rented van and immediately starts greeting people with big handshakes and bear hugs.

Suddenly, the energy seems cranked up.

"We managed to convince ourselves that it was under control," Ryan says, torching a cigarette as he addresses a group of mobile-team members. "Everyone's getting lethargic and exhausted. But we've got 17 people in the hospital now, and four new ones already today. We've got 45,000 people living in Pabo, and we can't afford to let it go. We can't take our eyes off the ball."

Waving his arms and bellowing, Ryan manages to get his audience guffawing, then he springs onto the porch. Just before dashing into the room, he turns and yells back at the group, loud enough for the entire parking lot to hear: "Let's keep our boots down on the neck of this bastard!"

At noon, Bob Swanepoel's team finally rolls out of Gulu for the Kalak Hills, escorted by 13 soldiers and an armored personnel carrier. They drive along the dirt roads, between walls of eight-foot-tall elephant grass, dodging bicyclists and pedestrians. Arriving at the refugee camp of Guruguru, Swanepoel negotiates with the villagers—two of whom say they dined on bats earlier that day—and sets out with a team of bat hunters and porters. In a scene that's vaguely reminiscent of some Great White Hunter epic, Swanepoel's party—soldiers, hunters, porters, and scientists—trudges over the hills toward the Kalak caves, trailed by an enthusiastic swarm of village children.

"It's very unlikely that we'll turn anything up," Swanepoel says, wiping sweat off his forehead as he walks. "You could test 100,000 bats for a virus before you find it; that's the sort of job we face."

Swanepoel decided a few years ago to shift his gaze upward, to arboreal virus carriers such as bats and canopy-dwelling insects, after exhaustive tests on ground-dwelling animals failed to reveal anything conclusive.

"At several points," he says, "bats have figured prominently in outbreaks of Ebola and Marburg. In some of those incidents, so have monkeys and chimps—but they died just like humans, so they can't be the reservoir. It has to be something that can carry Ebola without coming to harm. In the lab, when we injected Ebola into bats, we found that it could grow to a very high concentration, but it did not kill them. In fact, some of them excreted virus in their feces."

Arriving at the caves, Swanepoel assembles the lab on a large rock. The caves are narrow and steep, and the locals have been climbing in on rope ladders and using thorny branches to hook bats. But it's dangerous work; in the past year, more than ten residents of Guruguru have died in the caves, most by falling off the ladders. It's agreed that the bat hunters will work only in the most accessible caves to lessen the chance of anyone getting hurt. They head into the caverns, outfitted with nets and instructions to bring the animals back alive.

In Congo, Swanepoel used huge nets mounted on bamboo poles; in Gabon, he hunted with slingshots and live traps; in Côte d'Ivoire, he ascended elaborate walkways built in the treetops. He has used UV-light traps and fogging machines to collect insects. But today the expedition is decidedly low-tech, with teenage hunters wielding simple nets. As they bring in the bats, Swanepoel extracts vials of blood and puts the bodies in a freezer box for later dissection.

After four hours, the sun is moving toward the horizon, and the army commander indicates that it's time to go. The hunters have collected only nine bats, and Swanepoel is clearly disappointed. "To do this properly, you need hundreds, and you should really work at night. Like I said, it's a shot in the dark. I doubt we'll find anything—but we'll be back."

When the convoy pulls into town at dusk, Ryan and Kidega come out to the office parking lot, looking relieved. All afternoon, they've monitored radio reports of an ambush near where the expedition was working. The rebels attacked a vehicle, blowing it up with a rocket-propelled grenade, killing three people.

Just past sunset, most of the team gathers in the Acholi Inn courtyard.

After dinner, they linger under the trees, drinking Nile Specials and occasionally getting scolded for leaning on the hind legs of the chairs. The talk gets around to the first few days of the epidemic.

"This is the one that could have gotten away," Ryan says. "And it still might. But if we manage to contain it, we've got Matthew [Lukwiya] to thank. By the time we got here he was already mobilizing the community and building a containment operation, and that gave us a head start we haven't had in other outbreaks."

Looking back, Ryan says he's amazed by Lukwiya's instincts: "Ebola isn't the first thing you'd think about here; it's not even the tenth thing. But Matthew put two and two together—and he got *shite* for an answer. Had he not taken action when he did, I don't know what would have happened."

By all accounts, though, the first few days were shambolic. When Ryan arrived, he found Gulu in the grip of panic. Immediately, he began coordinating the multiagency, multilingual war against the virus, cracking jokes and chain-smoking cigarettes, winning the confidence and support of local health officials and military personnel. "We needed to train, to get equipment, to get people off 24-hour shifts," he says. "We stopped all IV interventions and cut down admissions to only the most life threatening. We needed to get simple things right, like standardizing disinfectant mixes and training people to use the protective gear."

Ryan orders another round. "When we arrived," he says, "there were bodies piling up at the morgue. It's an old brick building that sits in the middle of a field on the outskirts of town, like something out of a 19th-century horror story."

Once an isolation graveyard was established, several military personnel were assigned the grim, dangerous task of burying the highly contagious bodies.

"The first guys," says Simon Mardel, "when they saw us coming with the bodies, they ran away. We were yelling, 'Hey, at least leave your shovels!'"

"They were terrified," says Ryan. "They were convinced they'd get

Ebola if they got anywhere within an arse's roar of the virus. Simon and I realized that we couldn't expect them to do it if we weren't willing to do it ourselves. So we suited up and jumped in with the shovels. We were trying to joke with the fellows—saying things like, 'Hey, you just volunteered for the graveyard shift'—but they were pretty grim at first. In the end, though, they became the Olympic burial team; we wouldn't have had a prayer without them."

The next day, Mardel joins Lukwiya for rounds in the Lacor isolation ward. The two play a "good cop, bad cop" routine as they urge the more coherent patients to drink their rehydrating fluid. The majority of Ebola victims die of shock due to fluid loss; aggressive hydration is the only real treatment available for the disease.

Among the most serious cases on the ward are several nurses. Despite efforts to improve staff safety procedures and reduce fatigue, Lacor's nurses continue to get infected. But Marcel has a plan, and he tries to convince Lukwiya to buy into it.

"From now on, how about if we have the mobile teams bring all the new cases from the community to Gulu Hospital, to give your people a rest? We could still treat existing patients at Lacor, until they die or recover, and let self-referrals choose their hospital. That way, we keep all avenues of admission open."

Lukwiya says he'll consider it, but the following morning dawns with more bad news. Two nurses and a nun have died during the night, and the surviving medical-ward nurses walk out in frustration, grief, and terror. They assemble in a meeting hall and send for Lukwiya.

Lukwiya is calm and resolute as he walks into the room. For the past 17 years, he has been the stabilizing force at Lacor, the gentle but unyielding leader who has refused to let a civil war, a lack of resources, or anything else get in the way of helping his patients. A few years ago, on Good Friday, a band of rebels came to the hospital to take nurses as hostages. Lukwiya stepped forward and persuaded the guerrillas to take him instead. He spent a week on the move with them, treating their wounded soldiers, before they let him go.

Lukwiya tells the nurses of the plan to shift the bulk of the isolation work to Gulu Hospital and of his efforts to convince the government to provide hardship pay and compensation to the families of fallen nurses. He reemphasizes the need for full vigilance and adherence to the barrier-nursing techniques, especially at night, when tired workers are more likely to let down their guard.

"Those who want to leave, can leave," he finally says. "As for me, I will not betray my profession."

Lukwiya's words and the afternoon funerals, which take place in a downpour with lots of singing and praying, have a calming effect. The nurses return to work.

Lukwiya has seen more than a hundred Ebola patients, but none have developed the relatively rare severe hemorrhagic form of Ebola. Unfortunately, one of his nurses, 32-year-old Simon Ojok, is the first. Sanchez, who had begun to think that the stories of spectacular bleeding were "a bunch of crap," now sees it with his own eyes.

Ojok's condition deteriorates quickly, and in the middle of the night he starts thrashing in his bed, pulling off his oxygen mask and spraying bright-red, oxygen-saturated blood all around him. He stumbles out of bed, and, as night-shift nurse Stanley Babu pleads with him to stay put, Ojok walks out of the room, tearing away from his IV tube. Agitated and mumbling, Ojok stands in the hallway, coughing infectious blood and mucous onto the walls and floor. Terrified, Babu runs to Lukwiya's quarters and wakes him.

"Blood is pouring from his eyes and nose like tap water," Babu tells Lukwiya. "He is confused, fighting death. We are afraid to take him back to bed because he seems violent."

Lukwiya sprints across the compound and hurries into the dressing room. He can hear the commotion through the wall as he pulls on his gown, his boots, his apron. Then his mask, his cap, his two pairs of gloves. He does not put on his goggles.

When Lukwiya enters the room, Ojok has stumbled back into bed and is gasping for breath, wrapped in his blood-soaked gown and sheets. Lukwiya props him up to help him breathe and changes his gown and bedding. Just past dawn, as Lukwiya is mopping the floor, Ojok dies.

A few days later, Lukwiya sends for Rollin and Sanchez. Could they please come to his office—and could they bring their blood-sampling gear?

When they arrive, Lukwiya is calm. "I've developed a fever," he says. Rollin tells him that it's probably just the flu or malaria, nothing to worry about.

Rollin draws Lukwiya's blood, then heads to the lab, where he changes into a respirator suit with a battery-powered filter unit. He centrifuges the blood and generates a master plate, then dispenses a measured amount of the sample into the dimpled well of the plate. Pausing often to wipe the sweat from his face with the inside of his cloth hood, he deposits and rinses the various agents—among them are mouse and rabbit antibodies, horseradish peroxidase, and skim milk—in a strict order. Finally, some five hours after he began, he positions the pipette tip over the sample well and adds the final reagent, the telltale chemical that will turn green if the sample contains Ebola. The mixture doesn't turn green.

"Tony, he's negative," Rollin says. There's no sign of Ebola.

That night, Lukwiya vomits and develops a headache. When Rollin draws blood the next morning, Lukwiya's eyes are a ghostly gray. This time, the reagent turns a weak green.

OK, Rollin thinks, there's a 50 percent chance that he'll make it. The viral count is still low. Maybe he'll develop a mild case.

But the next day, the test goes a solid green, and Lukwiya asks to be taken to the isolation ward. "If I die," he tells the hospital's administrator, Dr. Bruno Corrado, "I only pray that I am the last."

He requests that his wife, Margaret, be told just that he has a fever and that she should not come up from Kampala. She comes anyway, of course, not letting herself imagine where she will be led when she walks through the hospital's front gate. Then it's as if she had practiced walking toward the building covered in plastic, practiced suiting up, practiced being strong and cheerful as she enters the ward to see her husband, dying of Ebola.

"Look here, Margaret," Lukwiya says when he sees her. "It is dangerous in here. Don't even come in." Then: "If you must come in, please stay for just one minute."

Wearing protective clothing, Margaret sees him twice a day for the next two days, unable to embrace or even touch him. Once, she breaks down.

"If you cry," Lukwiya says, "you'll rub your face, which won't be safe. Cool down, Margaret—and stand firm. Keep praying."

Simon Mardel and a Lacor doctor, Yoti Zabulon, team up to treat him, experimenting with aggressive interventions. As Lukwiya's breathing becomes more and more labored, they decide to artificially ventilate him.

His pulse returns to near normal, and his fever comes down. A second round of chest X-rays looks better, and the hospital announces that his condition has begun to improve. But later that night, he hemorrhages into his airway, and the doctors realize that what is happening to their friend is beyond their power to arrest, or even influence.

"There's nothing more anyone can do," Mike Ryan says. "Except say good-bye."

On December 5, at 1:20 a.m., Matthew Lukwiya, who fought so hard to keep the statistics down, joins the numbers himself, the 156th recorded victim of the outbreak.

The next afternoon, he is buried—in a tightly sealed coffin, with pallbearers wearing head-to-toe protective gear—in the shade beneath a mango tree in the Lacor hospital courtyard.

"I don't think he would regret this," Margaret Lukwiya says at the memorial service. "He knew the risk. He saw what was needed for his patients and he did it. That was him. Matthew was not for worldly desires."

Bruno Corrado says he sees Lukwiya's death as a symbol of defeat— a defeat made more painful by the hospital's initial success in containing the outbreak's first wave. "We all wanted Matthew to survive, not only because he was our colleague and friend but as living proof that this disease could be defeated," Corrado says. "We wanted to be able to declare that we fought against this thing together, and we won. But this is not the case. We did not defeat it."

Yet, by the time of Lukwiya's death, the epidemic was on the wane, largely due to his efforts during the first days of the outbreak. After a brief flareup, admissions slowed to just a handful each day, all of whom were now directed to Gulu Hospital. And although several workers temporarily left as a result of Lukwiya's death, the majority stayed on, inspired by his dedication. True to his hopes, Lukwiya was the last of the hospital staff to die.

On January 23, Uganda's last known Ebola patient was discharged, and the virus retreated back to nature, taking its secrets—including when it will come again—along with it. The international team scattered back to families and routines, in Geneva, Tokyo, Johannesburg.

In Atlanta, months later, Gulu already seems to Tony Sanchez like another life in another universe, a place that exists in flashes of memory and unaccountable longings—for that place where he dealt with things as they were, not as he wished they were; where he felt at once close to death and unimaginably alive. Sometimes, the place comes back in dreams, images piled one atop the other. In one, he is in the isolation ward, treating a terrified little girl not much older than his own daughter, whom he was afraid to touch for a few days after he returned. In the dream, sometimes, one girl becomes the other, and he's helpless—he can't soothe her with his touch, and he can't save her life.

But there are good memories, too. One night at the Acholi Inn, as bats swooped overhead, Mike Ryan held forth on one subject after another, a font of vinegar and piss. The waitress came out and scolded him for leaning back in his chair, and he apologized. Then he settled back squarely on the chair and requested another round of Nile Specials.

"Ah, the source of the Nile," he said when she returned. And he smiled mischievously and rocked back in the chair again, unthinkingly. And she smiled back, and said nothing.

A few minutes later, Simon Mardel and Cathy Roth said good night, and Ryan leaned back with his hands clasped behind his neck and let out a big sigh. "What a bloody ride this is," he said, looking up into the dark foliage overhead.

Like the woman and her exorcist, like the witch doctors in the villages and all the churchgoers in Gulu, like the doctors and nurses and virus hunters, Ryan imagined that there might be answers up there in the trees. But until someone manages to coax those answers out of the darkness, he and the others will be there to stanch the blood.

The truth is, you can't always slay the dragon. But sometimes, if you manage to keep your boot down on its neck long enough, you can quiet it.

The Climber Comes Down to Earth

by Daniel Duane

Conrad Anker in recent years has become
famous for finding George Mallory's body on
Everest and escaping the avalanche that killed
Anker's best friend, the legendary climber Alex
Lowe. Daniel Duane (born 1967) reports here
on the complicated life of a celebrity climber.

D rinking his third latte of the morning on our way to ski Alta, Conrad Anker looked, for a moment, content. I'd pulled him away from his glad-handing duties at the Outdoor Retailer trade show, and as we drove through Salt Lake City's suburban sprawl and into the frozen Wasatch Mountains, he seemed giddy at the prospect of some fresh air. Dark clouds hung low over the peaks, the snow-dusted road curved below shattered ribs of rock, and Anker, who lived nearby for a decade and a half, ripped apart a cinnamon bun and bubbled with nostalgia. Reaching across the dash, he pointed out an eagle's nest, then a mixed ice-and-rock route he'd once done in a single day, then a snow chute he used to ski in late spring— "Big GS-style turns," he recalled fondly, "not tips and tails."

A handsome, 38-year-old alpinist, with boyishly side-parted blond hair, close-set blue eyes, and a lantern jaw, Anker looks more like a high-strung surfer than a consummate mountaineer. With no hiker's thighs or gym-pumped muscles, there's a surprising lightness to his physique, and his head leans perpetually forward, as if straining into the future. A sometimes wry self-promoter who talks earnestly about saving the world, Anker also has the playful manner of the outdoors Peter Pan. Which makes sense, given that he has spent his entire adult life in a very particular America—an adventure-sports subculture in which status derives less from money than from talent at skiing, kayaking, and climbing, a subculture in which well-meaning environ-mentalist and anticonsumerist opinions make up an informal state ideology. Success begins with finding work flexible enough to let you play whenever the powder's deep, the ice is in, or the rock is dry. Greater success means making a living at some approximation of your game, like working ski patrol. True arrival means making a living doing the thing itself: travel, adventure, freedom.

Anker has been getting paid to play for most of a decade as a salaried, globe-trotting member of The North Face Climbing Team, and it's been a great ride. But lately he has been negotiating the tran-sition from being the favorite partner of some of the world's great expedition leaders to becoming a leader himself. At the same time, he has had a painful reckoning with the costs of playing one of the world's most dangerous games—costs that include his own brushes with mortality, the untimely deaths of his three closest friends in the high mountains, and the strange fallout that those deaths have had in his life.

Turning down the car radio, Anker gestured at a band of granite called Hellgate Cliff. He told me that together with his first serious climbing mentor, the legendary Mugs Stump, he established a notori-ously committed rock climb there, Fossils from Hell, in the 1980s. (Stump disappeared into a crevasse in 1992 while guiding clients on Alaska's Mount McKinley.) As we approached Alta, Anker remembered how he and another college climbing buddy, the underground hero Seth Shaw, had sometimes crammed an ice climb, a rock climb, and a few ski runs into a single day, even begged used lift tickets off skiers leaving Alta early. (Shaw was killed in May 2000 by falling ice, also in Alaska.)

"Wow!" he exclaimed as we rounded a snowbanked curve and a frozen waterfall swung into view. "Look at all the people on that ice climb! Wear your helmets today, boys!" Anker told me with evident pleasure that he and Shaw had held the round-trip speed record on that climb until Alex—Alex Lowe, Anker's best friend and a man once considered the best climber in the world—shattered it. In the fall of 1999, an avalanche struck Anker, Lowe, and a friend named Dave Bridges on the flanks of Tibet's 26,291-foot Shishapangma. Anker ran one way and survived, but Bridges, 29, and Lowe, 40, headed another way and disappeared. Lowe left behind a widow, Jennifer, and three young sons.

Even Anker's most famous achievement is shadowed by ambiguities. In 1999 he joined the Mallory & Irvine Research Expedition to Mount Everest. That May, just above 27,000 feet, he found the 75-year-old remains of the British climber George Mallory. The discovery shed new light on one of the great unsolved mysteries of world exploration— what befell Mallory and his partner, Sandy Irvine, during the third summit attempt on Everest. But for Anker, who has put up important first ascents from Antarctica to Baffin Island, and who has no particular preoccupation with history, it was more a quirk of fate than the kind of cutting-edge climbing achievement of which he is most proud. Nevertheless, he was lionized in newspapers and magazines the world over; he coauthored (with David Roberts) a book on the Mallory expedition; and he has been on a near-constant speaking tour ever since.

By far the greatest change in Anker's life came shortly after the October 1999 memorial service for Alex Lowe, in Bowman, Montana. In what must have been a bewildering and exhausting half-year, Anker had come straight back from Everest to spend five months cowriting the Mallory book, flown off to Shishapangma with Lowe, survived a battering in the lethal avalanche, and returned just in time to go on a book tour. Everywhere he went, according to Topher Gaylord, longtime director of The North Face Climbing Team, "people were giving Conrad so much support. But he had to go back alone to his hotel room every night, and it didn't bring Alex back, it didn't change anything. I think that's where Jenny and the kids became the best way of coping with losing Alex."

In a series of events that Anker understandably preferred not to discuss with a journalist, he eventually broke off his wedding engagement to an environmental lawyer named Becky Hall and became romantically involved with Jennifer Lowe. In December he proposed, and they plan to be married by the time this magazine arrives on the newsstands. Anker now lives with Jennifer and her sons in the Lowe home in Bozeman—finding himself, in other words, husband-to-be to his best friend's widow and stepfather to three boys who lost their father while he was climbing beside Anker himself.

In Little Cottonwood Canyon that day, Anker did not dwell on his own and his new family's losses, and this was only partly because he knew that I already knew all the details. He also resolutely insists on a life-affirming view of his profession. In his Mallory slide show—the story of yet another young husband and father who died climbing— Anker doesn't mention the half-dozen mangled corpses that he came upon on Everest and that he describes in his book. He never shows the macabre photographs of himself looming over Mallory's grisly body. (He criticized this magazine for running one of these shots on its cover.) He sometimes even tells audiences, in all sincerity, things like, "If I can motivate just one of you to go home and plan just one climb tonight, I will have done my job."

Anker is, of course, a paid spokesman for The North Face and a man who has never known much beyond extreme alpinism. But one senses, too, that he feels a great compulsion, even obligation, to argue aloud that his chosen profession has been worthwhile and that Alex Lowe did not die foolishly—that his life's foremost pursuit is still as it has always seemed: good for body, soul, and mind, and inspired by grand purpose.

As I clunked across the Alta parking lot in telemark boots, Anker instructed me, teasingly, on how to carry skis—over one shoulder, tips down—so as not to look like a dork. Once on the mountain, he humored me on the mogul-tree intermediate runs I'd said were my limit, but he dipped repeatedly off the trail, diving between steep trees and soaring, as airborne and playful as any teenager, back into sight. Anker has a reputation as a fantastic partner. Jochen Hemmleb and Jake Norton, for example, of the Mallory & Irvine Research Expedition, extol Anker as exceptionally hardworking and fun to be around, and all it took was a few runs that morning to see what they meant. When enthusiasm got the better of Anker, he steered me onto a series of experts-only bump runs through tight rock chutes, but I quickly forgot my irritation and terror in the sheer pleasure of watching someone ski the way you dream of skiing: as if your skis will never cross, your balance never falter, your reflexes never fail—as if the mountains, even at their steepest, are your best friends.

Indeed, Anker's two-page, single-spaced climbing résumé, with its emphasis on highly technical routes up good-looking mountains, must be the envy of all but a very small world elite. It includes a new route on the Russian Tower, in the Ak Su Himalaya, and desperate new big-wall lines both in Zion with Mugs Stump, and on Patagonia's Torre Egger with Yosemite hardmen Steve Gerberding and Jay Smith. The list goes on: Cerro Torre; Ama Dablam and Lobuche, in the Khumbu Himalayas; a first ascent, with Lowe and the writer Jon Krakauer, of Queen Maud Land's Rakekniven.

Anker may not be quite world-class at rock, snow, or ice climbing, but his combined skills at all three put him in rarefied company. As photographer and mountaineer Galen Rowell told writer David Roberts in 1999, "Conrad can ski down virgin faces of big peaks in sub-zero Antarctica, climb El Cap routes in a day for fun, sportclimb 5.12, speed-climb up Khan-Tengri in the Tien Shan taster than the Russian Masters of Sport, climb the north face of Everest or Latok, ice-climb the wildest frozen waterfalls, and run mountain trails forever. Plus enjoy hanging out with his friends talking about other things besides mountains." For this reason, Anker is a much sought-after expedition member: On both Everest and his recent re-creation of Ernest Shackleton's traverse of South Georgia Island for an IMAX movie, with renowned alpinists Stephen Venables and Reinhold Messner, Anker was the designated technical climbing leader. (Their film, *The Endurance: Shackleton's Epic Journey*, premiered in February.)

Late in the day at Alta, when light snow flurries turned into a miserably cold wind, Anker plopped beside me on a lift and told me something I'd heard him say several times before: that Stump, Shaw, and Lowe had all been better climbers than he. It's a frank self-assessment: Anker has tended to play lieutenant to bigger names rather than headlining expeditions himself. As a professional climber, he has also had to favor routes on which he has a reasonable chance of success and on which photographers and film crews can come along. Climbing's purist ideal—personified by Anker's very own mentor, Mugs Stump—is the two-man team moving fast with a minimum of gear, taking only enough pictures to prove what they've done, as Anker did for years with Seth Shaw. By contrast, caravan climbs like Anker's and Alex Lowe's National Geographic Society–funded first ascent of Rakekniven, with pressure for good photographs and a return on investment, require heavier anchors, more fixed ropes, and a slower schedule. Without criticizing Anker by name, last year's *American Alpine Journal* featured fierce denunciations of "Barbie mountaineering" and "business climbing."

Anker admits that professional climbers sometimes use power drills and fixed ropes with such abandon that it's akin to "hunting Bambi with a bazooka." He acknowledges that he and Lowe could have done Rakekniven in a single day, without drilling a bolt, instead of in four days with 28 bolts. But the role of alpha male is now wide open to Anker. He could easily pick one of climbing's "last great problems"—some hideous Himalayan north face—assemble a world-class team, and join the ranks of his sport's true immortals, climbers famous not just for stumbling across a dead guy on a trade route, but for hanging it all out in the most daring circumstances possible. Except, of course, that a lot of those immortal climbers have been turning up dead lately, and Anker now has the same incentive to stay alive that Alex Lowe did: Jennifer Lowe and her three sons.

As we rode Alta's Supreme lift for the last time that day, Anker's conversation reflected the painful complexity of this moment in his life. He remarked that he'd probably never have his own kids, then expressed his love for the kids he's now caring for—how he does homework with one, plays LEGO with another, does Brio with the third. Moments later, he mused on a high-altitude big wall he hopes to do this summer in Pakistan, then wistfully described the last time he'd skied Alta with Shaw. Such a bittersweet predicament: fame shadowed by loss, dreams seeming obsolete just as they come true, sudden responsibility but also love, and opportunities to weigh against the well-being of a still-grieving family. As we disembarked, I wondered aloud if Anker couldn't use a run to himself.

"You don't mind?" he asked.

I didn't, and as I shuffled toward a groomed slope, I watched him slip under an out-of-bounds sign, take one look off what I was quite sure was a cliff, and vanish.

Anker was born in San Francisco in November 1962, but he grew up largely abroad. Anker's father, Wally, was an international banker who moved his wife, Helga, and tour children first to Tokyo, then later to Hong Kong and Frankfurt, Germany. An avid mountaineer and skier, Wally also took the family on annual summer visits to Priest Ranch, the Ankers' California homestead, just outside Big Oak Flat, in the Sierra Nevada foothills. Later, in the mid-1970s, the teenage Anker boarded at the outdoors-oriented Colorado Rocky Mountain School.

Graduating in 1981, at age 18, he chose the University of Utah, at the foot of the Wasatch Mountains, and majored in commercial recreation. (Yes, the school's Department of Parks, Recreation, and Tourism really does offer such a degree.) Anker was more enthusiastic about fieldwork than homework and took seven years to finish his bachelor's degree. Along the way, he worked at the local North Face retail store and bicycled around Salt Lake City peddling homemade fleece hats to local shops for his fledgling outdoor-clothing company, Alf Wear. Anker took several semesters off to climb in Alaska with the soft-spoken, quietly driven Shaw, a classmate at the university. Starting in

1983, he also apprenticed himself to Terrence "Mugs" Stump, 31, a hard-living former college-football star (he played defensive back for Joe Paterno at Penn State before damaging his left knee) and one of the great American climbers of the period, renowned for his bold and visionary solos in the great ranges.

"I was like Grasshopper, listening to the master," Anker recalls. Up to that point, Stump was the most influential person in his life, "except for my parents," he says. For a time, Anker shared a house in Emigration Canyon, near Salt Lake City, with Shaw and Stump. Kevin Boyle, who started Alf Wear with Anker, recalls, "Their mentality was like, 'Hey, I can buy a bag of Bisquick, a thing of peanut butter, and I can live for a month and don't have to work, and now I can devote all my effort to climbing.'"

Out of college in 1988, Anker took Stump's advice and dedicated himself to life as a professional climber—a career that, in many respects, did not yet exist. He sold his interest in Alf to Boyle, switched from North Face retail clerk to product tester (meaning he got free stuff in exchange for telling them how well it worked), and made ends meet as a carpenter and high-access construction worker, scaling river dams and transmission towers. Like anyone who spends so much time in the mountains, Anker had his share of close calls. While attempting a new route on Alaska's Eyetooth in 1989, Anker and Stump, stormbound on a portaledge, suffered for a week without food until the weather lifted. Then, in April 1991, Anker and Shaw flew to Alaska and grabbed the much-coveted first ascent of Middle Triple Peak. During their descent, however, Shaw fell 80 feet to the glacier below, surviving only because he landed in deep snow. A moment later, Anker also fell. Both men walked away, and the route made Anker's name in the American climbing community.

In 1992, the year Stump was killed, Anker claimed first ascents in Baffin Island's Sam Ford Fjord and Antarctica's Sentinel Mountains. In 1993, he joined Alex Lowe in the Khan-Tengri speed-climbing competition, in Kyrgyzstan. They'd met as coworkers at the Black Diamond store in Salt Lake City two years before, and they now became close friends. Shortly afterward, The North Face made Anker a founding member of The North Face Climbing Team. By 1995 he was living in Oakland, California, and managing the team full-time. Just two years later, he decided business was taking too much time away from his real work. Giving up his apartment, Anker had all his mail forwarded to his family's Priest Ranch and began a relentless series of climbing trips that culminated, at the end of the decade, in the search for Mallory and the fatal avalanche on Shishapangma.

Until early 1999, relative youth and luck allowed Anker to focus single-mindedly on the positive, upbeat aspects of his sport. That May, however, he began a protracted confrontation with climbing's hardest truths. The Mallory & Irvine Research Expedition, led by Mount Rainier guide Eric Simonson, represented the latest in media-friendly commercial climbing projects: a demonstration of emerging technology that can broadcast events from remote corners of the globe and a chance to feed the ravenous appetite for tales of disastrous adventures. Invited along as the technical climbing specialist, Anker had never been above 24,000 feet. He jumped at both the free ride to Everest and the enormous career opportunity.

At 5:15 on the morning of May 1, Anker and four others left Camp V for the "search zone," high on Everest's northeast ridge. Wandering around at 27,000 feet looking for two dead climbers was novel enough, and even slightly bizarre, given that the usual goal at that fatal altitude is a dash to the summit and down again. The prior Himalayan snowy season had been the lightest in a hundred years, and almost immediately Anker and his companions came across what one of them, Tap Richards, would later describe as "a virtual graveyard of . . . frozen bodies, a kind of collection zone for fallen climbers." Anker encountered a corpse in a purple nylon suit with its face eaten to the skull by goraks (ravenlike birds that haunt the high Himalayas). Finally, at about 11:46 a.m., he came across Mallory himself, wool-clad, frozen into the scree, and preserved well enough that bruises still showed through his skin. While the others emptied Mallory's pockets for clues, Anker lifted the body. He wrote later that it "made that same creaky sound as when you pull up a log that's been on the ground for years. It was disconcerting to look into the hole in the right buttock that the goraks had chewed. His body had been hollowed out, almost like a pumpkin."

A few days later, after a short rest, Anker and his teammates headed up again, this time to tackle the question of whether Mallory, without modern equipment, could have free-climbed the Second Step, a crucial obstacle near the summit. (En route they found the body of a woman from Telluride whose family had asked that they unclip her from the fixed ropes so that future climbers wouldn't have to step over her). Anker's difficulty on the Second Step led him to believe that Mallory could not have gotten past it; after summiting, he returned to Base Camp convinced that the two British climbers had perished before reaching the top.

Five months later, Anker had a much more devastating encounter with mountaineering's mortal consequences. In early October, Anker, Lowe, and seven other climbers started up Shishapangma in an attempt to become the first Americans to ski down an 8,000-meter peak. According to Topher Gaylord, of The North Face (which also sponsored Lowe), Anker and Lowe had by this time become "the closest of friends—I mean true soul mates." For more than five years, the two had climbed together around the world and occasionally visited each other's families. Anker and Lowe were close enough in size to share climbing shoes, and they often zipped their sleeping bags together during bivouacs. Anker recalls that they also talked about becoming old men together. "You're going to come out to Big Oak Flat," Anker remembers telling Lowe, "and I'll come visit you, and we'll be in rocking chairs, reliving our youth." They shared the belief, Anker says, that "climbing's a wonderful thing, but if you don't come back again it's not worth it." ·

With every move documented in online postings and webcasts, the trip was precisely the kind of media spectacle that Anker and Lowe were tiring of, but they had so much fun together it hardly mattered.

They would wake in the wee hours to brew coffee, e-mail home, and talk. "We're so in synch," Lowe wrote in a dispatch to Mountain-zone.com, "words become superfluous—I'm awake—Rad's awake, my still, small voice speaks to me and echoes its words to Conrad. Partners are golden and Conrad's the motherload."

On October 5, 1999, the two partners, together with cameraman Dave Bridges, were crossing a flat section of glacier when they heard a crack high above. A huge avalanche began heading straight down toward the glacier. Lowe and Bridges ran downhill—Anker thinks they intended to jump into a crevasse—and Anker ran horizontally. Lying flat, he dug in his ice ax, only to be blown down the mountain. "It dragged me about 20 meters along the snow," Anker would later write. "It cut my head in four different spots, broke two ribs and stretched out my shoulder from the socket. During the course of this, I thought that I was going to die. Then light came and I realized I was alive." Holding his watch, Anker began searching for Lowe and Bridges, knowing that the last seconds of their lives were ticking away. Several hours later, Anker endured what he calls "the worst moment of my life." He used the expedition's satellite phone to call Jennifer Lowe.

Many career climbers, as they get older, yearn to come down off the mountaintop with something to say, some essential wisdom that will translate all those years of lonely, dangerous struggle into something of value to the rest of the world. Anker is no exception. Where most of the Shishapangma dispatches offer quick, sketchy impressions of the trip, Anker's tend to be thoughtful essays on moral matters—some serious, like his reflections on the Chinese occupation of Tibet, and some comedic, like his mock diatribe on the deplorable preponderance of fake plants ("*palm frondus plasticus, lilyus nylonus,* and *carnation impos-teroti*") in the LAX terminal. In *The Lost Explorer,* his Mallory book, Anker writes that he tries to use his slide shows and ski outings "to talk about being a good person, about how anger and hatred disrupt an expedition, about how sometimes it takes a little more effort to be pos-itive than negative, but that it's ultimately life-enriching."

Last November, Anker traveled to a Marriott conference center in San Ramon, California, a few miles east of San Francisco Bay, to give what he called the "state of the union" speech at a sales conference for The North Face. A poster on the ballroom's back wall featured the perpetual ghost in Anker's life, Alex Lowe, dangling from a Baffin Island cliff. Anker stepped to the podium and began his presentation, "An Alpinist's View of the Fall 2001 Selling Season," by projecting a slide of himself high on the Grand Teton. Leaning toward his notes and furrowing his freckled brow, Anker declared, "A lot of the things we believe in climbing are very similar to what is there in business. There's a good metaphor that goes with doing business: doing an expedition, doing a climb." The targeted summit, apparently, was $240 million in annual sales. Successive slides interspersed more glory shots of Anker with the motivational steps common to climbing and high-end retail fashion: Identify the Goal, Select the Route, Create Your Team, Climb, Believe, Summit.

Anker was, admittedly, just doing his job—thus the hokey nature of his speech—but a messianic side to his character does seem to have blossomed since Lowe's death. He talks a great deal about using his fame to spread his "message," a loose amalgam of Buddhism, environmentalism, and adventure-sports boosterism. I once asked who his heroes were, and Anker replied, "Reinhold Messner, of course—but that's just a sports thing. My real heroes are the guys getting change done, like Mother Teresa, the Dalai Lama, Martin Luther King, Gandhi." As evidenced by his North Face speech, Anker has also been drawn to that most enduring of aging-climber axioms: *I have gotten to one extraordinary summit after another by adhering to principles that will see you through to your own summits, whatever they may be.*

It seems both ironic and natural that the one struggle in which those principles cannot help Anker is the job of reconciling himself to what climbing has cost him. He told me, for example, that the turnaround moment in his mourning of Mugs Stump came during the Khan-Tengri speed-climbing competition, when Anker saved a Russian climber's life. "I felt then," he said, "that there's something good to climbing, there was a meaning to it." Anker has saved quite a few lives in situations that he could easily have ignored. But the tortured logic of validating one climbing death by preventing another exposes the limits of climbing as a universal metaphor. What kind of game is redeemed by the opportuniy it offers to save lives risked only in playing it?

Seth Shaw's death last May in Alaska, only seven months after the disaster on Shishapangma, brought Anker a new kind of regret. In a sense, he had long ago left Shaw behind. Shaw had stayed in Salt Lake City, working as an avalanche forecaster, and their near-fatal 1991 Alaska trip was the last time they climbed together. It was also, in the view of Durango climber Kennan Harvey, a good friend of Shaw's, "the last pure"—i.e., noncommercial—"expedition Conrad's done."

Anker was in Telluride, accepting an Adventurer of the Year award from Polartec, when he heard that Shaw had been killed. "Jenny and the little guys were there," Anker told me, "and at the time it was really hard to deal with it, because here I am—I've got the kids now, they want to go stay at a hotel with a swimming pool and watch the cartoons. And I realized how close Seth was to me, and we'd had a trip planned, and I'd backed out of it and decided to do a trip with Peter Croft and Galen Rowell instead . . ." Anker's attention wandered for a moment, perhaps distracted by what he'd implied—that he'd chosen a trip with a bigger-name partner and a bigger-name photographer.

Shaw, like Stump and Lowe, remains buried on the mountain where he died. Shaw's family and friends held a memorial service in Salt Lake City, planting a tree for him in Little Cottonwood Canyon near a taller one planted for Stump in 1992. By most accounts Anker gave a beautiful eulogy, but Harvey, who attended the memorial, feels that there was something detached, almost impersonal, in Anker's delivery. "Conrad was out of touch there, because he'd had to move on," Harvey says.

Doug Heinrich, another old friend of Anker and Shaw, considers Anker's dilemma just "part of being a star. Your career, to a certain degree, takes the place of a lot of what sometimes seems mundane, like your day-to-day interaction with your friends. And once that's gone, it creates a huge void, especially when your friends pass away."

• • •

A few days after his North Face speech, just before he flew back to Montana, I met Anker for breakfast at a café in Berkeley. He was unshaven and looked exhausted. Twenty years of mountain sun and a year and a half of personal upheaval showed in the wrinkles around his mouth and eyes.

After coffee and eggs took the raw edge off his mood, I asked him to talk about what Alex Lowe had been going through toward the end of his life. Lowe, he said, had grown tired of back-to-back climbing expeditions, their canned commercial agendas, and of the time they took away from Jennifer and their three boys. Lowe's Shishapangma dispatches make frequent mention of his family, and he muses several times about the relatively frivolous nature of climbing. No one is in a better position than Anker to understand the bitter irony—that Lowe was preoccupied with climbing's calculus of selfishness just as the self-indulgence inherent in the sport was about to exact its greatest toll.

Later that morning, Anker drove us to the Berkeley Marina. Sitting on a bench under a chilly blue sky, he acknowledged how devastating the first six months after Lowe's death had been. At the suggestion of a friend at The North Face, he'd spoken to a therapist. "It was worthless," Anker said with palpable contempt. "Maybe I was defensive or angry, but she didn't get where I was coming from." In his anguish, Anker turned to Jon Krakauer and confessed he'd had thoughts of suicide. "I said, 'Jon, it's fucked up,' and Jon goes, 'Yeah, it's normal. You're just angry, and you feel like your friend's been cheated, or you've been cheated, and you're wondering why did it end up like this.'"

A hard wind blew across San Francisco Bay. His hands deep in his pockets, Anker told me that he'd found the most solace in the friendship of Gil Roberts, a San Francisco emergency-room doctor who was a member of the 1963 expedition on which Jim Whittaker became the first American to summit Everest. Roberts had been walking through the Khumbu Icefall beside a friend, Jake Breitenbach, when Roberts stopped to wipe his goggles. Breitenbach took a few steps forward, a block of ice fell on him, and he was never seen again. Hearing about

Lowe's death, Roberts contacted Anker and talked to him about survivor's guilt—shortly before, as it turned out, Roberts discovered that he had metastasized melanoma and only a few months to live.

"Climbing is a good thing," Anker told me, switching abruptly from dazed emotion to his formal spokesman mode. "It's about the experience I had with Gil just before he died. We spent a day and talked about how death changes your view on life and makes you live life fuller."

It was an extraordinary thing to say: *Climbing is a good thing—it's about hearing a dying man's views on death.* And yet, why not? Climbing's relentless encounter with death appears to teach a twinned lesson. On the one hand, the sentiment captured in Psalm 103, which was read over the body of George Mallory high on Everest: "As for man, his days are like grass; as a flower of the field, so he flourisheth. For the wind passeth over it, and it is gone." On the other hand: Enjoy it while it lasts.

Bozeman, Montana, with snow thick on the surrounding Rockies and cottonwoods, and holiday lights on the eaves of all the Queen Annes just off main street, couldn't be a more picturesque mountain village. It also couldn't feel more like Alex Lowe's town. Barrel Mountaineering, down the street from the single-screen movie theater, has a kind of shrine to Lowe, with a signed poster hanging near a framed photograph of Lowe that someone has draped with white gauze. Barrel maintains a first-ascents binder in which local climbers, after establishing new routes, pen descriptions and attach photos. It might as well be Lowe's personal scrapbook. And when 1,400 people showed up late last year for Anker's Mallory slide show, it was a tribute to just how much Lowe mattered in the town in which Anker now lives with Lowe's family.

The boisterous audience quieted as Anker took the stage of the Bozeman High School auditorium. "As I'm sure some of you already know," he began, "Alex Lowe died in an avalanche last year." The auditorium fell silent, and Anker did a remarkable thing. "Alex died," he said, "and I survived, and I don't know why. By some miracle, I'm here, and in the memory of Alex, and of carrying on what Alex began with his family—Jenny and Sam and Max and Isaac—we're together." Anker paused then, as if to make sure everyone realized that he had just opened a slide show entitled "The Mystery of Mallory and Irvine" with a public declaration on the nature of his domestic and romantic arrangements. "And that's the best way that I can honor Alex . . . and I just thought that I'd say that and get that out there."

Shortly after Lowe's death, Anker talked about the loss of his friend with Tom Brokaw, on *Dateline NBC*, adding, "There's an unwritten thing that should one of the others make it through something, we would be there to help out." One can certainly imagine a warrior code by which duty demands that Anker look after Lowe's wife and kids. Anker has a strong desire to see—and to have others see—his actions as motivated by a clear moral purpose. I suspect that the appeal of climbing, for Anker, lies to some degree in its simulacrum of this clarity. When everything goes right, a climb can be very much the way he described it at the North Face sales conference—you always know exactly where you're coming from (the bottom), exactly where you're going (the top), and exactly what means you'll use to get there (gear, ability, and daring). But life has thoroughly undermined Anker's straightforward worldview, and no such surety is available in his current adventure, nor will it ever be again.

Anker later told me that Jennifer's once-skeptical friends were duly impressed by his words that night in Bozeman. (Jennifer Lowe declined to be interviewed for this article.) But who can really say if one best honors a fallen comrade by marrying his widow? Why even ask the question? Sir Edmund Hillary married the widow of a former expedition partner, and he ascribes the union to the very things that might well be drawing Anker and Jennifer together: mutual affection, common interests, a shared sense of loss.

The next day we spent the afternoon driving around town. Anker told me he'd been awake since 2:30 that morning—not the first time he'd alluded to missing sleep. He had a lot of organizational work to do for an upcoming Antarctica trip with Krakauer and a *NOVA* film crew, the subject of a PBS documentary on global warming scheduled to air in winter 2002. Around 8 a.m., Anker had walked the Lowe boys to school, and by noon, when he picked me up, he had already bought $800 worth of food for the expedition. The bed of his old Japanese truck—or, rather, Alex's truck, as Anker noted—sagged from piles and piles of plastic bags full of vegetable protein, nuts and dried fruit, brown rice, and black beans. We stopped first at a small sound studio where Anker recorded voice-overs for the IMAX film on Shackleton. We moved on to an office-supply store and then a mountaineering store. In each, people spotted Anker and asked about the Lowes. At the end of the day, we sat down in a bistro that hadn't opened yet. A waitress recognized Anker and gave us a booth.

Anker had been talking constantly about the Lowe boys. "One kid's one thing," he said, "but *three* kids, all boys and all hyperactive, bouncing off each other like neutrons—it makes a real challenge for Jenny. So Isaac and I do the alphabet, and Sam and I read, and Max and I do math, and it's a really good thing. I won't have children of my own, so that's . . ." His face tightened, and that "message" voice came back on again: "But overpopulation is the bane of our planet, and I'd always questioned the value of adding more souls to the world. So this is . . . These are good kids, and they deserve a chance to enjoy a normal childhood."

Someone cranked up "Jingle Bells" until it shook the empty room. When they'd turned it back down, Anker seemed slightly deflated. "I do feel bad leaving town now," he admitted, "especially over Christmas. You know what Max said, He's like, 'Dad was only here for two Christmases, and now *you're* going away for Christmas."

Daylight had faded from the snow-covered street outside. "We do talk about Alex every day," Anker said, "and things Alex did, and we do little special things for the boys, like work on the scrapbook and get out Alex's collection of old nickels." He added that he and Jennifer had been on a sort of tour of places she and Alex visited together—Telluride, Yosemite. "It's kind of taking the edges off," Anker said. "There's a lot of rough edges still . . ." His voice drifted, and he looked into his cup. "There's things that really set her off, and I could be wallowing in all this, but I've got to be a pillar of support to this family."

It occurred to me then that love, mourning, and Anker's ongoing life as a climber are all inextricably bound together right now. Anker has the difficult job of keeping his predecessor's flame burning for the family he calls his own—never will Anker be able to declare that he'd prefer not to hear about his wife's late husband again. After all, he too grieves for Lowe every single day. "For the first six months," he said, "it kind of felt like I'd lost my arm. There was this missing part of me. I would keep thinking, 'Well maybe the phone's going to ring and it's going to be him, saying, "Yeah, yeah, what's up?"'"

Anker had channeled his best memory of Lowe's voice, and it seemed to alarm him, as if he'd spoken Lowe back into being. "You know," Anker went on, "I still kept thinking, up until one year after the accident, that he was going to come back. I had these dreams that he would come back and he'd be like, 'What are you doing here?'" Anker's voice filled, for a moment, with genuine agony: "I'd go, 'Alex, man . . . *here*.'" With that, Anker leaned back and raised both hands in a resigned and desolate gesture of letting go, relinquishing any claim.

The waitress flipped over the "Open" sign, and I asked Anker if he'd ever thought about the disconnect between his turmoil and the picture of climbing he'd given to The North Face sales team.

"That's just the rosy side of climbing that people want to hear," he replied, shifting in his seat. "They don't want to hear that we all have demons somewhere driving us." Anker looked away briefly. "Putting yourself in that much harm's way, you've got to."

"To what degree did you feel like you were—"

"Lying through my teeth?" He laughed. "I don't think I was."

But could he ever communicate to such a group the things he's actually learned in climbing? About loss, loneliness, ambition?

"They wouldn't understand. *I* don't understand."

And how could he? Love is hard enough to find without questioning where we find it. Nobody knows an easy way to get over the deaths of people we care about. And while Anker does have a family counting on him for the first time in his adult life, he has also spent 20 years becoming a world-class climber. However he spins it in slide shows, his life has at its very core a deliberate dance with the reaper. "On Everest," he told me, "Death is right there. It's sort of like you're underwater, and there's this sort of semipermeable membrane, this gel that surrounds you, because you have warm boots and gloves and an oxygen apparatus. But you can kind of push through this thing, and there's death right out there. All your energy becomes focused on living, on surviving. That's the allure."

Anker says he wants to do more film and TV work. He has talked The North Face into moving its climbing-hardware division to Bozeman, which could provide him with long-term security. And he talks about staying off avalanche-prone 8,000-meter peaks. This will not be easy. Anker is coming into his physical prime as a high-altitude climber; on the very biggest mountains, experience and endurance count for more than fast-twitch muscle speed. He finally summited Everest on the Mallory expedition, his first trip into the so-called Death Zone, that realm where the air is too thin for long-term human survival. In the process, he proved what every climber hopes to: that his body performs very, very well there. The moment for Anker to make a permanent mark is now.

And even if he chooses not to defy the critics of risk-averse, high-publicity commercial expeditions—what is sometimes called "guaranteed-outcome mountaineering"—Anker will still make a good living as a member of The North Face Climbing Team. He loves the mountains of Antarctica, and he dreams of accepting an invitation to join his hero, Reinhold Messner, on Cerro Torre, where Messner wants to repeat the famous Ferrari Route. Talking about it, Anker's eyes lit up— the pure climber thrilling to the next great vision.

But Cerro Torre and Antarctica are, of course, both in the Southern Hemisphere, where the climbing season coincides with Thanksgiving and Christmas, the very holidays that Anker doesn't want to miss again. He also knows that none of his friends died pushing their limits. Stump, Lowe, and Shaw all vanished in unforeseeable mishaps on relatively easy terrain. Their deaths argue that it is not the difficulty level that kills the best climbers, nor the presence of film crews, but the sheer amount of time they spend in the high mountains.

Night had fallen by the time Anker and I stepped back outside. Just before we parted, I pressed him with a final question. How would he feel about dying on this trip to Antarctica? Would it seem an honorable climber's death?

"No," he replied, "it would be really bad. I would just have let people down. For the person who dies, it's like a lightbulb going out, but the pain for people who are still there . . . It would be really quite foolish." His intelligent eyes widened, as if the possibility were terribly real. Then Anker wrapped both arms around himself, looked away, and said, mostly to himself, "I've got to keep my ass really safe."

from Doctor on Everest

by Kenneth Kamler, M.D.

Microsurgeon Kenneth Kamler has taken part in six Everest expeditions, reaching 28,000 feet in 1995. His teammates on that trip included Sherpa Nima Tashi, walking on ankles Kamler treated after a 1991 accident.

The cold woke me up. In the dark I didn't know where I was or what was holding me here. As my head slowly cleared, however, the immediate mystery was solved. I was at base camp zipped into my sleeping bag, but I was certain that if I didn't fully awaken, I would fall asleep again and be back home when I really woke up. Instead I chose to stay where I was. I unzipped my sleeping bag, then unzipped my tent, emerging from both my shelters.

The larger mystery of what was holding me here would be harder to solve. It was 1995—my third trip. In two previous seasons, I had been on Everest a total of five months and now I had returned for at least two more. I knew that much of the time I would be cold, tired, and scared but paradoxically, Everest had come to seem like a protected place. It was a haven where I could lead a simpler life. Though death was always around us, it was in the background, happening to other people, not my friends, not my little group.

This year, as in previous years, I had renewed old friendships and made new ones in this isolated village called Everest Base Camp. Todd, Pete, and Frank were back, as well as our sirdar, Lakpa-Rita, and Ong-Chu, our cook. Newer additions were Wally Berg, an avalanche ski patrolman and mountain guide from Colorado, and Jim Williams, a geologist and mountain guide from Wyoming. Rounding out our group were some amateur climbers like myself including: Todd "Mook" Hoffman, an easy-to-like businessman whose personality undoubtedly contributed a great deal to his success; and Lily Leonard, whose excitement for adventure contrasted nicely with her training as a research biochemist. All together, it was a collection of levelheaded but somewhat aberrant people who were now making their way to the mess tent.

What was bringing us together this morning was a meeting to plan for the installation of some new GPS equipment at various points on the way to the top of the mountain. But, in a larger sense we were together because of a personal challenge each of us felt to try to reach the summit. That motivation, however, would seem a lot less compelling once death penetrated our little circle.

"Very good, Dr. Sab, Camp Three," said Kami as I entered the mess tent. He poured me some tea and gave me the thumbs-up sign. Kami was a new Sherpa in camp. I checked carefully: He wasn't just an old face with a new hat. Kami came from the same village as Lakpa-Rita, who had picked him as his protegé. He was given a job as cook-boy this year but was young and ambitious and wanted to work his way up one day to climbing Sherpa or sirdar. He was learning English, being helpful wherever he could, and seemed to be on the fast track.

The meeting had already started and I regretted being late, not because I missed anything, but because all the spots near the propane heater were already taken. We had been on Everest for five weeks already. The past few days we had spent high up on the mountain completing our second foray to build the upper camps and set up the route to the summit. This was our first day back in base, and maybe my confusion upon awakening this morning was due to oxygen intoxication from too much air. The trip had been successful for the team as well as for me personally. I reached Camp II without pneumonia or even undue shortness of breath. Feeling strong, the distance between II and III seemed long but not impossible any more. Whether my confidence came from better health or my strength was due to a better attitude, there was enough within me to reach Camp III. The Lhotse Face no longer intimidated me.

I was feeling positive and so was Todd. He said the weather continued to look good—cold and light snow don't count. There wasn't much wind or fog, and the jet stream was abating with no sign of the monsoon yet. The plan was to rest down here for about three or four days—eat, drink, relax, get our strength up, and then go for the top. If the weather held and everything went right, we could be on the summit in ten days. The possibility was exciting. In a few days, for the first time, I would be part of a summit team.

Incredibly, Nima Tashi would be part of that team as well. He had scrupulously followed my advice in the United States but then totally ignored it once he returned to Nepal. He went back to climbing his first week home and, despite his rigid ankle, soon regained his skill, strength, and prestige. His gratitude to me was limitless, and though Lakpa-Rita had hired him as a team climber, he was doubling as my personal Sherpa, attentive to little details like adjusting my pack straps and checking my rope. I was the only climber on Everest with valet service.

As the meeting broke up, the sun suddenly came out and I wanted to take advantage of it. My goal for the day suddenly became to take a shower and change my underwear. It had taken a few seasons but finally we had a shower that worked well. It was Liz's legacy. I was about to ask Ong-Chu for shower water when he came to me suggesting a starting time. Either he read my mind or I smelled worse than I thought.

Medically, things were also going well. The group was staying relatively healthy, though some people were hard to convince. Mook had an endless series of minor complaints and needed constant reassurance from me that he wasn't coming apart. I pointed out to him that his pulse was forty beats per minute less than mine and he almost seemed to be putting on weight.

The biggest medical problem so far was my own fault. I made the mistake of casually mentioning that I was taking diamox and maybe that was helping me to do better at Camp II and higher. Some climbers take it routinely, but until this year I hadn't taken it myself. Even though I'm a doctor I have a general philosophical belief that medicines are unnatural and, whenever possible, the body should be given a chance to heal itself without them. This year I concluded that there is nothing natural about being above seventeen thousand feet, so the body doesn't know how to deal with it and needs a little help. Such reasoning allowed me to compromise my principles without feeling guilty.

My casual comment had the effect of causing a run on diamox. Some climbers who didn't routinely take it and who didn't bring any along started asking for it. Having to supply two pills a day to three climbers over two months was seriously depleting my inventory of five hundred pills. Even with the need to maintain an emergency reserve, I figured I would just squeak by until Mook told me he "lost his supply in the tent." Knowing Mook was a smooth salesman, I wasn't sure whether he really lost them, or whether he wanted to double up on his dosage prior to the summit ascent, but feeling fresh from my shower and with the sun still out, I took a walk to the New Zealand camp to see if they had any pills to spare.

There was the usual boisterous scene that I had come to expect and enjoy and even at times to depend upon. Rob was there, as well as Jan and Chantal and a few other climbers, sipping tea and telling jokes. It turned out Jan had plenty of extra diamox. She needed some tetracaine and I offered to supply her with some. Problem solved, I leaned back to enjoy the tea, crackers, and laughter.

Chantal took the chance to tell me, in French, that since I saw her last she had torn a ligament in her knee and was using a brace. I had torn the same ligament years ago and was also using a brace. She asked if I wanted to see hers and I said okay, not realizing she was wearing it. She stood up and pulled her pants down. Eventually, I lowered my eyes to look at her brace. We had been conversing in French and I'm sure everyone else around the table must have wondered just what exactly we had been saying to each other.

I was late getting back to camp and returned in the middle of another meeting. Dave Mencin, a geophysicist familiar with our GPS equipment, had hiked into base camp to go over the system with us and to be around for radio consultations in case there was trouble setting up on the summit. He was giving a boring demonstration of how to bolt the stand into the ice. The group was looking for a little relief so I was immediately asked what was going on in the New Zealand camp.

I answered honestly: "Oh, nothing much. Jan and I shared some drugs and Chantal took her pants off."

The meeting droned on until Dave was satisfied everything was working. He was dithering too long with one dial and was losing his audience. A bored climber joked, "I bet I could learn to read that meter in five minutes."

"That's probably about right," Dave answered. "I could teach a yak to do it in two."

When it was finally over, he asked if there were any questions. "Just one," came the reply. "I'd like to ask Ken what color Chantal's underwear is."

Spirits were high. The weather was holding and soon we'd be leaving for the summit. Some climbers filled the time reading and listening to music while others took daily walks in the icefall to not lose their edge. Nima Tashi left for a quick trip to his village of Pangboché to get a blessing from his lama and to buy socks. Everyone prepared in his own way.

At first I firmly believed that I needed rest, but each time someone left for a hike in the icefall I looked on uneasily, fearing that he was gaining some advantage over me. Finally, I gave in to a group invitation to get in some exercise. I didn't have the confidence to resist.

The group had a head start, but as I caught up to them I could see that they had stopped to poke at something with their ice axes. They had come across parts of a skull—a human skull. I recognized the shape of the jaw and the teeth. I didn't have to tell them, though. We all realized it couldn't be anything else. No animal is foolish enough to venture this high.

Someone had gone into the icefall but hadn't made it out the other side. His name, nationality, and date and circumstances of disappearance will have been recorded in the history of Everest, but this area has the highest fatality rate and there would be a lot of possible candidates. We had no idea who the icefall was presenting to us, or why.

Oddly, we didn't talk about it once we left the site. The exercise session was definitely over, though, and we hiked out of the graveyard in silence. I sensed a tacit understanding that this would be something we wouldn't talk about, and try not to even think about, until the expedition was over.

I was wrong. Teatime came and went with no one mentioning anything, but then just before dinner I overheard one of my secret-sharers tell Todd he had a piece of a human skull in his backpack.

The smile left Todd's face. He said in a low, measured voice, "Don't bring it in the mess tent. Don't show it to any Sherpas. Don't talk about it. Just get it out of camp. It's bad karma."

I thought there wasn't enough smoke coming from the juniper fire that cold morning we started for the summit. I added some fresh branches and Ong-Chu nodded his approval. Once the smoke passed over me I threw a handful of rice at the lhapso and left base camp.

We reached Camp I, all of us tired but in pretty good shape. I thought: One hurdle down. Tomorrow is the Cwm. I'm getting closer to the summit. If I make it I'll never have to climb the icefall again. There's a big difference between wanting to climb Everest and wanting to *have* climbed it. I realized then that I was in the second category.

There is nothing colder than putting on a frozen climbing boot after you've slept all night on ice, except maybe standing around waiting to get going. I timed my routine the next morning to exit the tent the same time as everyone else—not too hard to do considering that except for my boots, I had slept with all my clothes on.

It got even colder when the sun came up and we started off into the wind that had haunted us in our tents all night. It blew unceasingly from the southwest, freezing the left side of my face. I moved up the Cwm wearing a down jacket, balaclava, and three pairs of gloves. With all the bulk, crossing crevasses was dicier than usual, especially when big gusts forced us to maintain our balance in midcrossing by leaning into the wind, out over the side of the ladder. Then, when the wind stopped, we'd suddenly find ourselves teetering over a yawning chasm. Each crevasse too large to cross on ladders was a welcome sight. It meant one less chance to be a weather vane and, since we had to turn to get around it, it meant a brief chance to get the wind off the west side of my face.

Just past the last crevasse was a flat where we usually took a break but it was so cold no one wanted to, except for one climber with diarrhea. I made him take a Lomotil pill on the spot and we continued on. We needed to keep moving to avoid hypothermia, but we also needed liquids to prevent dehydration. We made one quick stop to drink hot water out of our bottles, bundling down against one another like penguins in a roost.

My mouth was frozen by the time I reached Camp II, and I was afraid the hot tea that Dawa and Kami had prepared would crack my teeth. Along with some other Sherpas, they had come up the day before and had a fire going for us in the cook tent. I sipped the tea slowly and felt my mouth defrost.

In the morning, we all felt better. The sun was out, big and bright, and we were having trouble believing we were ever cold. Today would be a rest day. We had to make our final choices on what gear and clothing we'd be taking higher. Extra clothes mean extra weight. The closer you get to the top, the more it pulls you down. On the other hand, to have warm clothes but not have them when you need them is ridiculous, or worse. The memory of yesterday's march was not obscured by today's sunlight.

Todd and Pete held a briefing. The wind had blown most of the snow off the Lhotse Face, exposing the hard blue ice underneath. That meant tougher going; it's much harder to kick steps into ice than into snow. To use our energy efficiently, our crampon points would need to be extra sharp so they'd penetrate the ice easily. Todd also reminded us that, whatever clothes we chose, to avoid hypothermia we must make sure that all zippers lined up so that, when necessary, all the layers could be dropped and raised quickly. This was especially true for Lily, the only female in the group.

Nima Tashi hadn't made it back in time to leave base camp with the team, but he caught up to us at Camp II. I knew he was here because when I went out of my tent to borrow a metal file, I found that my crampons had already been sharpened. I went to thank him and ask if he had gotten the lama's blessing. He said, "Many times." He also had gotten his socks. I supposed we were all set then.

There was a hint of light in the sky when I awoke early the next morning but as the light increased, the air seemed to get colder instead of warmer. I was pleased tó not feel any wind as I came outside. The orange glow of the cook tent looked warm and I went directly to it, anxious to not get too chilled. Most of the climbers were there already and Dawa and Kami were earnestly serving up their attempt at porridge. It tasted as awful as usual, but at least I could warm my hands on the side of the bowl.

Once all the climbers had been served, Dawa and Kami took their leave, Kami being careful to leave some extra porridge in a pot in the corner in case anyone wanted more. They joined Pemba and the other climbing Sherpas who were going to Camp III on a roundtrip to drop off supplies. They were anxious to get an early start and left as soon as there was enough light.

We could linger in the tent a little while longer since we would be stopping at III and a later start would give us more light and maybe more warmth.

"Frank, how can you call yourself British?" I asked. "This porridge is an insult to the queen. It tastes like shit."

"I like it when it tastes shitty," he replied.

Secretly I admired a good climber's ability to eat anything. It was a skill I was unable to master.

Leaving our warm confines, we stepped out into the vast cold space outside the tent. In the early light the enormous face of Lhotse took on a blue glow, dominating the scene and our thoughts. This huge mountain would soon be taking our measure. Suddenly there wasn't much talk. We set off like a line of ants, taking microscopic steps and feeling humble and insignificant. I let my mind wander far from the trail. Often a song will come into my head—just one line over and over—and not a song I particularly like. In the company of Buddhist Sherpas I've come to realize that this is my mantra—a phrase of no emotional significance that's chanted continually. It lets the mind drift into a deeper level of consciousness.

It got colder and colder as we crossed the top of the Cwm, jumping over some small crevasses and probing for larger ones with our ski poles. The wind of the past few days had made our work easier by blowing off the superficial snow layer that often covers the crevasses. Despite two layers of gloves, my hands were tingling and I was having trouble controlling my ski poles. I withdrew my fingers into my palms so I could ball them up to decrease heat loss. It helped but it wasn't enough, and my hands soon were numb. We had been moving at a good steady pace, with no complainers, and I hesitated to be the one to break the rhythm but I had to get another pair of gloves on. I called a stop and as I took out my overmitts, almost everyone else reached for more gloves, a scarf, or an extra hat. I saw I wasn't the only one who was cold, nor the only one who didn't want to be the climber who called the stop.

The Western Cwm finishes at the world's most majestic dead end. Ahead of us was Lhotse; to the right, Nuptse; to the left, Everest: three points in a crown of ice over twenty-five thousand feet high. The base of Lhotse bends and cracks where it meets the Cwm. The crack was, for us, a huge moat too big to cross. We detoured around the crevasse, entering Lhotse at its far corner where a snow slope leads up onto the face like an outside ramp.

I was climbing well, I felt strong, and now I wasn't afraid to look up. At the start of the snow slope I tied my ski poles to an anchor. I wouldn't need them anymore. There were no more long flat spots between here and the summit. After a short break, Jim started up the ramp. I followed, with Nima Tashi close behind me. Pete and Wally brought up the rear.

The slope mounted alongside the base of Lhotse and gradually blended into it. We were on a ramp that got narrower and narrower until we were forced against the ice. It ended by diminishing into a ledge and then into just a series of footholds that led onto the sheer face of Lhotse.

Jim stepped out into the footholds, balanced on the front points of his crampons, then clipped into a dangling rope that disappeared over a protruding bulge of blue ice. The rope was the first in a continuous series of anchored lines which led straight up the 45-degree slope to Camp III, fifteen hundred feet above us.

I moved sideways to the end of the ledge, its width now less than the length of my boot. My forward crampons were solidly in the ice but my heels were hanging over the edge. I was waiting for Jim to start up the rope so that I could move into his position. Nima Tashi was on the ledge a step behind me, waiting to move into mine. There was no wind. There was no movement. We were suspended in a quiet moment of anticipation.

Suddenly, above us, there was a rumbling noise but our view was obscured by the overhanging ice bulge. It lasted longer than a second and then a body slid past us, skidding, tumbling, and then bouncing down the slick slope. In sheer horror, we watched as a human being with a face and a hat and a backpack and boots hurtled down the mountain at sickeningly increasing speed, catapulted over the crest of the huge crevasse and landed in the snow out of view on the other side. Jim cried out, "Oh, no; Sherpa, no!" From behind me I heard Lily scream, and then there was silence. Quietly, Nima Tashi said to me he recognized the red hat. It was Kami.

The three of us were on a precarious ledge, but no one moved. Jim radioed to Wally, who was the furthest one back on the slope. Wally hadn't seen what had happened, but while we waited he down-climbed to a position where he could look over the crevasse.

He came back on the radio: "I can see him . . . I don't see any movement." Kami had fallen to the bottom of Lhotse, in an area with hidden crevasses.

We backed down the ledge just far enough so we could stand, and waited while Wally and Pete slowly and carefully made their way over to where he lay far below us and out of sight. Nobody spoke.

It would be a lot easier for me if he was dead. The selfish, repugnant thought had surfaced immediately and I was ashamed to discover it within me. I couldn't allow it a chance to even fully form in my head so I quickly reburied it by focusing on how to proceed if he was still alive and by adding additional intensity to my hope that somehow he was.

The long silence was broken by Wally's voice on the radio. He said only, "We got to him." Nothing more. Kami's condition was obvious from what Wally didn't say. We all understood.

Slowly we down-climbed from the ledge, being more careful than we had ever been before, until we reached a flat spot at the bottom of the snow slope where we could stop safely. I was the last one down. Tears fell from Lily's eyes and her lower lip was quivering. Frank stood up and embraced me. He was crying too. We held each other a long time until he finally broke away, leaned down over his pack, and hit it. He said, "Why do these things have to happen?" and then hit the pack over and over.

One by one, people regained enough composure to start down. Nima Tashi got up as soon as he saw I was ready. I took a few steps down the slope before he caught up with me and handed me my ski poles. He remembered that I had tied them off on the way up and he had had the presence of mind to get them for me. Maybe I wasn't as composed as I thought.

Nima Tashi slowed his pace to keep me company, though we descended in silence. As we crossed below the giant crevasse, the lower slope came into view and we could see Kami's body at the end of a long streak of blood. Wally and Pete were standing there, unsure if according to Buddhist custom they were allowed to touch the body yet. Dawa joined them. He had raced up from Camp II with my medical kit in the hope that it might be needed, but there was nothing to be done. My job was easy. Recalling that repressed thought, I turned away with a pang of guilt, almost as if I had let him die.

Frank was the only one to not stop and look on the way down, and when I arrived in camp he was sitting on a rock. Each of us picked out a rock as we arrived. None of us was ready to be alone yet.

Behind us there was the slow procession of Wally and Pete and several Sherpas dragging a body bag across the Cwm and into camp. Later, Pete told me that when they got to Kami, they saw that his safety line was still attached to his harness, indicating he hadn't been clipped in. Wally said Kami's limbs were "at crazy angles" and his face was "mush." He used some of my bandages to cover the face before the other Sherpas arrived. "Even so," Wally said, "because we were dragging him there was a lot of leakage through the bag." When they got to camp, they put up a tent and put the body inside. We could smell the incense and hear the prayers.

Pemba and the other Sherpas who had left with Kami this morning returned from their roundtrip and joined us on the rocks. Pemba said that Kami had wanted very much to be a climbing Sherpa and this morning he raced ahead of the others to try to prove himself. He got to Camp III before anyone else and dropped his supply load. As Pemba and the others were still unloading theirs, Kami took off.

"I was just a few minutes behind him," Pemba said. "As I started off I could see the rope all the way down the face. Kami wasn't on it. I knew he must have fallen."

A lot of Sherpas don't clip in to the ropes. It takes time and they always want to show each other how fast they can go. They depend on a "Sherpa rappel"—twisting the rope around their arms and using the friction to hold them back. It's much faster but not very safe. Pemba guessed that Kami had tripped and his hand came free from the rope. Once you start falling on that steep, sheer ice, there is no way to stop. Judging by how soon he didn't see him on the rope, Pemba said he must have slipped right outside the camp.

A conversation ensued:

"He fell two thousand feet then."

"I hope at least he was knocked unconscious right away."

"He wasn't. I heard him scream as he flew by us."

"No, that was me," Lily said.

I mused sadly that Kami had wanted to be the first one down, and he was. This wasn't a tasteless joke, but rather an attempt to use irony to fend off an uncomfortable thought encroaching on me. Frank had asked why these things have to happen and then tried to beat the answer out of his backpack. But the answer wasn't in there. It was with the people who carried the packs. These things happen because we set the scene to make them happen. Once you decide that it's okay to pay people to risk their lives to help you accomplish a frivolous goal, you have to live with the consequences when the odds catch up with them. Kami was young, inexperienced, careless, and he didn't clip in. Todd had said, "At least it was no one else's fault." But it was. It was ours. It always feels better to blame the victim but we were responsible for Kami's death. Enticing these people to risk their lives for us is an abuse of power. We exploit them in the name of sport, offering them easy money and expedition glamour, and they don't stand a chance.

Yet it would be a mistake to blame ourselves entirely and not recognize that Kami's motivation had to be internal as well. He was responding to a deeply felt need to prove himself, impress others, taste glory, or whatever else it is that brings people to the highest mountains. In that way, he was no different than us. We had merely given him the opportunity to test himself—and to kill himself.

The rock I was sitting on was getting harder. I went to the cook tent for a cup of tea and some subdued lighting. The pot of porridge was still there that Kami had thoughtfully left in case anyone wanted seconds. Now I felt bad for not liking it this morning.

There are no set customs, no standard rules on whether a climb should be continued after a death. A decision can't be made until it happens because the effect on the expedition is the sum of the impact on each member. None of us had a sustained feeling to cancel the expedition. Nothing even as formal as a consensus was needed. There was just a shared understanding that we would continue. You can honestly consider people of all cultures to be equal, but it would be a lie to pretend you identify with them all equally. A young man cut down at the beginning of his potential is a universally understood tragedy. Our grief was real but the impact wasn't the same as it would have been were he "one of us."

A realistic and uncomfortable thought was easily avoided by invoking science. The GPS still needed to be put up and that was enough justification for being here and continuing on, though no one would deny that if it didn't have to be carried to the summit, we'd be a lot less interested in the project. We were here for the method, not the goal, but the GPS conveniently made it unnecessary to examine other motives which could prove selfish or egotistical.

In the morning, rows of prayer flags were strung up over the camp, a vibrant display in the early sunlight. The funeral procession, led by Todd and Lakpa-Rita, crossed under the colorful canopy, starting on its laborious way down the Cwm and the icefall. With the bright, cloudless sky, it was probably the nicest day since we'd been at Camp II.

Lakpa-Rita was crying when he left. He had taken Kami from his own tiny village of Tamé and had reassured his mother that he would take good care of her only son. Now he was bringing him back for cremation.

Todd felt strongly that as expedition leader, he had to go too. The descent would take three or four days. Then there were the ceremonies, after which he felt that out of respect he would need to stay a day or two before he could take his leave. But if we were to make another summit attempt, we'd have to start within the next few days. Our supplies wouldn't last much longer and the weather window would be closing. Todd knew as he left the camp that he was marching right out of the expedition.

The absence of Kami was obvious and painful as Dawa served us breakfast without his tentmate and assistant. Other climbers stopped by in the way one would expect when there was a death in the family, offering "condolences on the loss of your Sherpa."

Dawa was asked how he was managing. He said the cooking was okay but he had to change tents. "In my tent last night," he said, "there was too much imagination."

Fear of Falling
by Greg Child

Mountaineers can expect to encounter a variety of risks—from bad weather to rockfall. Greg Child's (born 1957) story tells how four young climbers who set out to climb Mount Zhioltaya Stena's Yellow Wall in Kyrgyzstan coped with a danger that took them entirely by surprise: terrorists.

The first shot hits the cliff at 6:15 a.m. The sun is rising over Central Asia, sending shafts of daylight through the gaps in a ridgeline of craggy summits, brightening the steep, shadowy Kara Su valley of Kyrgyzstan's Pamir Alai range. Deep in sleep, their two portaledges dangling 1,000 feet off the ground, the four climbers barely react to the thump of lead hitting granite. But when the second report echoes through the gorge, Jason "Singer" Smith bolts upright.

"What the hell was that?" he shouts, donning his helmet instinctively, assuming the rifle crack is the clatter of rockfall.

"We're being shot at, Singer!" Beth Rodden calls out in alarm from the other portaledge.

"That's irrational," Smith replies. "It's probably local hunters."

Then the third bullet hits right between the two platforms. Rock chips fly out of the crater, spraying the climbers.

"That was definitely for us!" Rodden shouts.

The climbers are bunked high on Mount Zhioltaya Stena, a 12,000-foot peak in this rugged former Soviet republic. It is August 12, day two of a planned four-day ascent of the 2,500-foot Yellow Wall, and they are making their way up to a sheer headwall, looking forward to sinking their hands into a highway of cracks splitting the face. The quartet represents a remarkable pool of American climbing talent, friends from years on the rock-wall circuit out West. A self-assured 22-year-old Utah native, Smith lives in his van in California. He has made a slew of notable ascents, including a 14-day solo of the 4,000-foot big wall of Mount Thor, near the Arctic Circle on Canada's Baffin Island. His nickname, Singer, is derived from his penchant for stitching up kitschy clothing on an old sewing machine. Lying beside Singer is Texas-raised John Dickey, the team photographer. Bearded, lanky, and at 25 the old man of the group, he's a seasoned world traveler and, since he moved to California six years ago, a frequent backcountry climber in the High Sierra. Rodden is a diminutive blond 20-year-old from Davis, California, with an angelic face that makes her look five years younger. Her appearance belies her toughness, however; she is one of the very few women—and the youngest—to have climbed at the top 5.14 rating of difficulty. Her soft-spoken boyfriend and bunk-mate, Tommy Caldwell, 22, is from Colorado. Built like a cross between a pit bull and a greyhound, he has laid claim to what is possibly America's hardest sport route, Kryptonite, a pitch near Rifle, Colorado, rated 5.14d. The group helicoptered into the Kara Su Valley from Bishkek, Kyrgyzstan's capital, two weeks ago, and they've got another good month of climbing to go. After they set up a base camp, Rodden and Caldwell began putting in this new route up the Yellow Wall while Smith and Dickey spent four days trekking down valley in an unsuccessful search for a telephone, to call about a lost duffel. Their journey had taken them past a Kyrgyz army camp and over a 14,000-foot pass, where they met yak herders who'd never seen foreigners.

The climbers peer over the edges of their portaledges and in the gathering light spot three men off the rubble-strewn slope below. The men wave their hands, gesturing that they should come down. The Americans yell to them to cease fire. Still sitting in their sleeping bags, they stare at each other with stunned expressions. Among them they can cope with any horror the mountains might dish out: avalanche, rockfall, stormy weather; surely this situation can somehow be worked out, too. Hanging here they are sitting ducks, so they start to draw straws to see who'll go down first to meet the guys with the guns.

Dickey steps up to the plate. "I'll go," he volunteers.

They tie their ropes end to end and Dickey clips his rappel device onto the nylon strand. He eases over the edge of the portaledge and swings into the void, carrying down a Motorola two-way radio. As he departs he blithely suggests he'll offer the gunmen a cigarette, a gambit that the laconic Californian has found useful in the Third World for defusing tense situations.

The climbers can't figure out what the trouble is. The area they are in—a complex of high valleys dubbed the Ak Su region—has been visited every summer for 20 years by scores of Russian, European, and American climbers. Renowned for its huge sheets of tawny granite, the Ak Su has been called the Yosemite of Central Asia. All that is required to climb here is a frontier permit from the government of Kyrgyzstan, which the Americans have.

Dickey spins slowly as he rappels down. Twenty-five long minutes pass before he reaches the slope. Through a 200mm camera lens, Smith watches the handshakes between Dickey and the gunmen, sees them reject the proffered pack of cigarettes. Then Dickey radios up.

"These guys want you to come down. They just, er, well, you better come down. They want to go back to our base camp for, er, breakfast." Smith knows Dickey well enough to glean from his quavering tone that something is seriously wrong.

Smith clips his rappel device to the rope and slides down. On the ground he is confronted by two men—the third has left the scene. Then are young; they wear fatigues and sport long black hair and beards. The men are packing Kalashnikov assault rifles, grenades, sidearms, and sheathed knives. Smith nervously shakes hands, and they trade names in a patois of gestures and the odd common word of English, Russian, and local dialect. The gunmen are Abdul, who seems to be the commander, and Obert. Smith sees that one is wearing a black Patagonia GoreTex jacket under his camo vest and a high-tech rucksack with a German label. Clearly these items were not mail-ordered; at the very least, the Americans figure, they are in the clutches of bandits. But Dickey also remembers seeing a short news story about Japanese geologists taken hostage here in 1999 by a group called the Islamic Movement of Uzbekistan, and the gunmen appear to fit the bill.

Rodden and Caldwell rappel down, and the gunmen indicate that everyone will head to the climbers' base camp, a mile down valley. Their tone is more matter-of-fact than menacing. They even smile occasionally. Yet there's no doubt who's in control. Half out of optimism, half out of a desire to suppress panic in the rest of the team, Dickey coolly reiterates that the gunmen just want some breakfast.

But when the climbers arrive in base camp they see that their tents, which they had sealed by tying the zippers together, are slit open at the walls. The third gunman—Isuf, or Su for short—is posted in the grassy meadow of camp, his weapon at his hip. He's wearing some of their clothing. A fourth man sits against a rock.

At first the Americans mistake this man for another bandit, until Caldwell and Rodden recognize him as Turat, a young Kyrgyz soldier who was friendly when he checked their permit a few days earlier. He's wearing civilian clothes now, and his face is stern. The Americans sit beside him, and when the gunmen aren't looking, Turat starts gesturing and scratching numbers in the sand. He manages to explain that he is a prisoner—taken off-duty, they judge from his dress. Next he holds up three fingers. Then he sweeps his hand across his throat.

"It wasn't hard to figure the math on this one," Smith tells me later. "There were three guys and one girl. I thought he meant that they'll take what they want from camp and then shoot the men."

"*Nyet, nyet,*" Turat insists when he sees the Americans' stricken faces. But the story he eventually gets across is hardly more encouraging: Yesterday he and three fellow soldiers were captured; the rebels executed his comrades, and they are keeping Turat alive as a guide. Turat points to his bloodstained pants—the blood of his friends.

Then Abdul summons Smith and Dickey to their big, yellow main tent. Inside, he and Obert are raiding the larder. They want to know the contents of each can and packet. A strange game of charades begins: When the rebels hold up a can of chicken meat, the climbers cluck "bok bok bok." When they point to a strip of beef jerky they intone "moo."

What the rebels don't want is anything that smacks of "oink oink." And, as Dickey has learned, they are not into tobacco. Turat warns them in a mix of Russian and English not to offer them vodka, either— the Muslims don't drink.

The rebels order the climbers to stuff four packs with about 30 to 50 pounds each of cans, candles, sleeping bags, and clothing. Then they confiscate their four two-way radios. As he packs, Dickey turns to Singer. A crooked, nervous smile contorts his lips.

"We're hostages," he says flatly.

This valley, these mountains, this country: It is all remote, but it was widely believed to be safe. As Lonely Planet's guide to Central Asia encourages, "Most travellers vote Kyrgyzstan the most appealing, accessible, and welcoming of the former Soviet Central Asian republics," touting the incredible peaks of the central Tien Shan and Pamir Alai ranges. Tourism, the book continues, "is one of the few things Kyrgyzstan has to sell to the outside world." Certainly Rodden, Caldwell, Dickey, and Smith had been welcomed warmly here, and their expedition, backed in part by The North Face (which sponsors Smith and Rodden), had not ventured far off the beaten climbing path. In fact, I had climbed here myself in 1995, on an earlier expedition sponsored by The North Face, with Lynn Hill, Alex Lowe, and Conrad Anker. We found a pastoral scene of verdant meadows and a scattered population of seminomadic Kyrgyz-Islamic subsistence farmers who come here in summer, tending yaks and cows. We also found a slew of virgin routes on the stupendous walls of Peak 4810, Peak 3850 (so called for their heights in meters), and Russian Tower. Two Russian teams and another

American group were also there, having helicoptered in from Tashkent, in Uzbekistan, and none of us encountered any hostility.

The next four years were equally calm, and Kyrgyzstan gained a reputation as Asia's hottest mountain playground. As recently as August 1999, the outfitter Mountain Travel–Sobek took trekkers to the same base camp where the climbers were kidnapped. But the frontiers of adventure, those last undiscovered and unspoiled places, are often the frontiers of political instability and civil conflict. They are often unspoiled not only because they are geographically remote, but also because they were historically frozen in place—for more than 50 years in Kyrgyzstan's case—by the geopolitical dictates of the Cold War. And now, as former outposts of the Soviet empire become hot zones of regional tension, they can also become dangerous to travelers. Fearing trouble, Mountain Travel–Sobek canceled its Ak Su trek this summer. And as Lonely Planet Online does warn adventure travelers heading for the boondocks of Kyrgyzstan, "There's a great temptation to hop off the bus in the middle of nowhere and hike into the hills, but this is not recommended if you value your life."

Indeed, Central Asia is a political powder keg—so much so that U.S. State Department officials refuse to even discuss the remote border regions of Kyrgyzstan, Tajikistan, and Uzbekistan on the record. But one official lists a Balkans-style litany of troubles: a five-year civil war that has killed 50,000 in Tajikistan; a weak Kyrgyzstan army; a repressive Soviet-style Uzbekistan government whose policies inflame the fundamentalist Islamic opposition. The most unstable element in this cauldron is war-torn, Taliban-controlled Afghanistan, now the world's greatest narco-state, churning out 4,600 tons of opium last year—even more than the Golden Triangle. Afghanistan is widely believed to be where militant groups like the Islamic Movement of Uzbekistan—the climbers' captors—get their training. Funding is handed out in the form of heroin. Rebels sell the drugs through pipelines to China, Russia, and Europe, and use the proceeds to buy arms from Russian, Chechen, and other sources. Much of this contraband is funneled across Central Asia's porous mountain borders, through high valleys like the Ak Su and Kara Su.

The IMU is a 1,200-man "cross-border, multinational fighting force," says Ahmed Rashid, author of the recent book *Taliban: Militant Islam, Oil, and Fundamentalism in Central Asia*. Mostly Uzbeks, the group's ranks include Afghans, Tajiks, Chechens, Pakistanis, emissaries from Saudi terrorist Osama bin Laden, and Filipino revolutionaries. The IMU, its Sunni Muslim membership having been repressed first by the Soviets and now by Uzbekistan's president-for-life, Islom Karimov, seeks to overthrow Karimov, who has detained up to 50,000 Muslim men from the country's Ferghana Valley. The ultimate goal is to create an independent Islamic state in the valley—one that, like Afghanistan, would adhere to the strictest eye-for-an-eye Sharia religious law. Led by Juma Namangani, an Uzbek warlord, the IMU operates out of the high mountains of Uzbekistan and Tajikistan, which embrace southwestern Kyrgyzstan from north and south. The Ak Su lies between their mountain stronghold and Ferghana, the object of their desire.

On August 23, 1999, IMU guerrillas poured over Tajik passes in the Pamirs into southwestern Kyrgyzstan, attached Kyrgyz soldiers, and seized four Japanese geologists. The hostages languished in Tajik camps for 64 days until their release. The Japanese and Kyrgyzstan governments claim that no ransom was paid, but as sources in the U.S. State Department and the independent Central Asia Institute confirm, several million dollars may have changed hands.

If ransom was paid, then the climbers who flock to the Ak Su would represent an irresistible cash crop. And since the Japanese incident, the State Department insists, it has posted explicit warnings on its Web site about fighting and kidnapping risks in the area. When Smith, Dickey, Rodden, and Caldwell left the States on July 25, the site displayed a "Public Announcement" dated June 15, 2000, and, as it does for every country, a "Consular Information Sheet." Dated November 17, 1999, Kyrgyzstan's sheet cautioned U.S. citizens "to avoid all travel west and south of the southern provincial capital Osh." But these alerts stopped short of a full-fledged "Travel Warning," which advises Americans to avoid a country completely. The climbers read some, but not all, of this advice, and they interpreted much of it as outdated. They did not contact the U.S. embassy when they landed in Bishkek. Their Kyrgyz travel agent, Ak Sai Tours, made no mention of danger, nor did the helicopter crew that flew them to the Ak Su, nor did the Kyrgyz soldiers who checked their permits.

At around noon on August 12, Abdul orders his five captives to dismantle the base camp. When Turat tugs a long, sturdy aluminum tent stake out of the ground, he feels the pointed end with his finger and catches Smith's eye. It is clear that Turat wants to use the stakes as daggers. Earlier, he furtively signaled that he will try to kill the rebels if he can, and that there are 15 Kyrgyz soldiers in the valley and 17 rebels. Fighting is imminent.

Seeing the desperate look on Turat's face, Smith scans the ransacked base camp and decides that the odds are not very good. The three men carrying assault rifles are alert and wary. "No way, Turat," Smith whispers, shaking his head. "No way."

The climbers pack their leftover gear into duffel bags, and the rebels conceal these under pine boughs. Abdul indicates to them that they should carry their passports in their pockets. That's a good sign, Dickey thinks; it means they want us alive. Still, as they prepare to move out, they are terrified; their teeth are chattering. Rodden, as the only woman, is particularly apprehensive, her mind racing, thinking, "What'll these guys do to me?"

As they pack, Abdul comes across a photo of a smiling Beth and Tommy, arm in arm. He points to the young couple, and in sign language asks if they are together. "Yes—married," Dickey says instantly. If the rebels think Rodden is married, he reasons, maybe she'll he safer.

Then the radio squawks—a message from Su's nearby position on the small rise. Abdul orders everyone to scramble under trees, and seconds later the windy roar of a Russian-made Mi8 gunship fills the valley. The climbers watch as the dronelike helicopter flies toward the Yellow Wall and rises until it is level with the deserted portaledge camp. Abdul sees that Rodden is distraught; he shakes his finger at her and smiles, signing, "Don't cry." The chopper hovers long enough to see that the platforms are abandoned and then retreats down the Kara Su Valley, seemingly in the direction of the Kyrgyz army camp, 25 miles away, that Smith and Dickey had seen on their trek.

Abdul barks orders, and they quit base camp hastily. It is clear they are going on a long walk—probably, Turat is indicating, all the way to Uzbekistan, 50 miles north. About a mile from base camp they near the confluence of the Kara Su and the Ak Su, at which point the two rivers form the Karavshin. Scouting for soldiers, the rebels creep from one boulder to another along the riverside trail. Suddenly the helicopter makes another sweep and the climbers are ordered into the bushes. Leveling his rifle point-blank at Dickey, Abdul screams that anyone who attracts the attention of the helicopter crew is dead. Again the Mi8 departs.

As they walk, Smith tries to reassure Rodden. "Your concern is no longer Beth," he tells her. "I'm thinking about Beth from now on. All you are thinking about is whatever these men tell you to do. If you see a helicopter I want you to play James Bond and jump headfirst into whatever tree these guys tell you to jump into. This is just a big giant video game and we are gonna turn it off in a couple of hours."

Quaking, Rodden nods.

The group traverses along the slope of a hill separating the Kara Su and the Ak Su Valleys. At this point Obert marches off down valley. At about 1 p.m. they stand 200 yards uphill front a mud-brick farmhouse. Beyond it a footbridge spans the Ak Su as it crashes downstream. Two Kyrgyz soldiers are outside the house, talking to the farmer. The rebels order their prisoners to sneak uphill through the trees; then Abdul urges them to run. When Rodden starts lagging under her pack, Smith grabs it. It is bright orange, a certain target. Twenty minutes later the group crests the hill. Gasping and sweating, they rest. Turat sits among the climbers, with the rebels watching from a few feet away.

"Over there," he signs to his fellow captives, pointing across the river. "Over there they kill me."

• • •

Sometime after 3 p.m. the shooting starts. The band of guerrillas and prisoners has stumbled downhill, across the bridge, and up the east side of the Ak Su Valley onto a steep, forested slope covered in boulders. The rebels have then split the hostages into two groups and hidden them under sprawling junipers. Another young rebel named Abdullah has joined them and the fighters have taken up positions among the rocks, laying, Dickey figures, an ambush. Everybody waits.

More soldiers are advancing up the hill, shouting to one another, when Abdul gives the order to fire. Within minutes two Kyrgyz soldiers are felled. Adbul's firearm is a cannon, a fast-action AK-74—more like an M-16 than the other rebels' AK-47s. Rodden, Caldwell, and Turat hunker behind a tree trunk, shielding their faces from the flying shell casings, ricochets, and rock chips. Ten minutes into the firefight Abdul scurries to the boulder and calls Turat's name. Turat is calm, Caldwell notices—"the toughest man I've ever seen," he'll say later—though it is clear the soldier is about to be executed. Caldwell has his arms around Rodden. She is weeping and shaking.

Turat turns to Rodden and, in the mix of words and hand signs with which they have learned to communicate, he tells her, "You, don't cry. I don't cry, and I am the one who will die."

Then he stands and walks toward Abdul, and the two disappear behind a car-size boulder 200 feet up the hill. The climbers hear two quick reports of a pistol, and then silence.

The battle continues, as Kyrgyz soldiers outflank the rebels. Abdul announces that everyone must move up to the boulder where Turat was taken. Dickey takes the lead, shouldering his pack and sprinting. The Kyrgyz soldiers draw a bead on him. Shots thump around his feet as close as nine inches. He sloughs off his pack and dives toward the boulder. The pack, lying on the ground, is riddled with bullets.

Smith runs to the boulder next; then Rodden. When she arrives, he twists her head away from Turat's corpse. Caldwell arrives last, chased by rifle fire, and wraps himself around Rodden like a shield. Behind the boulder now are the four Americans, Abdul, Su, and Abdullah.

"Abdullah was sitting against Turat's corpse," Smith will later recall. "He picked up Turat's arm and dropped it. Both he and Abdul laughed. Then Abdul kicked Turat's legs aside so he could make room to do his evening prayer. Bullets were raining over his head and he was kneeling, praying."

It is 4 p.m. when the first mortar round whistles in, exploding against the front of the boulder. The climbers huddle together in a ball of arms and legs. Heavy rifle fire zeroes in on them. When they look up they see Kyrgyz soldiers in positions 100 feet from the boulder. The whup-whup-whup of a helicopter, spotting overhead, adds to the noise. Smith is crouched over Turat's legs, wondering if he should pull the body over him and his friends. But the head wound is grotesque.

A third mortar round explodes 80 feet behind them at dusk, and Abdul makes them lighten their loads, ditching the packs and taking just a small sack with a few articles of clothing, credit cards, Turat's sleeping bag, a dozen PowerBars, and a handful of candy. This will be the total rations for six people for the next four days. At nightfall they run uphill, from tree to tree, through random fire. They march roughly four miles, heading north, downstream toward the Karavshin. They climb high on the tugged hillside to outrun the creeping light of the waxing moon, which backlights a skyline of shark-tooth peaks.

August 13, 3 a.m. The climbers have been moving for 18 hours. They shuffle forward like zombies. Abdullah has vanished into the night on another mission, and it is just Abdul and Su. At dawn the rebels stop beside a fast-flowing tributary of the Karavshin and order their hostages to crawl into two small caves.

Singer and Caldwell take one, with Su bedded down, gun in hand, at its mouth. Rodden and Dickey, with Abdul on guard, take the other. At first Dickey cannot believe that Abdul is serious when he motions them into "a small-ass little hole with a mud floor." The cave is 18 inches tall at its highest point. It is cramped for Rodden, who is five-foot-one, but Dickey, at six feet, can only lie with his knees to his chest. Spooning with Dickey, Rodden cries on and off all day. "Do you think anyone knows where we are?" she asks. "They're not gonna kill us, are they?" Dickey is as terrified as she. In the early afternoon, sun-warmed glacial melt swells the river, and the stream pours into the cave. Wallowing in four inches of ice water, in thermal undershirts, Dickey and Rodden shiver for 17 hours.

They emerge as the moon creeps over the opposite ridge. The food in their stomachs is long gone, replaced by lonely cramps; their captors are as hungry as they are. The rebels intend to cross the river, but fording it is out of the question—the rapids are Class IV. So Abdul and Su try to maneuver a log over the foaming torrent. They push the log halfway across; then it jams.

Suddenly Smith kicks off his shoes and wades into the waist-deep water. The current nearly overpowers him and the rebels call for him to return, shouting and gesturing, "danger, danger." Smith ignores them. He muscles the log toward the opposite bank, crouches atop a slick boulder, and steadies the log. Shouting above the roar, he motions for everyone to cross. Dickey goes first.

"What the hell was with that?" he asks.

"We gotta get out of here," Smith says.

Watching the rebels bungle the river crossing, Smith and the others realize that there are a lot of things they can do to help themselves. As Smith will put it later, "One: They should think we were 100 percent behind their cause. Two: We should show them we were tough as nails because for all we knew they might eliminate the weak; somebody twists an ankle, they would kill them. Three: It would help if we were super-cool and helpful to them, because that would lead to . . . Four: They could trust us."

And indeed, as Abdul balances across the wobbling log he pauses at the final hop onto the boulder. Smith extends his hand and—to his astonishment—Abdul hands over his rifle. Smith passes the weapon to Dickey, then grips Abdul's hand. There is only one moment to react: Smith must kick the log out from under Abdul and send him into the rapids, and Dickey must flip the safety on the automatic and drop Su. If the idea works they are free; if not, Su will kill them. But the moment passes and Abdul reaches the bank.

The guerrilla smiles and praises Smith's courage. "You soljah?" he asks.

• • •

Half a PowerBar per day, brown, silty river water to drink, and cold, tor-turously confined bivouacs take their toll on the hostages as they spend the nights of August 14, 15, and 16 marching around cliffs and steep rubble on the east flank of the Karavshin Valley. On the third night they only get 100 yards before Smith collapses. Rodden sees that he's exhausted, so she takes out their last candy bar, a Three Musketeers—how fitting, she thinks—breaks it into small chunks, and pushes it into his mouth.

They pass no huts, no farmers. None live this far up the steep hill-sides, and afraid of both the soldiers and the rebels, the locals give each faction a wide berth. Surreal moments abound. The whole valley, in tact, has turned nightmarish. On August 14 the hostages may have noticed the faint sound of a gun battle far down the Karavshin Valley. Rebel snipers had 30 Kyrgyz soldiers pinned in a crossfire in a narrow canyon. None survived. Later the Americans will pass that way and find blood-spattered rocks and a bullet-riddled field jacket. During the next two weeks the conflict will escalate all along the Kyrgyzstan-Tajikistan border. Firefights will claim up to 48 Kyrgyz soldiers, 12 antirebel Uzbek soldiers, and 75 rebels. More foreigners will be kidnapped. Else-where in the region, Russian border guards stationed near the Afghanistan-Tajikistan border will clash with rebels, and a passenger on a train leaving Tashkent bound for Kyrgyzstan will be arrested carrying 20 kilos of explosives.

But for all the climbers know, they are alone. Surely, they think, the Kyrgyz army knows they've been taken: Helicopters are ever-present, and one afternoon, as Rodden and Dickey lie hidden beside Abdul at the second bivouac, two soldiers walk to within a yard of them. Rodden's blond hair is visible through the pine boughs. The men say something in Kyrgyz and leave. But nobody moves: Abdul carries a grenade fixed to his belt; if someone makes a move he pulls the pin and everyone dies.

Killing has become the main topic at Smith and Caldwell's bivouac. Bashing in the rebels' heads with rocks, stealing their handguns, pushing them off cliffs, using choke holds and sharp sticks, punching them in the larynx, and strangling them with bootlaces are all discussed. Smith talks; Caldwell listens, quietly taking it in.

"How do you know all this stuff?" Caldwell asks.

"I hung out with thugs at school. I read *The Anarchist Cookbook*," comes the glib reply. Then Smith pauses and thinks about what is happening to his mind.

"Tommy, when I woke up today I realized I had lost all compassion for these men. I don't hate them. But I'm ready to do whatever it takes to get out of here."

Caldwell nods.

That day Smith begins working on winning Su's trust. When helicopters appear he nudges him awake and helps to camouflage their hiding places with more brush. On the move, he stops to lend his captor a hand on short cliffs, patting him on the back and telling him he's a "good alpinista," much to Su's amusement.

Su clearly defers to Abdul, who looks ten years older than his claimed age of 26. (The climbers doubt he's even called Abdul, in fact, as the other rebels carefully avoid addressing him by name.) But, Smith will say later, "At first Su scared me the most. He had a really blank look on his face. But soon I was doing things like showing him my passport, comparing ages and birth places with him. He told me he was 19 and came from Tashkent."

By the night of August 16, day five, the group descends the hillside back to the Karavshin. To their amazement they start walking upstream, toward their Kara Su base camp. During the five-mile march the rebels shift into battle mode and fan out in front. The Americans consider running, but they know that in their weak condition—they are now out of food—they won't get far before they are mowed down. Yet the rebels are getting lax.

They cross the bridge near the battleground and enter the Kara Su Valley. Abdul gives the order to bivouac—in another set of coffin-like holes in the riverbank—and signals that he'll go ahead and kill some soldiers to get some food. Before he leaves he pulls Dickey's boots off his feet and tries them on. They are too large so he tosses them back.

"You fucker," Dickey sneers.

Then Abdul makes Smith hand over his insulated coat, leaving him in a T-shirt, angry and freezing. But what catches Smith off guard is Abdul's parting message—a mix of words and gestures that clearly means, "Su will protect you." As if he were now one of them.

Before a storm, climbers always sense tension. The changing weather charges the atmosphere with a last-chance sort of feeling. On August 17, the sixth day of captivity, clouds fill the sky. The temperature is near freezing, the air damp. Something's brewing. Before dawn Abdul returned with two stinking, greasy 40-pound sacks. One contains salty yak butter, the other balls of congealed yogurt—Abdul and Su, as desperate and starving as their charges, start in on the provisions, most likely taken from a farmer. The Americans each force down one or two of the rancid balls. In his bivvy cave Smith sits on the suitcase-size slab of butter, insulation against the cold rocks. For the first time in a long time, Caldwell prays.

At dusk they get under way again. Abdul explains that they must climb the rugged west side of the Kara Su Valley to a plateau 3,000 feet above. There they will rendezvous, waiting several days if necessary, with Abdullah and Obert—who the Americans think must be dead, judging from their radio silence these last two days and several distant bursts of fire. Eventually they will be taken north, to Uzbekistan, the hostages are told.

Then Abdul turns away, signing that he will catch up after he heads up to the Americans' base camp, where the stashed duffels hold fresh radio batteries. It is 10 p.m. From where they stand, at the foot of a perilously steep climb that they'll have to tackle without ropes, it is an hour to base camp, an hour back. Su is now their only guard; the hostages will have most of the night alone with him. As they begin to climb the succession of slabby cliffs and steep grassy slopes, Dickey turns to his companions and says, "We gotta whack this guy, tonight."

Stifled by rain clouds, the now full moon rounds the mountainside and bleeds onto the group as it reaches a point 2,000 feet above the river. The Americans and their guard climb a moderately difficult rib, a series of 5.2 pitches, flanked by glacier-carved cliffs. Smith and Dickey shadow Su the whole way, openly talking about finding a place to push him off. But they are each burdened with the heavy bags of butter and yogurt balls, and Smith has Turat's sleeping bag draped clumsily around his shoulders, like a shawl.

"We had all been talking about killing someone for days," Caldwell will remember, clearly uncomfortable with the memory, "but Beth had said to me she just didn't think I could emotionally handle it. So I was staying out of it."

"Alpinista!" Su orders Smith to the front. He waves his hand at the cliff as if to ask, "Which way?"

Smith heads up the 60-degree face, pointing out the handholds to Su, urging him on like a guided client. Su slings his AK-47 over his shoulder and scrambles up. A shove here would be fatal, and Smith steps into position to body-slam Su off the ledge. But the rebel skirts around him, oblivious, and starts up another step of rock.

"OK, this is it," Dickey says in a trembling voice. He hands Smith the sack of yogurt balls and climbs into position, just below Su.

"Come on, do it, John," comes a collective murmur out of the night. But Su moves beyond Dickey's reach. It is now midnight. They are near the top of the last cliff. Somebody has to do something.

Caldwell is thinking his friends might not do it. And he starts worrying about how they would survive a storm up here, worrying about Beth, wondering what will happen to them all in Uzbekistan. He turns to Beth and asks, "Do you want me to do it?" She doesn't say anything. Then he starts moving toward Su.

Fueled by a wave of adrenaline, Caldwell scrambles across the ledge and up the cliff. He reaches up, grabs the rifle slung over Su's back, and pulls. A faint breath of surprise, a sound like *whaaa*, escapes Su's lips. He is falling.

The rebel arcs through the circle of the moon, pedaling air. The climbers see him hit a ledge 30 feet down with a crack. Then Su rolls off into the darkness, over the 1,500-foot cliff to the river below.

Caldwell is screaming. Clambering up the cliff in seconds, he curls up in a ball and begins gasping, "Holy shit, I just killed a guy."

Rodden reaches him and embraces him. "How can you love me now?" Caldwell sobs. "After I did this?"

"You just saved my life, Tommy," she answers. "I couldn't love you more."

Then Dickey is shouting, "Let's go, let's go!" But Caldwell, the one least likely to have acted on their talk of killing Su, is beside himself.

"Tommy, listen to me," Smith shouts into his face. "We did nothing wrong. We just saved our lives. When we get home we'll say we all did it, OK? But right now we have to get the fuck out of here. Go!"

They take off at a frantic pace, moving diagonally downhill, occasionally pausing to console Caldwell and catch their breath. Then the sound of rocks sliding behind them stops their hearts and they run again, stumbling over scree until, at 1:15 in the morning, they reach the Karavshin.

Beside the river is a well-worn trail that Smith and Dickey recognize from their trek; from here it is 10 miles to the Kyrgyz army camp. They are nearly hallucinating from fatigue, yet they keep stumbling forward. A herd of cows, moonlit in their path, frightens them: They mistake them for rebels. The climbers hug the shadows, running from tree to tree.

Hours later, they cross a footbridge near a bend in the river; now they are just a mile and a half from the army camp and a few hundred yards from a forward outpost. They're on the home stretch. But suddenly three men—rebels—materialize out of the forest, one of them just 15 feet behind them. One shouts something, then the muzzle flash and crack of AK-47s fills the night. Yellow tracers fly past their heads.

Dickey dives behind a bush. Caldwell and Rodden hide behind a rock. Smith starts running, dodging bullets, but alone and in front he suddenly feels naked, and he turns and runs back to the others. The four collide and then run together toward the outpost. It occurs to Caldwell that rebels might be manning that, too, but there is no turning back. Then shots from the front streak over their heads. Shots in front, shots behind. They are in no-man's-land. A figure stands in the doorway of a nearby hut, aiming a rifle at them. Army or rebels? They can't tell. They dive into the dark hut anyway.

Smith is first over the threshold. *"Americanski! Americanski!"* he shouts, holding his hands high.

All they see are gun barrels. Heaving with fear the four sprawl face-down on the dirt floor. Hands frisk them. Then one of the dark figures detects that Rodden is a woman.

"Oh, madame!" the man says, surprised. He removes his hands from her and steps back apologetically.

"We almost made it," shouts Rodden, confused, thinking Abdul will step forward any moment.

"We did make it, Beth!" Smith cries.

Minutes later Kyrgyz soldiers are thrusting cans of sardines and canteens of water into their hands. The soldiers have turned back the rebels. It is 4 a.m. on August 18. The climbers have escaped.

If their ordeal took place in a mountainous black hole, the four Americans now step into a whirlwind. A hurried hike with soldiers through the blood-soaked canyon gets them to a helicopter that whisks them to the town of Batken. That morning, the U.S. embassy learns for the first time that Americans have been kidnapped. Dressed in ill-fitting Kyrgyz army fatigues—their clothes are in tatters and they have lost all their gear—the climbers appear on Kyrgyzstan's state-run TV. They are hailed as heroes. They board the private jet of President Askar Akayev. They fly to Bishkek, where they are met by U.S. embassy officials and they make their first calls home. While in Bishkek they learn they weren't the only climbers taken hostage: Six Germans, three Russians, two Uzbeks, and a Ukrainian either escaped or were rescued in military operations on August 16. By September 5, Minister Councillor Nurdek Jeenbaez of the Kyrgyz embassy in Washington, D.C., claims that the rebels have been pushed out of the area by his country's forces. Abdul, Obert, and Abdullah have most likely died fighting or faded hack into the mountain passes of the Pamir. No one can say if Su's body has been found.

By August 25, all four climbers are home. When they hit the San Francisco tarmac, they slip back into their lives—or try. Caldwell and Rodden are reunited with their close-knit families, and Tommy is soon back up on the Colorado cliffs with his main ropemate, his father, Mike. Dickey and his girlfriend head to the Burning Man Festival in the Nevada desert. Smith returns to his Chevy van and to his job at The North Face, where he runs the A5 division, which makes high-end climbing accoutrements. And in press conferences, morning TV shows, and interviews, the four friends hedge around discussion of the death of Su. We all pushed him, they insist. That's the pact they had made; they would stick together.

Then one night Caldwell phones me from the Roddens' house in Davis. He has been reticent all along, reluctant to talk. This time, though, he sounds sure of himself. "This is the deal," he says. He takes a deep breath. "I was the one who pushed Su. It was something I wasn't prepared to do, so when I did it I was pretty shaken up. Jason and John said that we would say we all did it. That helped me a lot. I'm still coming to terms with it."

Smith is coming to terms with the experience in a different way. "When we reached the army camp," he tells me as we drive in his van to the Oakland airport in late August, "I said to everyone that if there was a week in my life I would want to relive, then this would be it. To experience every human emotion in such a short time, under those intense, life-threatening circumstances. I would gladly go back."

I have heard war veterans say such things. And I have said the same, in private, about peaks that took friends' lives and that I felt sure had been about to take mine. But veterans of combat and survivors of high-mountain accidents carry a burden that takes time to understand.

In the long run, Beth Rodden may be speaking for all four climbers when she admits to me, three weeks after their return to America, that she has begun having nightmares. "I see Abdul," she says. "I see weird concoctions of battles. My friends are in them, and I'm always running from something."

The rebel Su survived his fall and was made a prisoner of the Kyrgyz military. I traveled in March 2001 to Kyrgyzstan with the former hostages Jason Smith and John Dickey. We interviewed Su (whose real name turned out to be Rafshan Sharipov) in a prison cell in the head-quarters of the former KGB. He was awaiting trial on charges of ter-rorism. It was an emotional encounter for all parties. A Kyrgyz court in the summer of 2001 sentenced Sharipov to death, with the right to appeal.

—Greg Child

from Stolen Lives
by Malika Oufkir and
Michele Fitoussi

Malika Oufkir (born 1953) was the eldest daughter of a top aide to Morocco's King Hassan II. Malika's father was executed after participating in a failed 1972 coup attempt. Malika, her five siblings and her mother were imprisoned for 15 years. Finally, on April 19, 1987, Malika, her sister Maria and her brothers Raouf and Abdellatif escaped through a tunnel under the prison walls.

We had been living in the shadows for so long that our eyes had grown accustomed to the dark. We stood rooted to the spot, clutching one another, gazing at the night without any sense of fear. On the contrary, we were thrilled, exhilarated, convinced that the divine protection we had enjoyed so far would continue to safeguard us.

There was no sign of life from the guards' quarters, and we began to crawl across the damp field.

We could hear the barking of stray dogs. They were racing towards us, making straight for us, aggressive, starving and more ferocious than watchdogs. There must have been about ten of them, bounding through the dark behind the leader of the pack. They were getting closer and closer. We could feel their panting breath. Once again we huddled together for protection. Their leader came forward baring his fangs, growled and looked poised to attack. We froze, like statues, and held our breath, waiting for a miracle. Which, improbable as it seemed, was what occurred. The dog gave an unfathomable whine and slunk away, followed by the rest of the pack.

But the reprieve did not last long. Alerted by the dogs, the guards beamed their torches and floodlights onto the field. We froze again, praying that we would melt into the shadows. Certain of discovery this time, we stood there shivering, waiting for their shots to ring out.

The guards in the watchtowers exchanged a few words. At last the lights went off.

We stood there, unable to move for two or three minutes that felt like hours, then we set off again, crawling towards the right instead of going straight ahead. We were trying to move out of sight of the camp.

We found ourselves in a field of beans, closer to the barracks side. We needed a short rest, so we rolled over onto our backs and looked at the camp facing us for the first time. The full moon clearly picked out the top of the fence, the watchtowers and the walls. The rest was engulfed in a whitish halo of fog. It was a grim sight.

So this was the place where we had spent ten years of our life, where we had lost our best years, our hopes, our illusions, our health and our youth. In this death camp—there are no other words to describe our prison—we had been pariahs, cast out by the world, waiting for the end that was so slow in coming. Locked up inside, we had tried to forget where we were. But now, in that field, contemplating the place where we had suffered so much, the reality suddenly came home to us. And we were devastated.

I couldn't stop myself from sobbing at the thought and I wept even more when I thought of those we had left behind. I was so afraid for them. My heart contracted and a shudder ran through me. I heard the others crying softly; they all felt the same way.

We lay there for a moment, then we pulled ourselves together. The field was planted with broad beans, which we ate raw. Fresh, sweet and delicious, they tasted of freedom. Crawling, we set off again, and then, when we judged that we were far enough away from the barracks, we stood up and walked on in silence. The fields were so wet that we were soaked from head to foot.

In the pitch dark, with no landmarks and no signposts, we quickly realized that we were going round in circles. It was as distressing as being lost at sea or in the desert.

There was nothing to give us any clue where the road was, and none of us had a good sense of direction. Mother had taught me to read the stars, but I must have been a very bad student as I couldn't find the Great Bear, or Cassiopeia, or the Evening Star.

We continued to wander aimlessly.

A cough sent a chill down our spines. It came from overhead. Looking up, we saw a watchtower: we were back at the camp.

We didn't hang around, we turned on our heels and ran. We began to feel desperate. Tired, with dread in the pit of our stomachs, we stopped and lit a precious cigarette that we had carefully saved for this occasion. We smoked in silence, our hearts heavy, still thinking about Mother and the others.

We weren't on safe ground yet. We didn't know which way to turn. Then I asked Abdellatif to guide us.

'We are adults,' I said to him. 'We may have committed sins, but not you, you are so pure . . . if there is a God, he'll take pity on you. You will lead us to freedom.'

We followed him without a word. Our bodies were aching and our clothes soaked through, but we had to keep going.

'Kika, come and see, there's something hard. I don't know what it is.'

Abdellatif had never walked on asphalt. We rolled on it and kissed it. We felt like cosmonauts venturing their first steps on the moon.

We went back into a field to change into our 'civilian' clothes. I put on a long dress that Mother had worn in the Seventies, a cashmere print in autumnal shades. The others slipped on plain trousers and sweaters. They were a bit outmoded but were supposed to make them look 'normal'. We wore our Vuitton boots and we dumped our combat gear in the fields.

We set off again. As leader of the band, I accelerated the pace, exhorting the others to keep up. They trailed behind dragging their feet, they were so tired. Raouf laughed at my manic speed. He put on a

German accent and urged me on, saying, 'Go, Jeanne, go,' a subtle allu-
sion to my Alsatian governess.

Eventually we came to a large building, a dairy cooperative. We con-
ferred and decided to try out our first scenario. Maria and Abdellatif
hid. Supported by Raouf, I launched into a Moroccan-style screaming
fit, invoking Allah and the Prophets.

This brought out a guard, armed with a stick. He wore a jellabah
with a hood. I crumpled into his arms without waiting for his permission. He had no option but to support me.

He looked at Raouf suspiciously and asked him what was going on.

'My wife had a miscarriage last week. She can't get over it.'

The man was doubly suspicious.

'I didn't hear any noise. Where have you come from out of the blue,
in the middle of the night?'

Without giving him time to ask any more questions, I fell to the
ground again, pretending to writhe in pain. With many polite phrases,
Raouf asked him for a glass of water. He explained that we had come
from Belgium and hadn't been back to Morocco for fifteen years.

'Our car has broken down,' he added.

The guard was suspicious, like all Moroccans who have learned to
survive under a regime of terror. He did not believe Raouf and questioned him closely, trying to catch him out. But he did fetch me some
water.

During the conversation, I managed to slip in the fact that we were
related to Driss Basri, the Minister of the Interior, which had the
desired effect of intimidating the guard: the man calmed down a little.
We tried to get him to talk, we wanted to know where we were. He suggested we wait for the dairy truck that was going to Bir-Jdid, the nearest
town. At last we had the information we so badly needed.

We waited forty-five minutes for the truck, terrified that the man
might raise the alarm, but he had no telephone. The dairy gates
opened, the truck came out . . . and drove off without stopping to pick
us up.

We were frantic. It was already four o'clock in the morning, we had been going round in circles since eleven o'clock at night and we had just wasted another three-quarters of an hour waiting for the truck. The only positive thing was that at last we knew where we were going.

We set off down the road again, our spirits at a low ebb. We must have formed a strange procession in the dawn glow, two boys and two girls walking like robots, with halting steps, and staring straight ahead. But we didn't have time to think about our appearance; we had to keep moving.

After a few kilometres, we came across one of those local buses that stop in all the villages. The farmers thronging around the bus stop carried bulky sacks, and there were chickens and sheep milling about.

We joined the fray. We felt awkward, convinced that everybody was staring at us. Until then we had been protected by the dark, but now it was daybreak and the dawn light made us feel exposed.

Raouf offered to pay the driver with the nameplate from my father's identity bracelet. The other passengers paid for their tickets with eggs or hens, bartering as hard as they could. The driver was wary, and refused. He wanted cash and nothing else. We gave up the idea of the bus and set off again on foot.

A truck drove past and I stuck out my thumb. The driver, a friendly hippie type, gave all four of us a lift without any questions. He simply warned us that at the entrance to Bir-Jdid we were likely to encounter a police roadblock but that we could avoid it by following a little path where he set us down.

Luckily, he was wrong and we reached Bir-Jdid without seeing anything resembling a roadblock.

The town was tiny and extremely poor. The road was lined with a few neglected houses, cafés and butchers' shops, and that was all. It was half-past six. The cafés were just opening, and through their doors radios blared out deafening music. The waiters bustled about and customers ordered coffee or mint tea. Life was there, unchanging, resuming its course as it had done each morning that we had been excluded from it.

The street felt strange to me, and it took me a few minutes to realize why. I was no longer accustomed to noise. The shouts, the voices, the hooting, the oriental songs, the tyres screeching on the road . . . all those sounds grated on my ears. Raouf and the others were in a similar state. The light hurt our eyes, and our heads throbbed.

Frightened by so much commotion, we stared eagerly about us and people stared back. But, even though we cut a wretched figure, we did not look out of place in these surroundings, especially Raouf, who was as toothless as the peasant farmers, as a result of abscesses and beatings.

At the end of the village was a collective taxi stand where a dense crowd was milling around. Raouf went ahead as a scout and when he came back, he told me that the taxis were headed for Casablanca. He went off again to negotiate with one of the drivers, and their discussion lasted a good twenty minutes. I was anxious, I was sure his plan would never work; and so when I saw him waving excitedly, I didn't realize straight away that he wanted us to join him. But another miracle had happened: the driver had agreed to take us in exchange for the gold nameplate.

Two men were sitting in front next to the driver. The four of us got in the back, and the taxi roared off. We were silent and pensive. I thought of Mother and my sisters with a heavy heart.

My gaze rested on Abdellatif. For the first time in ages, I realized just what a terrible state he was in. He had been incarcerated since the age of three and a half. He was outside for the first time in his life, at the age of eighteen. My little brother sat open-mouthed, watching the road fly past, a glazed look in his eyes. Bewildered by so many new sights, he was like a zombie who had just climbed out of the tomb.

He had been in a car only two or three times in his life, and then only to be shunted from one prison to another.

My sister Maria weighed barely thirty kilos. Her huge dark eyes devoured her tiny, gaunt face. Raouf was as thin as she was, but bloated from water retention. He was pale, feverish and toothless.

Nearly fifteen years had gone by, fifteen years of torture that had scarred us terribly. But, when I studied the three of them closely, I would catch an expression, mannerism or smile that reminded me of the children they had once been.

I felt responsible for their condition. I cursed prison for what it had done to them, what it had done to each one of us.

I will never forget my shock on our arrival in Casablanca, as we drove through the working-class district. I had completely forgotten what the city was like. The crowds walked hurriedly, jostling, filling the pavements and rushing across the road without looking. It made my head swim, the screech of brakes, the cries of the street vendors, a horse-drawn barouche, two women arguing, a policeman blowing his whistle at a speeding car. I inhaled the smell of petrol and the aroma of food coming from restaurants and stalls.

It was the first time in fifteen years that I had seen so many people at once, that my ears had heard so many sounds, and my senses had been assailed in this way. It seemed to me that the population of Morocco had tripled. Everything was bigger, newer, more modern. There were more women in the street, dressing in European-style clothes and make-up; they were well groomed.

This continual procession of people walking with their heads down, not seeing where they were going, reminded me of Chaplin's *Modern Times*. I felt curiously sorry for them. All in all, they were more to be pitied than I was. Perplexed, I mused: 'So is this life, is this freedom? They are just as much prisoners as I was . . .'

Myriad details that I had never been aware of in my previous life jumped out at me: the apartment blocks like rabbit hutches, the vacant stares, poverty, exhaustion, needless stress.

My companions were probably not thinking along those lines at all, or at least not in so many words. Abdellatif's jaw dropped in amazement, Raouf and Maria were silent. The taxi was driving too fast. I was afraid every time it suddenly braked. After all the trouble we had gone to, this was not the moment to die in an accident.

The driver began to complain. He was suspicious of us and wanted to go to the police.

'I'm not allowed to take you into the centre of town . . .'

Raouf managed to sweet-talk him into it. After all, we had given him a little piece of solid gold, the equivalent of two thousand five hundred dirhams, for a journey that was barely worth fifty.

Raouf gave him the address of Jamila, his teenage sweetheart, in the residential district of Anfa. While the driver was looking for the street, I stared out without recognizing anything. I felt as though I had landed on another planet. We were like the Lilliputians arriving in the Land of the Giants in *Gulliver's Travels*. Anfa had always been like a miniature Beverly Hills with its neat rows of immense villas. Some looked like palaces. They had swimming pools, tennis courts, golf courses, striped lawns and flower beds that were a riot of colour. In the garages stood dozens of gleaming cars. Armies of chauffeurs, gardeners, butlers and maids attended to their masters' comfort.

But fifteen years later, the houses looked even more luxurious to me, the gardens even more impressive and the display of wealth even more ostentatious. And, indeed, this was probably true. There was no possible comparison between all this luxury and the sordid prison we had escaped from.

The taxi dropped us off and left without waiting. Jamila had moved. We felt marooned but I didn't want to dwell on this painful feeling. I told the others to wait outside while I went up to one of the villas. A gardener in a white apron was watering the lawn.

I greeted him haughtily and asked him to call the mistress of the house, claiming I had an appointment with her. He looked me up and down and then brandished his hosepipe and threatened me with it, ordering me to leave.

'Get a move on or I'll call the police. We don't want your sort around here.'

Without waiting to hear any more I ran to join the others. I was mortified, humiliated. In the days of the old Malika, that man wouldn't even have dared talk to me. And now he was chasing me away as if I were a poor beggar . . .

• • •

We continued walking, at a loss as to what to do. At random I chose a villa with a beautiful wrought-iron gate and rang the buzzer. A woman's voice replied. I asked her for a glass of water. Moroccan custom demands that you never refuse a beggar a glass of water.

A stunningly pretty maid in a pink apron and a little cap perched jauntily on her neat hair came out of the house. I stared at her, envious of her appearance, before starting to talk to her. My demented expression must have frightened her because she recoiled.

Then I launched into my story: Belgium, fifteen years away, the miscarriage, and asked her if I could make a telephone call. She began to warm to me but replied that she would have to ask her employer's permission.

She closed the door. I signalled to the others to stay hidden behind the bougainvillaea hedge.

A few minutes later the door opened again, revealing a tall, handsome man of about fifty with salt-and-pepper hair. He was wearing a towelling bathrobe. I had probably disturbed him while he was dressing, for he was holding an electric shaver. He smelt nice and was well groomed; this man was on a different planet from me. He winced at my poverty-stricken appearance.

My eloquence saved the situation. I immediately spoke to him in my most elegant French, with judiciously chosen phrases. My language no doubt reassured him and he began to address me as '*chère madame*'.

'My maid tells me that you've had a miscarriage. I hope you're not haemorrhaging? I'm a doctor, I can take you to hospital.'

I stammered a vague explanation, repeated my Belgium patter, and then, before he had a chance to think, I asked him if I could use the telephone. He said yes and invited me in.

His house seemed like a palace to me, and yet there was nothing luxurious about it. But it exuded order, cleanliness and middle-class comfort with its white walls, red hexagonal floor tiles, and plants in the windows. The telephone was on a pretty little table next to the phone directories.

I hadn't forgotten how to use the phone, but my heart started thumping as I picked up the receiver. I felt as though I were in *Hibernatus*, that film with Louis de Funès, where the hero comes back to life after being asleep for many years and mustn't give himself away. Like Hibernatus, I couldn't help making blunders.

My grandfather's phone was continually engaged. Dr Arfi—for that was how the owner of the house introduced himself—pointed out that you had to dial six numbers whereas I kept dialling five, as in the old days.

'Oh yes,' I said casually, my heart pounding as if it would burst at nearly having given the game away, 'I know. But it's always like this, even when we call them from Brussels. They're always on the phone . . .'

He offered me a coffee. At that point I told him that I was accompanied by my husband, my sister and my brother-in-law. He seemed unfazed, so I signalled to the others to come in while he went to get dressed.

The maid arrived, carrying a tray covered with delicious food: exquisite-smelling coffee, cakes, bread and jams. We looked at one another in silence. We were so hungry we couldn't touch a thing, otherwise in a few minutes we would have devoured the lot—the food, the carpet, the furniture and even the dog. Abdellatif was fascinated by the animal, for he had never seen a pet dog before. It was a playful little cocker spaniel that licked him and stood on its hind legs in its excitement. My brother was torn between delight and fear.

We sat in the lounge, holding ourselves bolt upright, careful not to dirty the white carpet with our pitiful shoes that were covered in mud and wet from the dew. After an eternity, the doctor joined us. He wore a suit, a clean shirt and tie, which for us was the epitome of elegance.

He began to converse in an urbane manner while offering us coffee. I told him that we had friends in Casablanca, I mentioned the B— J—s and the B—s, two bourgeois families. His face lit up. He was on familiar territory.

'Incredible,' he said, 'they are friends of mine too.'

Reassured to discover we had mutual acquaintances, he offered to drive us over to the B— J—s.

They belonged to a family of Casablanca bankers. One of the sons, Kamil, had been considered the handsomest boy of his generation. His younger brother, Laarbi, had been one of my close friends. During my last holiday in Kabila, just before the coup d'état, I had organized a birthday party for him at our house. I used to see them every day and I was very fond of them.

When the doctor dropped us off outside the house, I told the children to hide again and I walked straight in without ringing the bell. I just pushed open the door. Suddenly it was as if those fifteen years had melted away. I recognized everything, the furniture, the paintings and the familiar smells. My head swam.

The house seemed empty. I stroked the dog who was overjoyed to see me, then I walked through the house to the kitchen. I saw a telephone. Without thinking, I dialled a number, my grandfather's. Each time, a stranger picked up the phone and answered 'hello' in a gruff voice. I was terrified, but I kept trying.

Eventually I realized that it was an internal line and then I recognized the voice. It was Laarbi's. I asked him to come downstairs without telling him who I was. He did so, grumbling.

When he walked into the room, I was taken aback by his appearance and it took me a few moments to recognize him. I had known him as a slim twenty-five-year-old, and now before me stood a portly, greying forty-year-old. We greeted each other. He didn't seem to know who I was.

'I am Malika,' I said.

'Malika who?'

'Hadji's daughter.'

Hadji is an honorary title for someone who has made the pilgrimage to Mecca, like my father.

I was unable to utter my surname. I was afraid of stating my identity, a fear that stayed with me for many years.

'I don't see . . .'

Not without effort, I finally managed to stammer my name:

'Oufkir, Malika Oufkir.'

He was rooted to the spot.

'What do you want?' he asked me in a tone that was both brusque and haughty.

I told him that we had been released and that I was with Raouf, Maria and Abdellatif. I was shaking with fear, and worst of all I didn't know where I stood. During all those years in gaol, we had thought of ourselves as innocent parties, convinced we were in the right. We were victims, not culprits, as Laarbi's reception implied. Never could I have imagined that our own friends could display such total amnesia.

Laarbi had just given me my first slap in the face.

I swallowed my pride and forced myself to think of the others who were waiting for me, and of everything that lay ahead of us.

'I need money,' I said dryly. 'And I would like you to drive us to the station.'

I had learned of the existence of this new railway line from the taxi driver. In my day there was no train from Casablanca to Rabat.

Without saying a word, he left the kitchen and came back a few seconds later holding out three hundred dirhams—about twenty pounds. That seemed plenty, a royal sum even. I was unaware that the dirham of 1987 no longer had the same purchasing power as before.

Laarbi gave me a little moralizing lecture forbidding me to go near his elder brother who had been suffering from depression since the death of their uncle. Kamil, I was certain, would never have treated us as Laarbi did. He had always been kind, humane and sensitive. And loyal. But I didn't have time to check this out. Laarbi took the car out of the garage. He eyed the others with a mixture of contempt and fear, without a trace of pity for their wretched condition, then he motioned us to get in. He dropped us like bundles of dirty washing outside the station.

This encounter had shaken me but I didn't want to brood over unpleasantness. With my dirhams in my pocket, I felt rich, and my first purchase was for Abdellatif. I bought him *l'Equipe,* a sports paper. He had discovered football thanks to the radio, and he could recite the names of all the players in the French and Moroccan teams as well as the results of all the matches.

We stocked up on cigarettes, thinking of Soukaina. She loved smoking so much that in Bir-Jdid she would dry the grass and leaves gathered by Halima in the courtyard, and then roll them in paper salvaged from the bread boxes or in saffron wrappers.

Buying tickets was more of a challenge for us. We were afraid of the crowds, and especially of the uniformed inspectors. The giant portrait of the King hanging on one of the walls induced a fresh panic attack that sent us rushing outside, panting and trembling, as if Big Brother himself were after us.

Of course it was stupid, but we couldn't help it.

We finally boarded the train, conscious of our bizarre appearance and aware that people were staring at us. We settled down in the compartment, ordered coffee and lit our cigarettes, experiencing, for the first time in hours, a sense of freedom. But when the inspector came in to check our tickets, we began to shake from head to foot again.

Next to us, a French couple was berating the corruption of the regime, the excesses of Throne Day, the expense involved and the fact that tourists had been turned away from La Mamounia, the famous luxury hotel in Marrakesh, even though they had reservations, because the government had requisitioned the rooms for the occasion. The conversation reassured us that we were not the only ones to criticize the authorities.

From time to time the French pair glanced over at us, intrigued. We had a desperate urge to talk to them, to tell them about our fate. They seemed friendly and open, but how did we know they wouldn't inform on us despite their fine words?

We had become too suspicious.

We swallowed our appeals for help.

Abdellatif was in a state of shock that intensified with each new discovery. He had never seen a newspaper in his life. He stared, gaping, at the photos of the players with their footballs. The only football he had ever seen was the one we had made for him in prison.

His amazement grew when the train pulled out of the station and began to go faster and faster. His mouth fell open and he gazed wild-eyed at the landscape. Raouf tried to relax him but to no avail. To our dismay, Abdellatif was an *enfant sauvage*, a wild child, bewildered by the avalanche of new experiences and sensations.

During our five days on the run, he continued to feel that he was riding on a moving train. Later, in Tangier, in the bar of the Hotel Ahlan, which we made our headquarters, he asked if the train was ever going to stop.

With a feeling of dread in the pit of our stomachs, we walked through Rabat central station. Had the alarm been raised? Would we be arrested on the platform? Or outside? But no, nothing seemed out of the ordinary, there wasn't a policeman in sight. We hesitantly made our way towards the taxi rank. This station was much too big, much too new and much too busy. The crowd jostled us, people seemed to be in a hurry. They knew where they were going. But nobody was waiting for us.

Raouf and Maria got into the first taxi and I took another one with my little brother. It was nine o'clock in the morning. We were to meet up at the French embassy. A Moroccan policeman was guarding the entrance. I faltered for a moment then I went up to him.

'I want to go in,' I said.

'The embassy is closed,' he replied, as if it were obvious.

It took a few minutes for it to dawn on me. It was Monday 20 April, in other words, Easter Monday. Despite our carefully laid plans, we had overlooked this important detail. Who knows what would have happened if we had escaped one day later?

Raouf came over and tried to engage the policeman in conversation, but he looked at us suspiciously. It didn't take him long to realize there was something odd about us. He bombarded us with questions, and even asked us if we were on the run. His eyes swept over us with contempt, from the top of our balding heads to our muddy shoes.

Without giving him time to question us further, we climbed back into the taxis. The driver also glanced at me suspiciously when I asked him to drop us outside the American embassy.

It was our only back-up plan in the event that our request for political asylum at the French embassy was refused.

'Why do you look as if there's someone after you?' he asked me. 'Where are you from? There's something odd about you. You look like a European, but no, there's definitely something strange about you . . .'

We didn't answer. He asked more questions as he drove, but we held our tongues. We pulled up in front of the American embassy, and I decided to try my luck alone. Another Moroccan policeman stopped me at the entrance and asked me to put down my bundle. It contained the revolver that Abdellatif had made that looked so authentic it could be mistaken for a real one. I was afraid of being taken for a terrorist.

I stammered that it contained my brother's toys. But the man snatched the bag from me, flung it into a corner of his sentry box and told me to pick it up on the way out.

I was despondent. We had been so confident of success at the French embassy that it had not occurred to us that we would have to improvise in the event of failure. Nor did we have the moral strength. In our agitated, bedraggled condition, executing a finely honed plan that we had been preparing for weeks and learned by heart was still feasible. Coping with the unforeseen required an effort that was beyond us.

I was disoriented.

Trembling, I walked down a ramp to the embassy offices. On the right, there were two uniformed GIs in a glass-walled office, watching the comings and goings on their surveillance monitors. Facing them, on the left, a Moroccan in a suit and tie stood guard in front of the chain barring the entrance to the offices.

I requested immigration forms from the Moroccan and asked him how to fill them in. As he replied, my mind was racing. All I had to do was thrust aside the chain and I would be on American territory. On the other side, the officials went about their business. I tried to attract their attention, imploring them with my eyes, but in vain.

A man came over to the Moroccan orderly. He showed him his badge and the orderly raised the chain. I dithered again as to what I should do. Should I rush after him, jump over the chain and yell that I wanted political asylum? But if they accepted me, what would become of the other three? Would they be turned away? Denounced? Arrested?

If the Moroccan had been American, I would have stepped over the chain without any qualms. He would have represented deliverance, America, the Rights of Man. But could I trust a fellow Moroccan? Supposing he barred my way?

When I finally decided to act, it was too late. The GIs in their glass office had become suspicious. They spoke to each other in English, pointing at me, then barked into their PA system, telling the Moroccan that there was something odd about me. One of them came out and walked towards me.

I panicked. I gathered up the forms, retrieved my bundle and ran away, my heart pounding as if it would burst. I rejoined the rest of the little group in the taxis. It was a disaster. Our only hope now was the British embassy or the Spanish embassy. But they were closed too. We were utterly at a loss.

There was someone else who could help us, a friend of my grandfather's, a fellow Berber. One of his daughters had been at school with me at the Palace. We asked the taxis to take us to the Agdal district, where he lived with his family—his wife Lalla Mina and his daughters, Latifa and Malika. In the old days, the Agdal consisted entirely of charming little villas. But all the houses had been pulled down and replaced by apartment blocks.

We didn't recognize anything. The taxis drove round in circles, and we were increasingly disoriented. Then I remembered that their house was next to the post office. Luckily, it was the only one that had not been demolished.

The concierge asked me who he should announce. I told him I

wished to speak to Lalla Mina, that I was Malika, Hadji Fatima's daughter.

He came back and told me with an air of distrust:

'She doesn't know anybody of that name. If you don't get out of here straight away she'll call the police.'

I pleaded with him.

'Tell her I'm Malika, Oufkir's daughter.'

He stopped in his tracks, surprised, almost frightened.

'Don't insist,' he said at length, 'there's no point. She doesn't want to know.'

But he gently shut the door between the living room and the hall, and threw me a curious look. I asked him where Latifa lived.

'She lives in Agadir.'

Malika, her sister, lived on the other side of the street. I had known her well; she had been a teacher when she was younger. In the days when my father was still head of national security, she used to come to the house and give private lessons to the children. Now she was married to an entrepreneur and had children of her own.

Without much hope, I decided to try my luck. We stood outside the building and waited for her. Around half-past twelve, we watched a car draw up. A plump woman got out followed by four children in single file, like a mother hen with her chicks. Malika must have put on ten kilos with each pregnancy.

I approached her. She stared at me, and her expression froze. The closer I got to her the more flustered she became.

In the end, she grimaced, stepped back and began to cry.

'But why me?' she screamed. 'Why do this to me? You don't have the right . . . Children, go inside quickly,' she went on, on the verge of hysteria.

She continued to distance herself, shooing me away as if I were a leper.

We went back to the city centre to send our letters from the main post office. We had written about twenty, to politicians and personalities from the entertainment world, including Alain Delon, Simone Signoret, the former President of the European Parliament Simone Veil, Robert Badinter the former lawyer now President of the French Constitutional Council, and José Artur. We also wanted to make some phone calls. We shut ourselves in a telephone booth but we couldn't work out how to operate the phone.

Each time somebody approached, we rushed out of the booth as if we were going to be pursued. Although we were afraid, we had a good laugh, which allowed us briefly to forget that we were fugitives. But we didn't manage to dial a single number.

The hours were ticking by. We had to find shelter somewhere. The only people we could turn to were our childhood friends, and one of them was Reda, a close friend of Raouf's. In the old days he used to live nearby, in the Allée des Princesses. To reach Reda's house, we had to go past our own old house. I had always promised Abdellatif that I would show it to him one day. He had no recollection of it, but he loved to listen to us wistfully talking about it.

It was now or never.

I arranged to meet up with the others outside Reda's house, and Abdellatif and I turned off towards ours.

I dreaded what I might find, what changes might have been made by the new tenants. Would they have kept it the same? Was my room still there, between the swimming pool and the sauna? And what about the garden? Would it still be full of the flowers I so loved?

When we arrived at the gate, I thought I'd come to the wrong address. Instead of the majestic red ochre villa surrounded by a lush green lawn, there was nothing but a wasteland. After our departure, the house had been looted. Our former hangers-on had helped themselves to the furniture, the paintings, the carpets, my mother's jewellery, the photo albums, trinkets, clothes, mementoes . . .

Then Hassan II had ordered the house to be razed to the ground. It no longer existed, just as we no longer existed. Through this brutal act, he had obliterated us.

I reeled under the blow. That house had been terribly important to me. When I lived at the Palace, it had always been at the centre of my thoughts, the symbol of a normal, happy home, the haven of peace I craved.

During all those years in prison, I had clung to it. I could visualize it clearly. At night, before falling asleep, I would wander through all the rooms, drinking in every detail. It was my umbilical cord, my last link with my father and the long-lost days of happiness.

With its disappearance, I had lost my anchor. I felt sullied, violated, crushed. Alone in the world, once again. Nothing made sense any more. I didn't want to upset Abdellatif, so I pretended that I was lost and couldn't remember where the house was. He meekly swallowed my lie.

We got back into the taxi and set off for Reda's house. A gardener was standing outside the door.

'Reda?' he said as if talking to an idiot. 'Reda got married. He doesn't live here any more . . . His parents? But they're in France . . .'

When pressed, he grudgingly told me that Reda now lived in the Zawha apartment building. We clambered back into the taxi, more downhearted than ever. At the entrance to the building, the concierge stopped us. He was suspicious, nosy and probably an informer, like most concierges in Morocco.

I affected a casual tone and asked him where Reda's apartment was. I picked my way there with great caution, as if crossing a war zone. I felt as though I were passing a dangerous frontier, and might be stopped in my tracks by a bullet at any moment.

I rang the bell. A maid opened the door. Reda had just left, and she wouldn't tell me where he was having lunch. I asked her for a glass of water, and begged her to let me use the phone.

I wanted to call José Artur at France Inter. His programme had comforted us so often during our captivity that I was certain he would help us . . . but she refused my request and showed me the door.

I was about to start pleading when I heard the familiar drone of a helicopter in the sky. I took Abdellatif's hand and rushed down the stairs. Maria and Raouf, who were waiting for me at the entrance, also began to run.

The craft was flying so low that we could clearly see the soldiers sitting inside, cradling their machine guns. The four of us kept running until we found a hiding place behind some cypress trees. We huddled together, quaking. We had no idea that our grandfather also lived in this apartment building and that this was the first place the police had searched.

Then Raouf had a brainwave, another one, but at this stage we weren't going to argue. Next to the Zawha residence was the villa of some other childhood friends, Patrick and Philippe Barère, a Moroccan French family. We had always been on good terms with them and we were fond of their parents, especially their mother, who was a real mother hen, always fussing over her offspring.

After a few minutes' walk, we came across their enchanting little house set among trees and lawns.

A maid opened the door.

'We would like to see Mme Barère. Please tell her Malika and Raouf Oufkir are here.'

She shut the door again. We were prepared for anything: to be driven away like thieves, insulted, despised and denounced. We were exhausted, hungry, numb and desperate. Incapable of taking another step.

Then we heard running footsteps in the hall and the door flew open. Michéle Barére stood before us, weeping.

She was crying so hard she was incapable of speech.

She flung open her arms and embraced us, murmuring:

'My children, my darling children, how wonderful.'

She showed us in. We felt safe for the first time since our escape.

from Flags of our Fathers
by James Bradley
with Ron Powers

James Bradley's (born 1954) father helped raise the American flag on Iwo Jima's Mount Suribachi. The younger Bradley's book describes the bloody fighting his father's Easy Company endured to take the mountain.

A storm lashed in from the ocean; blasts of wind; the surf at six feet. But this was nothing compared to the hell-storm about to erupt on the southern neck of the island. At eight-thirty a.m. a thin line of unprotected American boys would arise and rush directly at the most fortified mountain in the history of the world. Almost one third of them would be killed or maimed. But not in vain: Their charge would mark the beginning of the end for "impregnable" Suribachi—and thus for Iwo Jima itself as a factor in the war.

Soaked, cold, and fatigued, the Marines awoke and gazed toward the primitive mass of rock that held their fates. In the tense silence as first light broke, Easy Company lay poised for action on the 2nd Battalion's right flank. Easy faced a long, lethal gauntlet on the volcano's northeastern side. Dave Severance's boys would have to rush across two hundred yards of open terrain toward the mountain's base, with very little cover of any kind.

The guns trained down on the two hundred yards between the 28th Regiment and the mountain's base would soon make those yards the worst killing ground in the Pacific. Only after the battle would Americans grasp the full extent of what had been concentrated against them. Suribachi's interior had been hollowed out into a fantastical seven-story subterranean world, fortified with concrete revetments and finished off with plastered walls, a sewer system, and conduits for fresh air, electricity, water, and steam. As many as 1,300 Japanese soldiers and 640 navy troops filled each of the various rooms and tunnels. They were armed with guns of every conceivable size and design.

The terrain below this fortress—the ground between the Marines and the mountain—was not only barren of natural cover, it lay in the teeth of overlapping ground-fire. At the mountain base stretched a welter of reinforced concrete pillboxes and infantry trenches. The firing ports of the pillboxes were angled so that the Japanese shooters could see one another and offer mutual support with their spewing machine guns.

At a little after seven-thirty a.m. the Marines' own artillery opened its earth-shattering barrage. Hot "friendly" metal streaked low over the Marines' heads, splintering the rock on the side of the mountain. The boys on the perimeter ducked under the lethal salvos; shrapnel was a fickle friend. "Ask for all of it!" Harry the Horse had yelled at his operations officer. There was no reason to hold back; after this day, there would be no space between the Marines and the enemy to aim shells. The combat could be hand-to-hand.

Toward the end of the barrage, forty carrier planes screamed in low, drilling the mountain with rockets that exploded at an earsplitting pitch. Some of the bombs landed a football field's length away from the crouching Marines.

The planes pulled away; H-Hour drew near: eight a.m. The boys braced themselves for the cry of "Attack!" that might usher in their last moments on earth.

But no attack order came.

The problem was tanks. Colonel Liversedge had expected several to arrive to cover the assault, but none had appeared. Rearming and refueling problems and Japanese mortar harassment had kept them pinned down. Harry the Horse delayed the assault until eight-fifteen, hoping that at any moment the mechanized monsters would grind into view.

Nothing.

At eight-thirty, Colonel Liversedge made a harrowing decision. Despite the crucial absence of armor to cover the charging boys, he could afford to wait no longer. He gave the order to go.

An electric current of pure terror pulsed across the regiment. The Marines could see that the tanks were not in the field. No tanks; no large bulky shapes to protect the boys against fire from the pillboxes as they ran. No tanks; nothing but bodies against bullets. A certainty of death filled the air. No jaunty war cries came from the veterans. Richard Wheeler experienced a pang of utter hopelessness: "I could feel fear dragging at my jowls." Lieutenant Keith Wells would later admit to a memory from his boyhood in his father's slaughterhouse: an awareness, among the cattle, as the doors closed behind them, of what lay in store.

And then the heroes of the day began literally to stand up and be counted.

One of the first was Lieutenant Keith Wells of Easy Company's 3rd Platoon. Wells did not tell his men to follow him. He simply got to his feet, waved his gun toward the mountain, and began running. "I just thought it was pure suicide," he later recalled.

His mute example stirred the troops. Behind him, hundreds of scared boys stood up, leveled their rifles, and advanced against the mountain. To the left of Wells's 3rd Platoon (with Doc Bradley) was Lieutenant Ed Pennel's 2nd Platoon (with Mike, Harlon, Ira, and Franklin) matching Wells's advance step-by-step.

The mountain exploded back at them, a screaming death.

Harlon, Doc, Ira, and Franklin swept forward with the rest of Easy Company, in the vanguard of the attack. Immediately, Japanese shells and bullets began cutting the Americans down. Amidst the din, the air was cut with kids' strangled voices calling, "Corpsman! Corpsman!"

Officers and enlisted men crumpled together under the hail-stream of steel; were blown to bits; were machine-gunned where they crouched; were sliced open by hot shards.

Clusters of men were raked, and raked again. In Corporal Richard Wheeler's area, a mortar shell killed Corporal Edward J. Romero, an ex-paratrooper from Chicago. Wheeler dove into a crater and had scarcely recovered his wits when another shell exploded, ripping the future writer's left jawline apart. As the blood spurted, Corpsman Clifford Langley—who had treated a jaw wound on D-Day—hurried to Wheeler's side and applied compresses. Then Langley gave aid to a wounded man nearby. As he was closing his pouch and preparing to leave the crater, Wheeler's rifle in his hand, yet another mortar shell burst upon them. This one ripped Wheeler's left calf apart and drove shrapnel into Langley. The young corpsman ignored his own wounds and once again dressed Wheeler's laceration. Then they both realized that the shell had done its worst work on the wounded man nearby; both his legs had been ripped open, and he lay on his stomach, conscious but slowly dying.

It wasn't over yet. Now a fourth mortar hurtled in; it landed with a thump—a dud. Had it been live, it would have killed everyone near it.

Corpsman Langley—his clothing now soaked with his own blood—once again methodically closed his pouch, grabbed Wheeler's rifle, and went on his way.

William Wayne saw a bullet take a buddy's face off. "His teeth were just lying there," Wayne said. "If I'd thought about it at the time it would have driven me crazy."

Yesterday's heroes became today's dead. Don Ruhl's eccentric bravado finally got the better of him. It happened early on. Ruhl and his platoon guide, Sergeant Henry Hansen, were in the forefront of a charge that reached the brushy fringe of the mountain's base. They rushed past bunkers that had been blasted by the bombing, but soon found themselves at close quarters with active defenders. The two leaped atop a disabled pillbox and emptied their rifles into a cluster of Japanese who were hurling hand grenades. As they blasted away, a grenade chinked down between them.

Eyewitnesses recalled that Ruhl, who was near the roof's edge, could easily have slid over the side and escaped harm. But that was not his nature. He sized up Hansen's position—helplessly isolated near the center of the roof—and acted: With a shout of warning—"Watch out, Hank!"—he flung himself on the charge.

Sergeant Hansen recalled seeing the charge land, realizing he was trapped, flattening himself out ("hoping the fragments would pass over me") and hearing Ruhl's warning almost in the same instant. "I heard [the] muffled explosion," Hansen said in his official report of the incident. "I pulled Ruhl off the bunker, but he was dead. I am positive that had it not been for the self-sacrifice of his life, I would have been killed or seriously wounded."

Among the first to reach Ruhl's body was Doc Bradley, who held the dead boy in his arms while he examined him for signs of life.

For his bravery, Don Ruhl received a posthumous Medal of Honor.

The chain reaction of slaughter continued on. When Wheeler received his jaw wound, a comrade named Louie Adrian, a Spokane Indian, scrambled out of that foxhole and dove into another. There crouched his best buddy, Chick Robeson. The two Washington boys had enlisted together, traveled to Camp Pendleton together by train, and shared a tent in training. On liberty in California one night, feeling no pain, they fell asleep on a beach; they awoke when a huge wave crashed over them.

Now the two comrades were shoulder to shoulder, firing and tossing grenades, taking turns popping up and down in the cold, driving rain. "I came down to reload and Louie went up," Robeson recalled. "Then a bullet got him right in the heart. He fell and turned yellow with death. Louie was my best friend. My link with home. I was staring at him when our corporal yelled, 'Move, Chick! Move! Move!'"

And so seventeen-year-old Chick Robeson stood up and charged forward. He was a Marine, and he had work to do.

The 2nd Platoon, fighting hard on the left, found itself under a concentrated mortar barrage. Ira, Franklin, Harlon, and Mike zigzagged from one shell hole to another as they bore forward, looking for any sort of protection. Around them, their friends were suffering and dying as Easy took a cluster of casualties. A mortar round blew two boys to hits. An artillery round landed near Tex Stanton. The concussion blew Tex ten feet in the air; he fell to earth with deep burns on his legs and hips.

And still they advanced. Even as their casualties mounted at a rate that would have caused panic and retreat in nearly any other attacking force, these Marines remembered their training at Camps Pendleton and Tarawa and kept moving forward. Stoically, they followed their assigned rules and maintained the intricate teamwork of the great assaulting organism. The riflemen and machine-gunners who survived the charge aimed their fire at individual blockhouse ports, often mere slits in the hardened igloos. And as the enemy ducked (if the enemy ducked), the surviving demolition squads and the flamethrowers moved in through the chattering cross fire to get close enough for extermination.

In the midst of the carnage, Doc Bradley ran through the chaos, doing what he could in this landscape of blood. Just thirty minutes into the charge, the wet terrain was strewn with American bodies. Now the peaceable newsboy ignored the bullets and tried to save lives.

He watched a Marine blunder into a cross fire of machine-gun bursts and slump to the ground. Doc did not hesitate. His telltale "Unit 3" bag slapping at his side, my father sprinted through thirty yards of saturating cross fire—mortars and machine guns—to the wounded boy's side. As bullets whined and pinged around him, Doc found the Marine losing blood at a life-threatening rate. Moving him was out of the question until the flow was stanched. The Japanese gunfire danced all around him, but Doc focused his mind on his training. He tied a plasma bottle to the kid's rifle and jammed it bayonet-first into the ground. He moved his own body between the boy and the sheets of gunfire. Then, his upper body still erect and fully exposed, he administered first aid.

His buddies watching him from their shell holes were certain that he would be cut down at any moment. Bur Doc Bradley stayed where he was until he thought it was safe to move the boy. Then he raised a hand, signaling his comrades not to help, but to stay low. And then my father stood up into the merciless firestorm and pulled the wounded Marine back across the thirty yards to safety by himself. His attention did not flicker until the Marine was safely evacuated.

This action—so heroic that two sergeants and Captain Severance came forward to report it—earned him his Navy Cross, an honor he never mentioned to our family. It was one of the bravest things my father ever did, and it happened on one of the most valorous days in the history of a Corps known for valor.

Among the many heroes on the field, none surpassed the sustained courage of Lieutenant Keith Wells, Don Ruhl's 3rd Platoon leader and the man who had stood up to inspire the initial charge.

Wells took a terrific hit in the early fighting. It happened as Easy, slogging with ferocious intent toward the entrenched defenders, outpaced the unit on its right flank and began taking fire not only from the front but from the side as well. Soon the company was pinned down by grenades and bullets from a blockhouse in its path. Worse, it came under a pinpoint barrage of close-in mortar fire. Two kids volunteered to the rear for more grenades; they were gunned down from the blockhouse. Flamethrowers Chuck Lindberg and Robert Goode rushed to the scene but could not get through the mortar fire to the emplacement. Then a shell burst near Lieutenant Wells, wounding him and four other men, including William Wayne.

Wells suffered shrapnel wounds to his legs and lost some of his clothing. Doc Bradley darted to his side, injected him with morphine, and told him to get the hell to the rear. Wells would have none of it. His unit had begun the morning with forty-two men; twenty-five now remained. No one could be spared. The feeling had returned to his legs and he decided to stay in the field, in command.

Lieutenant Wells's determination drove his men to new heights of valor. Lindberg and Goode arose with their deadly flamethrowers and, ignoring the sheets of fire directed at them, stalked toward the pillbox. Soon the two were squirting their molten fire streams in all directions. They not only incinerated dozens of Japanese—the smell of burnt flesh floated on the damp wind—their liquid fire turned several pillboxes into infernos, causing Japanese ammunition to explode in great bursts.

Chuck Lindberg later recalled the hazards of lugging a tank that carried seventy-two pounds of jellied gasoline—napalm—under twelve hundred pounds of pressure. "The shot only lasted six seconds," he recalled. "We fired in short bursts. It was dangerous work. A lot of guys bought the farm trying that." Lindberg's steely calm and ferocious concentration led him to heights of accomplishment that few others attained. His day's work earned him a Silver Star.

The roar of tank treads now competed with the din of artillery all along the Marines' front, as dozens of them belatedly joined the front line. Shielded by the armored bulk, infantrymen could rush ever closer to pillboxes and bunkers without being exposed to fire. The inhabitants of those hovels—those who were not gunned down or scorched to death—began to flee toward the mountain. The Japanese first-line defenses were crumbling.

But the price of this victory remained high, and heroes continued to suffer. Five of the flagraisers fought side by side, led by Lieutenants Wells and Pennel. And now Pennel himself was a lacerated casualty, needing rescue. He was dashing from shell hole to shell hole when a shell landed between his legs and blew him a distance of thirty feet. His left heel was blown off, his right buttock and thigh gouged out, and his left shin pierced by shrapnel. Half a century later, Pennel told the story with detached humor:

"I was semiconscious. I heard someone screaming. Then I realized it was me. I felt liquid running down my butt and I thought my life-juices were running out. I looked between my legs to see what I had left. It was OK. It was my damaged canteen leaking.

"A medic came by and gave me a brandy and a shot of morphine. I took my helmet off and put it over my genitals. I laid there in a depression like a soup tureen for hours—parts of my body blown off, no clothes, helmet over my privates. I laid there with everything exploding around me."

An amphibious tractor tried to reach him. It hit a mine and blew up, killing the boys inside. Several hours later, four Marines approached him with a poncho. They rolled him onto it, each grabbed a corner, and they set off for the beach. A bullet wounded one of the carriers and Pennel toppled heavily to the ground. The remaining three men dragged him to the beach.

He lay there on a stretcher until darkness. "I felt exposed," he said, "like I was on a platform for all to see. Those flat-trajectory shells would skim straight in, making a roaring sound in the dark: *Foom! Foom! Foom!* Guys were being killed all around me. It was complete chaos."

Finally Lieutenant Pennel was loaded with some other wounded boys onto a long pallet. An amtrac rushed them to an offshore hospital ship, where the pallets were hooked with wires and winched up to the main deck. "A wire broke that was pulling the pallet just before mine," the lieutenant remembered. "Those guys screamed and just sank to the bottom."

Lieutenant Pennel's ordeal was not yet over. As a doctor examined him, a Japanese shell crashed onto the deck and skittered into the fuel bunker. The doctor turned and stood with his stethoscope pressed to the bunker, listening to the shell as it rolled around, doubtless wondering whether he and everyone nearby was about to be blown up. But it was a dud.

"It had been a long day," Ed Pennel told me later.

Soaked with blood, nearly immobilized by pain, Keith Wells continued to direct the 3rd Platoon's attack through the late morning. But he grew weak. He fell once, dashing to elude gunfire, and reopened his festering wounds. Immediately Doc Bradley was at his side. Doc dosed him up with morphine again, meanwhile screaming, "Enough! Get out of here!"

Wells willed himself to stay in the field another half hour, directing assault groups and rallying his men. Finally, half delirious with pain and confident of victory, he turned his command over to Platoon

Sergeant Ernest Boots Thomas and made for an aid station in the rear. He got there by crawling. He was awarded a Navy Cross.

As rainy morning wore into afternoon and the fighting bogged down, the Marines continued to take casualties. Often it was the corpsmen themselves who died as they tried to preserve life. William Hoopes of Chattanooga was crouching beside a medic named Kelly, who put his head above a protective ridge and placed binoculars to his eyes—just for an instant—to spot a sniper who was peppering his area. In that instant the sniper shot him through the Adam's apple. Hoopes, a pharmacist's mate himself, struggled frantically to save his friend. "I took my forceps and reached into his neck to grasp the artery and clinch it off," Hoopes recalled. "His blood was spurting. He had no speech but his eyes were on me. He knew I was trying to save his life. I tried everything in the world. I couldn't do it. I tried. The blood was so slippery. I couldn't get the artery. I was trying so hard. And all the while he just looked at me, he looked directly into my face. The last thing he did as the blood spurts became less and less was to pat me on the arm as if to say, 'That's all right.' Then he died."

The near-misses were nearly as ghastly, especially the ones that resulted in other deaths. Donald Howell's buddy Walter Gust took a piece of shrapnel in the side of the head. It did not fracture his skull, but for a moment he was incoherent, flailing around. Howell and some buddies tackled him and were taking him to a corpsman when another round exploded, blowing Howell into the air and nearly taking Gust's arm off. The Marines reloaded Gust onto a stretcher; then a machine-gun burst killed the stretcher-bearers and ripped apart Gust's other arm. "I was watching this," recalled Howell, "and there was nothing I could do about it. Walter survived. He lived near me for years. I was the best man at his wedding."

By late in the bloody afternoon, the conquest of the mountain seemed within the Americans' grasp. Marine discipline and the sacrificial bonding of ardent young men was prevailing over concrete, steel, and thick volcanic rock. But the Japanese—even as their ingenious fortifications crumbled or were scorched hollow—were not quite done with their own desperate resolve. As the 28th continued to inch forward, Navy observation planes above the battle radioed that a swarm of Japanese had emerged from inside the mountain and was forming up for the dreaded banzai attack.

Within minutes, American planes were swooping in low to strafe the area. Their tremendous roar, and the concussion of exploding rockets, reverberated among the close-by Marines.

Finally the planes banked and vanished, and for a few moments the battlefield was silent, tense with expectation.

It was Sergeant Mike Strank, with the 2nd Platoon now on the left side of the line, who broke the spell. Leaping to his feet, the Czech-born Marine bellowed: "Let's show these bastards what a real banzai is like! Easy Company, charge!"

With that, the bone-tired, battle-scarred Marines got to their feet and once again slogged forward into the line of fire. To the right of the 2nd Platoon, the 3rd, commanded now by Boots Thomas, joined the footrace to Suribachi.

Boots Thomas was the next hero to shine. With rough terrain stalling the tanks some seventy-five yards to the rear, the twenty-year-old Floridian saw that his riddled unit was grievously exposed once again. In the thick of battle, a daring solution came to him. He sprinted back, through fire, to the nearest tank, and, still out in the open, directed its fire against the stubborn pillboxes. Then he dashed back to the front to exhort his men. A bit later he headed for the tanks again. He repeated this action several times.

His example paid off. The 3rd Platoon virtually annihilated the very enemy that had been massing for devastation of its own. As darkness on this triumphant, bloody day was setting in, Thomas himself identified the weak spot in the defensive line and personally led the breakthrough to Suribachi's steep flank, waving his knife aloft in victory. Boots was recommended for a Navy Cross, which was awarded.

• • •

Suribachi had not fallen, not quite, not yet, but victory now seemed inevitable. The wet day ended with the 28th Regiment poised in a vast semicircle around the battered volcano's base, gathering its strength for the finishing assault, expected to come the next morning. For Easy Company, it had been a day of grievous loss and historic valor: For its day's work, the badly decimated unit would receive a Medal of Honor, four Navy Crosses, two Silver Stars, and a number of Purple Hearts— one of the most decorated engagements in the history of the United States Marine Corps. These honors were paid for in blood: Casualties for the day amounted to thirty percent of Easy's strength.

Easy Company had actually moved a little too far and too fast for its own nighttime protection. Dave Severance's boys had penetrated past some active Japanese units, and spent the night isolated from the battalion. They huddled on a strip of jagged, rocky terrain at the southern base of Suribachi, the roaring surf of the Pacific below them on the opposite side. Dave Severance set his command post as close as possible to the mountain, so that he would have a line of sight up its flank. In the late evening, searchlights from the offshore destroyer-escort ships revealed something that looked like Japanese moving into view above Easy. As the ships began tattooing the volcano's flanks with 40mm shells, Captain Severance moved his command post back thirty yards to the water's edge, for a better view of the volcano's slopes. It was a good thing he did: The next morning's light would reveal that the original CP site lay buried under several tons of rocks from a bombardment-triggered slide.

Low on ammunition and food, Easy's troops munched what was left of their chocolate bars and waited for yet another dawn on Iwo Jima.

The Marines had paid for their advances across all fronts on the island with heavy losses. Official casualties for the battle now stood at 644 killed, 4,168 wounded, and 560 unaccounted for. Howlin' Mad Smith himself was sobered by what he had witnessed. "Watching the Marines cross that island," he later told a newspaper reporter, "reminded me of the charge of Pickett at Gettysburg."

But the horrors of this day's fighting did not end with the darkness.

Just as dusk fell, an air raid signal alerted the ships offshore. To Don Mayer of Portland, nineteen then, it made a spectacular show: "Every ship was firing thousands of tracers," he said. "It was more beautiful than any Fourth of July you've ever seen."

To the boys on board the task force ships, the sight was not quite so beautiful. Cecil Gentry, a radio operator on the USS *Lawrence Taylor*, could not move when the order to "Hit the deck!" came from his captain. "I was transfixed," he said. "I just stood there. One plane flew right over my head. I could see the face of the Japanese pilot. You could see the fear of death on his face. His lips were pulled back over his teeth."

This pilot immolated himself against the USS *Bismarck Sea*, adjacent to the *Lawrence Taylor*. Four of the ship's own torpedoes detonated in the concussion, and the great ship exploded in huge sheets of orange flame and rapidly sank, its bow turning straight down as it slid under the rough waves laced with rain. The men of the *Taylor* managed to rescue about 120 of the 800 crewmen from the water. Other rescuers managed to save hundreds more. Cecil Gentry recalled watching corpsmen amputating sailors' legs with razor blades, saws, and meat-cutters from the galley. But more than 200 were lost as the Japanese planes strafed the waters.

Back on land, the chilled, hungry, and exhausted Marines faced a different kind of nocturnal menace. Fear of infiltrators—the fear of the dancing shadows—had preoccupied the Americans on each night since D-Day. On this night, the fear took on more justification than ever before. On this night, the madman in the haunted house unleashed all his ghouls.

"Prowling wolves" was the name that General Kuribayashi had given his teams of stalking, crawling night-murderers; now, desperate to save their mountain fortress, they crept out in force.

At around nine p.m., up north with the 26th Marines, Thomas Mayers of the Bronx was surveying the terrain from his foxhole when a flare exploded in the mist. It illuminated a horrible sight, accompanied now by screams: Two Japanese slashing two helpless boys in the next foxhole with bayonets. Their names were Crull and Dortsch. Mayers and his buddy leaped to their feet to take action. One of the "wolves" wheeled and hurled a grenade at them; it was a dud, but it struck the other Marine in the head and knocked him unconscious. Mayers squeezed off one round before his rifle jammed. The predators were now advancing on him. The twenty-year-old private groped for his hand grenades. The Japanese were so close that throwing the explosives was out of the question; Mayers ripped out their firing pins, scattered them at the edge of his foxhole, and ducked.

The enemy soldiers howled and collapsed, their legs full of shrapnel. Mayers climbed from his foxhole, and with his knife cut their throats. Then he sprinted to the other foxhole. Crull was dead. Mayers shouted to the lacerated Dortsch: "Do you have any guns?" "Yes," the boy murmured. "Crull has a .45 in his shirt." Mayers snatched the weapon. It was slathered with Crull's blood and would not fire.

Two more Japanese were now upon Mayers. He rolled a few more grenades at them and ducked through the explosions, and then finished them off with his knife.

Thomas Mayers received a Navy Cross for his actions. He has never forgotten the moment-to-moment sequence of that bloody episode. Crull, a freckle-faced Irish boy not more than eighteen years old, was screaming as he died. And his words would forever haunt Mayers: *"Mom! Mom! He's killing me! Mom, he's killing me!"*

from Facing the Congo
by Jeffrey Tayler

⸙

Jeffrey Tayler in 1995 set out to navigate an 1,100-mile section of the Congo River—from Kisangani to Kinshasa—in a log canoe called a pirogue. Here Tayler and his guide Desi are about to enter an especially dangerous stretch of the river.

I n the cool of a saffron dawn we broke camp and abandoned our little Eden, paddling hard, energized by the hope of reaching Bumba by midday. Bumba! What was Bumba to us? Bumba was not just a town on the river—it was the end of the first segment of our journey, and reaching it marked incontrovertible progress toward Kinshasa. For Desi it was more: it was where he would see his wife and daughter.

But as the day wore on the clear sky became our bane; the razoring rays of the sun wearied us and slowed our advance. The water lane that had granted us swift passage on robust current debouched into a pool sluggish and choked with algae. The air grew pungent with the scent of water hyacinth blossoms and marshy vegetation, with the fetor of swamp weeds. Black swarms of bees hurled themselves through the harsh light like flying buzz saws, and we wished for the saving cool of dawn. Yet around noon, on the distant bend, where the river deflected south toward the equator, we made out the whitewashed walls and red-tiled roofs of ruined villas. Bumba.

Desi took his shard of mirror in hand and began primping, combing his hair and examining his teeth, then lathering up with toothpaste and shaving away his fleecy beard. Finally, he donned his tracksuit and ten-gallon hat. All in all, he cut a dapper figure.

He checked the ride of his hat in the mirror. "My wife and baby—I have to look good for them."

"You want the Polaroid?"

"Yes, please."

I gave him the camera plus a pack of zaires as a present for his family. He accepted the money without thanking me. It was, I now saw, part of my duties as a (supposedly rich) *mondele* to make such gifts to him.

"Remember," I said, "we have to be out of here by three at the latest. We want to be deep in the islands by nightfall."

"No problem."

Hoping to avoid detection, we landed at a deserted beach at the edge of town, but within minutes a boisterous crowd of raga-muffin children and smiling teens appeared and came slip-sliding down the steep clay bank to gawk at us. Under their curious eyes I gave Desi money for a sack of charcoal, a crate of Cokes, some kerosene, and a few other things we needed; this was, first of all, a supply stop. He draped the Polaroid around his neck and jumped ashore, zipped up his tracksuit, and was gone. I sat down and watched the children cartwheel along the bank and dive somer-saulting off a nearby rise into the river. They were amicable and well-formed youngsters, all laughs, and we often exchanged smiles. Many were Lokele.

Desi stayed away a long time, missing his deadline by an hour. When he returned, he came loping down the bank in a happy-go-lucky mood, accompanied by more children and a porter bent under a load of supplies. Desi said his home visit had gone well, very well, and he was *très, très content.* That was all fine, very fine, I replied, but I looked at my watch. What about our deadline, and (I glanced at his acquisitions)—*sacrebleu!*—had he forgotten the charcoal? Holding his cowboy hat to his head he scampered up the bank and ran back into town.

We ended up pushing off just before sunset. Desi paddled with particular urgency, declaring that we had to move well out of the range of Bumba's thieves, and *fast*, as though this were a risk of which he thought it best to remind me, lest I forget, river-naive *mondele* that his tone implied I was. With the mosquitoes soon to descend and Desi's cheerful tardiness alternating with his oddly didactic exhortations to paddle hard, with the coming inconvenience of having to pitch camp in the dark, and with the possibility that someone might indeed have followed us (for who had not turned up on the bank to stare?), I felt rancor rising in my throat. Although an hour in Bumba would have sufficed, I had offered Desi three, he had taken five, and now we were at risk.

Yet presently a look of melancholy mixed with fatigue stole over his face. "You know what?" he said, "I'm tired." He put down his oar, and reclined.

I kept rowing, but the pirogue spun lazily out of control, unmanageable with me paddling at the bow alone. I could hold in my irritation no longer and thwacked my paddle down.

"Desi, look here. You're in my employ and you know our security depends on our taking certain precautions. You were late today and now"—I swatted mosquitoes off my cheeks and caught my faltering balance in the wobbling scow—"now, look at us! You're resting and it's almost night and we're nowhere near a campsite and God knows who could be following us!"

My outburst caught him off guard. He looked at me perplexed for a moment, as though attempting to divine the ravings of a lunatic. "Why are you so upset?" he asked. "Jesus is looking out for us. Jesus—"

"Desi, come on! Don't change the subject."

"You don't have faith in Jesus?"

"Faith has nothing to do with this!" I was suddenly sick of this Jesus talk: it was an excuse for sloth and irresponsibility. But I did not want to get into that. "Another thing! You've been so lackadaisical the past couple of days. What's wrong? If you're sick we should find you a doc—"

"I am *not* sick! And I don't go to doctors!" He jumped to his feet. "*I have faith in Jesus—Jesus!*—and He's looking out for us! I pray for His help!"

"'*His help*'? Isn't there a line in the Bible about God helping those who help themselves? Just do your job!"

"You are *scolding* me!" he thrust out his shoulders, addressing me for the first time with the informal *tu*. "*Why?!*"

"I want to get to Kinshasa in one piece, that's why!"

We stood glaring at each other in the waning light, the sun dropping blood-red behind the forest. The sounds of the night-time jungle—the alarm calls of kulokokos, the hoots of owls, the weird buzzings of giant nocturnal beetles—were slowly creeping out onto the river. It was useless to continue this argument. I stomped and shook the mosquitoes off my legs. I ripped open my duffel and threw on my long pants, I splashed repellent over myself. "We need to find a campsite before it's too dark to see."

Glaring at me, Desi slowly picked up his paddle.

We floated toward a cliff about ten feet above the water. In the dark its altitude would make us invisible to passing pirogues. We pulled up to the shore beneath it and I got out, slipping on the root tangles, and clambered up its face. We erected a rudimentary camp—no tarp, no tent, just nets—on the lumpy, root-covered eminence, ground that even with our foam mattresses was going to make for poor sleep. As soon as the nets were set up we climbed inside, assaulted by mosquitoes, hungry and unbathed.

I lay down and gruntingly tried to position myself so that the roots wouldn't poke me. But it was futile. Desi lit his lamp and started reciting a passage from the Bible, then thumbed through his *Code du Travail* and perorated a subclause on a worker's right to advance notice in the event of untimely dismissal. That led him, somehow, back to a verse from Isaiah, and he flipped pages and cross-referenced the two.

As I listened to him read I thought, *How little I understand this guy!* His thoughts never matched my thoughts; I could never foretell his responses. But more than just culture and upbringing separated us: our purposes in traveling the river put us at odds. For me, everything here was new and urgent and unique; for Desi the Congo was a harsh and ancient waterway out of which to wrest a meager living while he battled constant fatigue from worms or fevers or whatever it was that was afflicting him. He would not hurry because, danger or no, this river was his home and he lived by rhythms that allowed him to conserve his strength, enjoy himself when he could, and go on.

It was wrong of me to lose my temper, and I regretted my sharp words.

"Desi, I didn't mean to yell at you. Just let's be more careful next time. Maybe it's the nine days of river travel that are wearing on us. Why don't we rest an extra day in Lisala?"

He halted his reading and sat up in his net. After clearing his throat, he clasped his hands and raised his head. "O Lord Jesus! Watch out for us on this huge river! Great dangers are ahead! And please watch out for Monsieur Jeff's woman in Moscow. O Lord Jesus! Watch out for Monsieur Jeff so that he can go back to Moscow and have many, many children with his woman and be very happy there! Amen!"

No sooner, it seemed, had I suffered my way into a spell of fitful sleep than the sun was beating down through my net. We had overslept by an hour. Without having breakfasted, we decamped, sore and grimy, poked tender by the roots, and poled out into the rushing current. But shortly the river widened from three miles across to six, and the current whisked us into a wild profusion of isles and jungle alleys. I asked Desi if he knew the way to Lisala from here; we didn't want to end up on the wrong side of an island and shoot past the town without realizing it.

He listened to my question and said, in a disoriented voice, "I feel dizzy."

"*Dizzy?* Desi . . . Desi, I'm asking you how well you know the river here. If you have any doubts, we should stick to the north bank, so we'll be sure to see Lisala."

"I know the river. But I'm tired."

• • •

The morning wore on, growing overcast and humid. We skirted a finger of land and startled a villager in a cove: a stubble-bearded man in his forties with unkempt hair and a goiter the size of a pomegranate was standing there fixing a fishing net. As though I were carrion, he flinched at the sight of me. But he had a fat capitaine on a rope and we needed to eat. Desi called out a greeting and offered him ten thousand zaires for the fish, an acceptable price; he uttered a curt *te,* and demanded thirty thousand. Desi made a counteroffer. Shaking his head *(Te! Te!),* the fisherman refused to come down. We handed him thirty thousand, took the fish, and paddled off, with him shooting deranged looks at us.

"What's his problem, Desi?"

Desi was fully alert now. He shifted around on his seat and watched the man watch us as we made our way downriver. "I don't know. He's not of my people. I don't know what tribe he's from."

By noon the river on which fishermen had hitherto passed by four or five times a day was flowing empty, and there were no villages. The open and swampy forest around Bumba had metamorphosed into a dark and snarled wall of vegetation, of serried gum trees and teaks and bombaxes rising hundreds of feet into the sky straight from the banks. A headwind wearied us, blowing hot and wet from the equator, where battlemented clouds of gunmetal blue massed above the jungle. Lightning tore loose over the horizon.

"Should we pull ashore?"

"We should not stop," Desi said, working his paddle hard. "Not here."

Soon the clouds were lowering, the palm fronds were hissing, blowing backward and showing their pale undersides; the wind was frilling the slate-colored water with white. We were approaching a forested peninsula. A long rumble of thunder broke into pealing explosions. We *had* to take cover. I looked back at Desi.

His eyes widened. "A boat!"

Rounding the cape at high speed was an oil-carrying barge, its deck manned by Bangala soldiers bearing automatic rifles. It came crashing through the storm-roiled water, and we ran lurching through its wake. As we regained our balance, two pirogues came around from behind the barge and shot toward us. The pilots—two men in each—were in rags, but they were muscular, paddling in unison, pitching and rolling expertly with the wake. They came alongside us, one port and one starboard.

"*Mbote!*"

"*Mbote!*"

Greetings were exchanged all around, but smiles were not, and no handshakes followed. One of the men put down his oar and shouted to Desi in Lingala. "We are *matata* [vicious]! Give us food! Give us cigarettes! You have a *mondele* with you—you have food for us!"

I looked at Desi. His face went blank and his eyes darted to the feet of these men, where there lay glistening machetes, heavy and murderously sharp.

"*Pesa ngai mbongo!*" (Give me money!), the leader shouted, growing impatient. He started leaning toward his machete.

"*Problem eza te,*" Desi said calmly. Take what you want.

The leader paused and, turning away from his weapon, began rifling through our provisions. The others held our pirogue firmly to theirs. We were being robbed.

Desi bent over as if to help him find what he wanted, but instead he reached under his bag and drew out the shotgun. He straightened up, expressionlessly waving the barrel back and forth across the four brigands. We bobbed on the waves, we drifted; thunderbolts broke free of the clouds to the south, flashing and crashing into the forest; wind gusted up the river. We swayed and tried to keep our balance on the mounting surf.

The robber abandoned our sacks and smiled. Desi smiled, too. I smiled. The brigands began half-bowing, rapidly uttering a supplicatory Lingala. Ngombe was mentioned over and over, as well as *likama* (danger) and *matata*. We were drifting toward a few huts under giant trees, and there were people outside them. Women picked up their children and ran off, and four or five men in rags came out to the bank.

"Come and shelter in our village," the leader said. He pointed at the sky. "*Mbula.*"

Desi kept the gun trained on them. "No, thank you."

"Please, you and the *mondele* are welcome."

"*Te.* We thank you very much."

The leader shouted to the men on shore and one of them went running to the huts. A blast of wind hit us, and we all nearly toppled over. The man came running back with a handful of smoked catfish and crashed out through the water to the brigands' pirogue. We were directly opposite the village now, ten feet from the bank. The brigands took the fish—three shriveled black things—and passed them to Desi, who adjusted the gun in the crook of his arm and accepted them, nodding thanks.

At this point the leader began pointing at the forest and the river, gesticulating with passion, speaking loudly and with nasal flourishes, over and over saying *matata* and *likama* and Ngombe and much more than I could follow. Desi listened, his face a mask betraying no emotion, his gun remaining trained on them. Finally, they picked up their paddles and rowed back upriver toward their village.

Desi kept his eyes on them until they had vanished behind the trees.

"They warned us that they're Ngombe, they're vicious robbers and proud of it, and we're in their territory. We will have problems. No one who's not an Ngombe enters Ngombe land, and even the barges speed through, because Ngombe use gaffs to snare people off the decks. If we're seen we'll be robbed or worse. They told us to avoid showing ourselves to the villages ahead. And if Ngombe fishermen come up to us, they're not really fishermen—they're robbers. They said to shoot in the air or into the water when they approach." He held the gun high and gave it a proud pat.

"Our gun is a dud, Desi."

He lowered his eyes.

"But," I said, still not yet fully feeling the fear I knew would come once I had digested the incident, "no one has to know that. So, we have to hide from the villages?"

"Yes. We have to hide."

"Do you know where the villages are?"

"I . . . no, not exactly."

Any minute the storm would hit, and holding to midriver, which would help us conceal our identity from those on shore, would not be possible. I sat down in a clammy sweat. There weren't supposed to be Ngombe until *after* Lisala. I picked up the map. It seemed to show that we were following the bank of an island that terminated near Lisala— but then there were more islands here than anywhere we had been before, and the profusion of waterways could have confused us. The more I tried to make what we had seen today jibe with what was on paper, the less certain I became of our position.

Then I harked back to my pretrip readings. Stanley had described the tribes in this section of the river as "powerful, well-equipped, and warlike . . . hideously bepainted for war . . . remarkably superior . . . [entertaining] a singular antipathy toward strangers," but could his words really apply to the Ngombe of today? I also recalled the hierarchy and territoriality of the tribes he encountered, most of whom were cannibals. Many forbade strangers to enter their land—which accounted for much of the hostility with which he and his crew were met, hostility that resulted in some forty battles on the way downriver and dozens of deaths. But that was all a hundred and twenty years ago! Could there still exist such people in the Africa of today? After all, barges passed through here. Isolated tribesmen did see outsiders; in fact, they relied on them for medicine and manufactured goods. How could it be—*could* it be?—that they were still so dangerous, as *matata* as the brigand declared? Then it occurred to me: if violent robberies were so common in Kinshasa, why wouldn't bands of thugs also roam the river?

I put away the map and started to paddle. Thunder broke once, twice, then lingered. Or was it thunder?

Desi froze. "Drums!"

Beats ominous and deep reverberated across the water. We listened.

"Could they be saying something about us?" I asked.

"I don't know. I don't understand the message. They are not the drums of my region."

"We have to stay away from their village, but where is it?"

The forest amplified the drumbeats and bounced them all over. They could have been coming from anywhere.

"There!" Desi whispered.

Smoke was billowing out from behind trees twenty yards ahead. It was too late to take evasive action: we would pass within ten feet of them. We quietly placed our paddles in the pirogue. Desi grabbed the gun, I seized the machete. Without steerage we started rotating, looping down along the bank.

We ducked. We revolved past the fire—but it was unmanned. The drums were resounding from somewhere else.

Rain began falling in heavy, single pellets. A terrible mountain of black thunderheads firing yellow bolts of lightning into the jungle filled the sky to the south, moving along the equator. It was three-thirty. We needed to find a secluded place to camp, and fast.

Despite the clouds, we coursed far out into midriver to avoid showing ourselves to a village on the left bank. The islands now were too numerous to keep track of: each had its own dark waterway with its dense jungle and kulokoko sentries. Conical wasp nests hung from high branches but there wasn't a wasp about. "The storm," whispered Desi. "It will be bad. Everything is hiding."

The rain was dappling the water with frothy ringlets of white, but the wind had died down; the storm was passing south of us. We drifted by a cove accessible through a narrow break in the trees—a perfect hidden campsite. We pulled up to the bank, and I stepped out and dragged the bow chain.

There was a gunshot. We ducked. Then another shot.

"Get back in! Let's go!" Desi whispered, "Let's go!" He dug into the water with his oar, I pushed the bow back out and splashed along, trying to catch up to it, my bare feet slipping over the roots on the bottom. Cringing, I jumped aboard and we both began paddling. We saw smoke—the gunshots were from the opposite bank—and shouts of "Eeyaaah! Eeyaaah!" rang out from up and down the river. With these cries villagers alerted one another to approaching barges, to the unexpected presence of strangers.

We stayed within a yard of the bank. The rain turned heavy and gusts came rolling upriver, slowing us, raising breakers—it would soon be too rough to continue. We reached the rear of the island and started down the alley between two others.

We spotted a secluded glade at the far end of an island. It would afford us a with a view of the south bank, of the approach from the villages we had passed, so we chose it and set up camp in the soaking but now thunderless rain. We camouflaged our tents with tree branches, we dragged our pirogue behind the foliage, we abstained from lighting our lanterns or playing the radio. We spoke in whispers—when voices carried across the river we held our breath, and Desi tried to discern what was being said. But they were speaking Ngombe, and he could not understand.

I was determined not to give in to panic or break our routine. We had hundreds of miles to go to Mbandaka, and we would have to remain composed or we would destroy ourselves. I therefore shaved and bathed, albeit in the rain, and Deli did, too, and we felt better. At four-thirty in the afternoon I crawled inside my tent, Desi into his net. Desi spoke in a low voice.

"I'm a stranger here. If they see me, they will think I've come to steal, and they'll kill me. These people are robbers and killers."

I did not know what to say to him.

Later there was a rustle, sinuous and faint, coming from the forest behind us, moving slowly and surely toward our camp. I held my breath and sat up. It grew louder and more distinct. The rain plopped from leaf to leaf, splattering onto the ground, into the river; the river was now an expanse of running pewter glimmering through the trees. I gripped the gun, squeezed its iron barrel, and I waited, sweat pouring off my brow, for whatever it was to come into view.

A python, ten feet long and as thick as a human thigh, scaly and slimy, muscular and mottled brown and black, slithered by my gauze tent door. It wended its way around our gear, slithered past us, its tail slightly raised in a curl, and, at last, was gone into the brush.

I relaxed and lay back, still listening but now breathing freely, as the light failed and darkness, sultry and suffocating, settled over the forest. Rain continued to fall in maddeningly resonant drops, dripping down from the treetops.

Around midnight it ceased. For a while there was not a sound, but slowly the forest began echoing with cries and wavering hoots, with screeches that rang with the numbing terror we felt as trespassers in this wilderness. We heard crashes in the bush, the snapping of branches in nearby glades. Every snap or crash *could* indicate the approach of an Ngombe murderer, but each time silence followed, a tense silence, as if the forest, frightened by an intruder, were holding its breath. I woke up over and over again, unaware of what had roused me, experiencing only a residue of fear without knowing its cause.

Desi's cool and quick thinking during the attempted robbery had saved us. But it occurred to me: might the Ngombe brigands, in their chest-thumping explication afterward, have exaggerated the danger for some purpose unbeknownst to us?

I pondered this during the long, long night, and waited for dawn.

At five in the morning we slipped out of our tents, tossed the camouflaging brush from our pirogue, and shoved off, soundlessly regaining the current, the sky hunkering low above us a black cauldron of cloud. As day broke a headwind arose, rifling through sopping leaves. Silently and assiduously we worked our paddles. Lisala had to be at the end of this island, it *had* to be. Noting that villages tended to appear in the southern reaches of the river, we stuck to the northern bank. The isle went on and on, and the sun came out, driving away the clouds and whipping up a headwind. We strained with each stroke of the oar, the calluses on our hands degenerating into blisters, then bloody-watery sores.

We passed only one village. The men came out and shouted, "Is that mondele alone?"

"No," Desi answered. "There are more coming behind us. Touris."

They laughed and shouted a response in brazen Ngombe.

I looked back at Desi. "That was clever. Let them think we're carrying a veritable armory of Motorolas!"

Just then we floated by a cove. Two youths brandishing machetes came running out of the forest, leapt into their pirogue, and cast off, all in one balletic, lethal rush.

A surge of adrenaline coursed through my heart and I plunged my paddle deep into the muddy water. Desi scrambled and pulled out the gun. As the pirogue overcame us, he trained it on the youths.

"Ah, you and the mondele have a gun!" one shouted to us. "You win! We would have robbed and killed you both, and who would have ever known!" Laughing, they dropped back and returned to their cove, their laughter mocking and following us as we sped away down the bank.

We lunched on the capitaine and the smoked catfish the Ngombe had given us, adding rice and canned tomatoes. This simple meal did more than nourish us—it distracted us, it gave us something on which to concentrate besides our wearying fear, and Desi's face showed fear as clearly as mine must have. I even managed to ponder for some time the putrid flavor of the catfish—which tasted the same as catfish I had eaten in the States. It took me back to the canal on which I used to fish as a boy; to mornings on the Potomac River; I recalled high school and friends I had not seen in years . . .

There was a glint in the distance far ahead of us, as of polished steel over water. Two pirogues were coming with three men in each. But as I bent around to warn Desi, who was washing his plate, I caught sight of two other pirogues approaching from the rear. He saw the look on my face, grabbed the gun, and shoved a cartridge in the chamber.

"That will do us a lot of good," I said, laughing.

"We have nothing else."

We were going to be ambushed. I could slash with the machete, I could strike with my oar. I could stuff a rag in the kerosene can, light it, and toss it like a Molotov cocktail. Desi kept the gun in his hands, his finger on the trigger; he steadily repeated a verse from the Bible. We were both going to remain calm. Until . . .

The sun gilded the river; a breeze blew cool and fresh; the coruscations ahead were rhythmic and slashing.

"I hate strong sun, Desi. I prefer the clouds. That's one reason I love Russia. The sun is soft there in the summer. In the winter, the sun is rare and welcome."

"Winter?"

Each set of pirogues was now twenty yards equidistant from us.

"When it snows."

"When it *what*?"

"Haay! Whooa! Whooa!" the men in the pirogues were shouting.

The pirogues from the rear reached us first. They paddled alongside us; their pilots, lanky youths, greeted Desi and ignored me. Then the pirogues from up ahead passed us, filled with families. The "machetes" turned out to be wet oars reflecting the sunlight.

In two craft next to us sat six people, men, women, children; in one, fish was being smoked in a miniature hut of bamboo sheltering a fire burning on a pile of earth. They had started out in Bumba and tried to catch up with us to warn us about the route we were taking, but they lost us in the islands. Desi told them about our troubles.

The senior youth astern shook his head. "You are lucky to be alive. Anyway, what are you doing out here, Lokele? You're crazy to come out here with just a *mondele*. You need protection. You need to travel with Bangala or Ngombe. The people in these parts are *matata*."

He jumped aboard our pirogue. His head, wrapped in a turban, was angular, his jaw square; he was long-limbed and sinewy. He took my paddle and motioned me to rest, then turned to Desi. "And what is this *mondele* doing here? Looking for diamonds?"

We bucked heavy waves and a headwind. Tsetse flies, swarming above the hyacinth, dove into the air pockets formed by the gunwale of our pirogue; they tormented us, biting us behind the knees, on the backs, wherever we could not see to swat.

But it did not matter. In the company of others a millstone of fear had been lifted from our hearts. The youth said he and his companions were Bangala fishermen from near Mbandaka. Bangala! He would know about the abattoir—the place of slaughter—that the SNIP colonel in Lisala had told me lay between Lisala and Mbandaka. I interrogated him and Desi translated. The youth said he had seen two *mondeles* murdered in pirogues south of Lisala, and had a lot to say about the region. "It's very dangerous. We Bangala don't care for life. If we see a *mondele* many of us think only to kill him and take his things. After the murders I saw the whole area became a scandal for Zaire. Mobutu sent in troops and they wiped out the villages that killed them."

"Can we make it through?" I asked.

"You'll need to fire your guns. When the pirogues appear, shoot in the air before they approach you. You must scare them first, make them afraid. You will have to be alert and very careful, or you will have problems."

The day aged, the sun described its arc across the cerulean-sky, the banks lifted the forest higher and higher. Lisala was not at the end of that island, or the next, or the next. At five, however, the youth announced we were drawing near.

I started getting ready. I put on the fresh Oxford shirt and trousers I had stashed in the bottom of my bag; I combed my hair; I checked my *lettre de recommandation* and passport and placed them in my breast pocket. Just before the sun fell Lisala appeared on the ridges ahead, and atop the ridges children popped up, running along and chanting *"Mondele! Mondele!" Mondele* rang out from hut to hut, along with cries of "Eeyaah!" The children raced the pirogue, shouting and skipping, now and then tossing stones at us. We paddled hard, riding the current, which was frothy and fast here.

The beach came into view. Soldiers were hoisting their guns to their shoulders and loping toward us, stumbling down the steps of the landing, their boots untied and flopping, their guns swinging. The youth hopped back into his own pirogue. I thanked him and he nodded farewell, then he and his company veered off downriver, leaving us to face the soldiers alone.

"Come here! Hey! *Le Blanc!* You come *here!*"

Like a ragtag lynch mob drunk on whiskey, seven or eight soldiers came bounding down the bank toward us, shouting in French and tripping on their bootlaces, waving their guns. As at Ngobila Beach, so here, there was something almost comic in the mix of swaggering bravado and exaggerated, no doubt, staged rage to which my appearance provoked them. But their sloppy speech told me they had been drinking booze or smoking *mbangi,* and they pointed their guns at us, which was not funny.

I stopped paddling and stood tall, preparing to ham-act here as I had done in Lokutu. We coasted up to the beach and the pirogue's bow scraped its way up onto the sand. The soldiers were dressed in khakis and yellowed T-shirts. They were enlisted men, and there was no sign of an officer among them. I stepped out, and they closed around me.

A man in full uniform shoved through the mob, kicked the last private aside, and thrust his face in mine. He was almost Arab in complexion, with a mustache and a long, stubble-encrusted mug. Epaulets on his shoulders marked him as an officer. Still, *mbangi* was on his breath and his eyes were murky red. His tongue moved around in his mouth like a squirming clam.

"Sh-show me your—"

I held out my *lettre de recommandation.* "I am on a mission sanctioned by the Chief of Staff of Military Intelligence of President Mobutu, as it says here. I will speak only to the Lisala base commander."

The officer shifted the gun under his arm. He squinted at the letter and reached for it, but I pulled it away. "I *said* I will speak only to the base commander," I repeated, staring hard into his sodden eyes.

He stepped back and dropped his gaze, and so did his men, who lowered their guns. He made a wary welcoming gesture toward the stairs leading up to the town. "No problem, *commandant*. After you."

Desi set about unloading the pirogue, and the officer and I started up the steps. The other soldiers tagged along, lagging well behind, as if I might crack a whip or kick an ass, and I tried to look as though I would. But along the way, still more soldiers fell in with us, and in no time we were leading a procession of slovenly, stoned, or drunk Zairean warriors swinging their taped-up rifles, scuffing their boots in the dust, nagging me for *mbongo*, beer, *mbangi*, or whatever *cadeau* they could cadge; they grew so insistent, pulling on my sleeves and whining, that I snapped to the officer, "Do something about these ridiculous men!" He flailed his gun at them and they dropped back a few paces, but followed us just the same.

We were in Lisala to hire a soldier for protection. I suddenly envisioned myself sharing the same pirogue with one of these louts, eating and drinking with him, and most absurdly, relying on him to protect my life.

Lisala was a torpid town with no charm. Its center was a mess of concrete buildings on dusty earth diminishing to huts with African-style courtyards in jungly suburbs. At the military base we were told that the commander was not in, that we had to come back in the morning. But on our way out we ran into the chief of SNIP, a potbellied colonel in his fifties wearing a Hawaiian shirt. Ignoring my proffered hand, he did not slow his pace to greet me, but instead pointed to a fellow waving at me and running up the road. "This man will take care of you," he barked, turning away.

The waving man, also dressed in a Hawaiian shirt (I was beginning to recognize a certain style of Hawaiian shirt as the Polo of the Zairean elite), grabbed my hand and pumped it vigorously. "Oh, pew! Hot today, isn't it? Well, I'm the adjutant. I got the letter from Kinshasa. I'm responsible for your security. Anyway, welcome to Lisala! We have reserved suites for you! Where is your gear? At the beach? Ah! *Après vous!*" He grandly motioned me ahead, but then took my arm anyway and pulled me along in search of a pickup truck that could transport our belongings to the hotel.

The adjutant was sportily coiffed, and his wingtips were polished; he had an air of pleasant alacrity about him that contrasted with the malign torpor of most Zairean officials. His diction was clipped and suggested efficiency. All of this set me at ease and made him seem worth the price he was sure to demand.

Later, up at the no-name hotel to which he took us, Desi and I settled into our "suites." There was no water or electricity and the doors had no locks; in fact, most of the rooms had no doors. There were curlicues of feces scattered across the bathroom floors—only the toilets were clean. But the staff, a friendly family, did their best to make us comfortable, bringing water from the well for our baths and providing us with kerosene and kitchen space.

Night fell. Lisala after dark was all smoking middens alternating with the pale yellow flames of kerosene lanterns that illuminated the larval wares of sidewalk vendors. But it was not quiet: the air rumbled with generators powering the air conditioners and fluorescent lights of villas belonging to the local Big Men. Lisalans, Bangala, for the most part, were aggressive and blustering, and they made Desi and me nervous. It was not a friendly place, and we kept off the street.

Morning sun flooded through the window panes, flies buzzed in the dusty checkers of light falling on the floor. Mobutu looked rather peeved and put-upon in the portrait on the wall of the base commander's office, slumped on his throne and clutching his chief's staff, his Hawaiian shirt buttoned up to his neck and pinching him in the armpits. The commander, a clean-shaven man in spotless khakis, shook my hand and ignored Desi, and gestured to me to take a seat. Both Desi and I sat down in front of his desk.

"It is kind of you to receive us, Commander," I said. "I know you are very busy. I appreciate the time you will spend accommodating us, and I would like to present you with a token of my gratitude." I placed a brick of zaires—twenty dollars' worth—on his desk. (Desi suggested the amount and the wording of this address beforehand.)

His eyes on mine, the commander took the brick in hand, opened a desk drawer, and dropped it in.

"We will need a soldier to protect us on the way from Lisala to Mbandaka."

"There is no problem," he said flatly. "We have been informed by Kinshasa. The adjutant will find you a suitable man."

"Thank you."

I started to stand up and so did the commander. But Desi, slouched in his chair, did not move. He interrupted our rise. "Now wait ju-u-ust a minute. About this soldier. He must not be just *any* one of your men. He must not drink and he must not smoke. He must be a God-fearing Christian. He must love Jesus, and show that love in his deeds."

The commander furrowed his brow and eased himself back into his seat, as did I. He addressed me, as though I, not Desi, had just spoken. "Well . . . I don't see what Jesus or smoking has to do with your expedition. And I'm no less a military man for having a beer now and then . . . anyway, you talk to the adjutant."

Desi continued. "He must not smoke or drink because—"

I stood up and cut in. "Thank you for your time. We'll have the adjutant inform you of our progress." I grabbed Desi and led him out.

At that moment the adjutant came sauntering into the waiting room. He was beaming. "I have found *the* soldier for you. Meet Henri. You can reach an agreement with him right now!"

Henri was one of the *mbangi*-head privates who had pestered me on arrival. He was a runt with a pinched oily face—he looked like he needed a good scrubbing with antibacterial soap. He averted his eyes from mine and spoke only to Desi. I heard numbers being bandied around. Next thing I knew Henri was shaking my hand.

Desi was triumphant. "Henri has accepted your offer of two hundred and fifty thousand zaires."

"My *offer*? What are you talking about?"

"Well, the adjutant has approved him."

"I haven't made an offer. I don't know the first thing about this guy." I turned to the adjutant. "With all due respect, I decide here."

The adjutant opened his mouth, but Desi cut in. "Okay, what do you need to know?"

I was still upset about Desi's meddling in my talk with the commander. "Desi, you're not to talk on your own. You're acting on my behalf. Well, first of all, can this . . . Henri . . . swim?"

Desi asked him in Lingala. Taking a deep breath, Henri muttered an answer.

"No. Henri fears the water."

"Well, that's not good news if he'll be in a pirogue for the next two weeks, is it?"

"He knows that. He's very concerned. So he has raised his fee. To four hundred thousand."

"What happens if he should drown?"

"*Drown?*" Desi turned to Henri and translated my query. Henri protested, spewing forth verbiage in agitated Lingala, his forehead beading with fresh oil and more sweat. Desi relayed his words to me. "If he is going to drown he must raise his fee. He will now accept eight hundred thousand."

"Desi, I'm not hiring anyone who can't swim."

This truly upset Henri, who raised his rate to 1,500,000.

Desi grew grave. "You're frightening him with all this talk of water."

"Oh, for God's sake, he's fired!" I responded. Henri dropped his fee to 350,000. No. He then asked for severance pay. No again.

Desi turned back to me. "You are worried about his drowning. For your information the *Code du Travail du Zaire* states that the life of a soldier is worth the lives of one hundred and fifty civilians or fifty thousand U.S. dollars."

The adjutant perked up. "Is that so? Fifty *thousand* dollars?"

If I had had a club I would have clobbered Desi, and I told him so with my look.

The adjutant's eyes sparkled. "Fifty thousand dollars. Fifty *thousand*! But of *course*!"

"I'm not paying anybody fifty thousand dollars. No one is going to die on our expedition. We need a soldier who can swim and accept the risk in return for a suitable salary, food, and, if he does his job well, a healthy bonus." The salary alone that I would offer was more than twice as much as a soldier would normally receive in a month. It would be a good deal.

"You don't care about the life of a soldier?" Desi asked, frowning.

The adjutant interrupted. "You don't have to. You can simply pay an insurance premium and be absolved of responsibility if anything should happen."

"What sort of 'premium'?"

He darted into the commander's office, whence a bout of excited whispering issued. He darted back out. "Five hundred thousand zaires. Payable to the base commander through me. In advance."

"What sort of policy papers are involved?"

"Why, none at all! Just pay us cash—in advance!"

"With all due respect, no."

"But the commander has accepted your offer!"

"I haven't made an offer."

Desi took me aside. "You're acting as though Henri's life means nothing to you. You are acting *méchant*. You're—"

"Desi, please, stay out of this." Obviously the premium was a scam, and I wanted to talk no more about it. I addressed the adjutant. "Listen, if something happens to this soldier it will be in the line of his official duties; I have authorization from Military Intelligence for his services. In truth, I shouldn't have to pay him anything at all because he's still going to get his salary and he's simply doing his duty—the duty you are assigning him to carry out by ordering him to accompany me. Remember, my *lettre de recommandation* orders you to assist me. But I'll be generous with him—and with you—if this can all be satisfactorily arranged. And I'm not taking anyone aboard my pirogue who can't swim. Period." I walked to the other side of the room and looked out the window.

"*Bon*," said the adjutant. "Okay. Wait here a minute." He hurried out the door, and Henri, realizing his services would not be wanted, slunk away.

A little later the adjutant appeared with another soldier in tow, a genial fellow who was just over five feet tall. His name was Amisi. Amisi held high his seventy-two-caliber FAL automatic rifle (a Belgian version of the M-16), and his uniform was buttoned and pressed. He could swim and knew Lingala and Swahili (he was a Swahili speaker from east of Kisangani), and not much French, he said, but he managed to converse well enough in that language that I got an idea of his character. He was not the fierce-looking guardian I had imagined, but he seemed trustworthy and that sufficed. I hired him on the condition that he sign a contract stating our terms. I wanted no misunderstandings to arise between us, and I wanted us both to operate on the assumption that we were mutually accountable. He heard me out and pensively nodded his assent.

The adjutant *après-vous*'d us into his office. "Yes, a contract! Now let's discuss the terms. The first term is that his entire salary is payable in advance. To me."

Desi rubbed his chin. "Sounds reasonable."

"Desi! I'm sorry, Adjutant. I will pay Amisi half his fee before the trip and the other half when he successfully completes his mission."

"Then pay me his bonus now."

Desi's forefinger stabbed the air. "Good idea!"

"Desi! I will pay *him* as I've said, Adjutant. The bonus will depend on an outstanding performance, as our contract will stipulate." I knew nothing would stop the adjutant from taking a cut later, but this was the most I could do now.

"Oh, his performance will be outstanding," the adjutant asserted crisply. "You can be assured of that! All the same, it will save us time if we dispense with the bonus and fee issues now, before such a dangerous journey."

"As I said, we will sign a contract and I will pay him as I've specified. That's my last word."

He fell silent, the pleasant expression on his face withering as he digested my intransigence, and, to be sure, the loss of the soldier's salary, which no doubt he would have simply seized for himself if I had paid it through him. "Listen," he said, "I absolutely *must* receive his salary in advance, or you can't have him. Your trip is too dangerous for us to wait until Mbandaka."

"Fine. Then I will call the Office of the President and tell him you are preventing me from carrying out my mission."

His smile returned, albeit in a somewhat sourer version. "Okay! All right! *Pas de problème!* Outstanding performance and a contract! *Mais oui!*" The adjutant rustled through the things on his desk and presented me with a sheet of paper and a pen.

Ten minutes later I had written out a straightforward contract in French. It stated that Amisi would receive his pay, his food, his return fare on a barge to Lisala, plus, if he did a good job, a hefty bonus. I would give him half the salary before we left so that he could go home and deliver it to his family. We would depart in the morning.

Amisi signed it, and I pulled the cash from my pocket. He took the money from me and looked at it, he *glowered* at it, as if it were an insult, then raised his eyes and glowered at me.

Why?

He again stared at the bills and recounted them, as if suspecting I had shortchanged him; then, apparently satisfied that he had indeed received half his salary, he hoisted his gun to his shoulder, paused, and walked out.

The adjutant stood expectantly with his hands in his pockets.

"You have helped us a lot," I said, offering him a modest brick of zaires. I was not lying to be polite: I had expected far worse. He was just another basically capable man warped by this horrible system. He accepted the money with a dignified bow and agreed to send a driver to pick us up at the hotel at five-thirty in the morning.

Later, after we returned to the hotel, I fell ill in the debilitating heat of late afternoon. Tormented by nausea, my intestines tightening into knots, I rolled from side to side on the lumpy mattress in my green room, weak and clammy, listening to the lizards crawl up the walls and the parrots squawk outside my window. My hands were blistered from paddling, my nose was burned from the sun, my tsetse bites itched. On the river I had held myself in check; here I could relax, but I felt that I might collapse into a mass of maladies.

The last days on the water had been frightening; the worst, I quailed to think, was probably ahead. Desi's meddling during the day's negotiations had puzzled and irked me. How was he reasoning? Why was he siding with everyone against me? If I needed his loyalty in a tough parley on the way to Mbandaka, would I be able to count on him?

His talk of drowning and the Zairean Code of Labor served to introduce a valid point, one I truly had not addressed in my bargaining: what if the soldier were to die? Fifty thousand dollars or a hundred and fifty civilian lives—could this be true? And what if Desi were to die? What would happen to his wife and daughter in Bumba and his family in Lokutu? And how was I to interpret Amisi's angry look on taking his advance? Could I trust him? There were too many questions to answer, and I turned away from them in that hot room, in my damp and suffocating net, feeling pain knife its way through my gut.

I suddenly found myself fantasizing about finishing the trip and freeing myself of Desi and the soldier and all the fears I had lived with for the past six months. And then Tatyana came to mind and memories of her were too evocative to dwell on. It was incredible to think I was putting myself through all this, and I could not imagine why I should go on.

There was a knock on my door. I dressed quickly, hurriedly putting on my dollar-packed money belt beneath my pants, and answered. It was Desi. He had a towel around his shoulders; he had just bathed.

"Bonsoir."

"Bonsoir."

He tilted his head back and looked at me. "I want more money." His eyes were narrow and adamantine. "I have been thinking about it. It cost you millions to fly to Zaire from your country. You had money enough to buy a pirogue, and a good pirogue at that. You had money for a gun. You had money enough for charcoal and Cokes in Bumba, you have money for supplies in every town. You have money for a soldier. You have money for the base commander. You have money for the adjutant. You have much, much money. I want more money."

He poked his forefinger into the money belt bulging on my waist. (I had not had time to put it on properly.) "What is this? Your money?"

I stepped back, unsettled. "Come inside, Desi." I caught my breath, feeling the need to lie. "Most of my money is in the bank in Kinshasa. I would have been crazy to come out here with a lot of cash. The amounts I'm giving out are the amounts I carefully estimated in advance."

"Estimated?"

"I mean I have enough to get us to Kinshasa, and not more."

"So . . . can I have more money?"

"Desi, you signed a contract for a specific amount and I have given you half already, as we agreed. You will receive a bonus, too, as we agreed, once we get to Kinshasa."

"You are very harsh," he said, raising his head again, giving me his stony glare. "You were harsh with the adjutant. You were harsh with Henri. You seemed *méchant*, not wanting to buy him insurance. As if you didn't care if he lived or died."

"Desi, that insurance bit was just a ruse—a trick to get money from me. Couldn't you see that?"

"Well, I see how rich you are." His bony feet spread on the dirty floor. "I'm not rich. This trip is not so easy for me."

"You've done a good job, and if you keep up the good work I'll reward you well. In Kinshasa."

"Will you give me the pirogue?"

"Probably, but I'll decide that in Kinshasa."

"And all the things you've bought for the trip?"

"I'll decide that in Kinshasa. If all goes well, I'll be very generous with you, but in Kinshasa, as we agreed, and as is stated in the contract we both signed."

He mopped his forehead with his towel and sat down on the bed. "You are very harsh," he said again. With that he seemed to be saying, *Your world is your world, my world is mine. You are rich and I am poor. Have pity on me, because that will never change.*

I stepped back and looked out the window into the yard. In the lot stick-figure toddlers were running around naked, and a woman was pounding manioc root with a pestle, her arms little more than bones in loose dark skin. I had understood that Desi might not have had a clear idea of what signing a contract meant, but putting things in writing was the only way I could think of to prevent misunderstandings. I didn't want to give him more money (or not now, at least), and not because I was greedy: it was a matter of limits. I resisted giving more under pressure like this because I didn't want to look weak and invite further pressure, pressure to give *beyond* my limits. I had a certain amount of money on me, and there was no way in this wilderness to get more, if we should actually need it. But he might not believe me.

Then I thought again. Desi had just poked my stash of cash. He had watched me dole out *matabiches* to corrupt officials while he was used to living hand to mouth. I had everything I needed to survive in my world, but I was risking my life for nothing in his, and spending what to him looked like obscene amounts to do so. And in the end he would stay here and I would fly out. What loyalty *should* I deserve from him?

"So can I have more money?"

"I think you'll do all you can to get me safely to Kinshasa. In view of the dangers we're facing I'm doubling your pay." I could not refuse him, and not only out of pity. I *did* pity him, I *did* see how hard he was trying to do his job, but I also feared that if I appeared to be a greedy ogre, his loyalty would waver, and with the most treacherous stretch of river ahead that was not a pleasant prospect.

"Okay," he said in a low voice. "Okay."

I looked at him, at his bony feet. He was not just lanky—he was rail thin, and the skin on his legs was flaky. Had he grown this emaciated on our trip? I asked how he was feeling: fine, he answered. He didn't need any more worm medicine.

I wanted to cheer him up. "By the way, is there anything in Lisala you would really like to eat during the days ahead? Is there monkey here?"

"There's better: there's goat. I would really like some good goat."

"Then buy a goat so that we'll have meat on the river for at least the first couple of days." I handed him a wad of zaires. "Now, I'm tired and we depart early in the morning. We should get some sleep."

He walked out and I collapsed into bed, weak and shivering, and turned to face the wall. I found myself wanting to call off the trip. But it was easier now to just go on to the end, whatever that end would be.

Healed and refreshed by the night's sleep, I got up before dawn and knocked on Desi's door. He had not, it turned out, been able to procure a goat the previous afternoon. In a groggy mood he threw on his tracksuit and set out to find one. I sat down on the porch and waited.

Five-thirty passed and there was no sign of the adjutant or his truck or Amisi or Desi. By eight the sun was mounting a cloudless sky, searing Lisala with incandescent light; pedestrians trailed keen black shadows on the bleached dust road. I paced the porch, a feeling of queasy unease spreading through me and mingling with discomfort from the heat: we would not get out of here in time to avoid detection. To distract myself, I took to double-checking our gear and studying the map.

Finally Desi came jogging up the steps holding chunks of goat wrapped in damp paper. "This is good goat. It will keep us strong."

But the sun grew hotter and hotter, driving away thoughts of food, and still there was no truck. We set the goat in the shade, and slumped by our things, weary already, and waited.

It wasn't until nine-thirty that a pickup truck came careening down the road to the hotel. Soldiers, mostly the louts who had harassed us on arrival, were seated in the rear, guns raised. The truck skidded to a halt, and its dust trail floated ahead to settle on our gear. The adjutant, wearing a fresh Hawaiian shirt, stepped out and waved. *"Bonjour! Allons!"*

He shouted in Lingala at the soldiers, who climbed down and snatched up our gear and loaded it onto the truck. Ten minutes later we were careening back down the street toward the landing. The late hour, the rumors circulating in town about who we were and what we were up to, and now this less-than-discreet ride to the river assured that our departure would be no secret; in fact, they guaranteed it status as the public event of the day. Near the landing we slowed and began fording a crowd. Half of Lisala had shown up to see us off.

Our pirogue was still there, locked by the bow chain to a mooring post, half-beached, the green river rushing frothy white around its wagging stern. Under the hectoring supervision of the adjutant, the soldiers started unloading the truck, grabbing our things and jogging them over to Desi, who packed them to make room in the middle for Amisi.

And then Amisi appeared at the edge of the crowd, staring disapprovingly at this mayhem, his FAL rifle sagging heavy on his left shoulder.

I went up to him. "Good morning. Are you ready?"

"Yes," he answered glumly.

"Ever been in a pirogue?"

"No. But I'll do all right."

Half an hour later, after having shaken fifty hands, paid the soldiers for their porter services, thanked the adjutant for his good offices, and seated Amisi in his chair, I poked my paddle into the sun-warmed sand and shoved off, and, with Desi's assistance, poled the pirogue out through the shallows. At the channel, the current picked us up and buoyed us downstream. Children followed us along the bank, shouting farewells, shouting and cavorting and cheering in the razoring, midmorning light.

The river, studded with clumps of water hyacinth, spread glaring and glassy, surging southwest at the same time as it appeared to embody the very essence of equatorial torpor. We paddled slowly, overtaking and parting the hyacinth floes with our bow, sending the bees on their blossoms into angry flight, stirring up black flies and butterflies. The forest here was of palms; their fronds drooped, white with glare, heavy and still in the heat. We soon relinquished our paddles and retreated beneath our umbrellas. Ten miles out of Lisala the crumbling brick walls of an abandoned Protestant mission emerged on the north bank, covered with creepers. Even here there had been missionaries.

A screech shattered the tranquillity. "I once was lost but now I'm found . . ." Between verses Desi cleared his throat and piped his voice to decibels and notes it had (mercifully) never before attained on our journey.

I suffered the tune, but it grew more vigorous and intolerably strident, and it well seemed he might have the energy to wail on for hours. We needed to keep a low profile here; caterwauling like this could alert Ngombe to our presence miles in advance.

When I could stand it no longer I swung around. "Desi!"

"Quoi?"

"Desi, for the love of God, we're sailing into cannibal territory here!"

"You are right! Only with the help of Jesus shall we survive!" He laid his paddle in the bottom of the pirogue, and stretched his arms skyward. "Lord God! Listen to the words of Your humble servant! God, You love us! Jesus, You love us! Give us Your protection as we travel forth down this perilous river! Stay at our sides, be our light in the darkness of this jungle! Spare us from the dangers ahead! And save us from temptresses! Amen!"

He stood at the stern as if crucified on an invisible cross, then lowered his head and muttered a private prayer. Amisi, unmoved, shifted in his cramped quarters.

A word lodged in my mind's ear. "Desi, what was that about 'temptresses'?"

He grabbed the goat, unwrapped it, and with his machete started hacking it into bloody chunks. "Why, women have the powers of sorceresses—don't you know? When I'm away from my wife I always ask God to keep an eye out for the women."

"I see."

"Satan does his work through women. Satan comes to man through woman. I fear being alone with a woman."

I asked Amisi if he agreed.

"I don't fear anything. I'm a soldier."

Desi dropped the goat into the boiling *bambula* and sifted in rice. "I'm surprised you ask these questions. It's your prophets who tell us that Satan comes calling when an unmarried man and woman are alone together. But there are many kinds of sin. Amisi, you're a soldier. Soldiers rape and pillage. In God's eyes that is also sinful."

Amisi looked back at Desi and raised an eyebrow.

Desi stirred the *bambula*. "Do you follow God, Amisi, or do you pillage?"

Amisi said something under his breath, then, adjusting himself in his seat, picked up an oar and tried to paddle. "Amisi is trying to change," Desi said. "He does not agree with the ways of his fellow soldiers."

"So he doesn't rape and pillage?" I asked.

"No."

"That's comforting."

I suggested we tell Amisi about the problems we expected during the two weeks ahead, and Desi repeated the words of the fisherman from Mbandaka, with his own minor but colorful augmentations: "Mobutu sent his Division spéciale to punish the Bangala tribes here for murdering *mondeles* . . . the tribes had been cutting mondeles into little pieces . . . this was giving Zaire a bad name . . . the Division wiped out whole villages, killing and burning and looting everyone . . . the Bangala are thieves and murderers . . ."

Amisi listened but said nothing, his face remaining inscrutably blank.

By noon the heat exceeded anything we had experienced since Bolobo; the glare burned us from every angle. The *bambula* bubbled over, and Desi pulled it off the coals. The combination of the gamy aroma of goat meat and sweltering heat killed my appetite.

Desi ladled a fatty gobbet onto a plate.

"It's ready!"

He served us all. I took it and let it cool off under my seat, then, bite by bite, forced myself to eat every bit. Aroma or no, and notwith-standing a gag here and there, it was tasty, and most important of all, nourishing. Amisi enjoyed his portion. Desi, however, ate but a little, then put his plate aside, having trouble swallowing and complaining of nausea.

After the meal we returned to the shade of our umbrellas, pulling our limbs within their protective and soothing circumference. We let the pirogue drift, and it performed lazy rotations among the hyacinth. As somnolent and serene as a Louisiana bayou, with the progress of the day the river shaded from green to satin blue, blue as the sky. Soon, my eyelids grew heavy.

But I struggled against sleep—this was not the time to drop my guard—and sat up. "Amisi, you should keep your gun on display. And Desi, raise the barrel of the shotgun so that it sticks out above the hull. Let no one doubt that we're armed."

Amisi sat alert with his gun on his knees; Desi dozed, his shotgun lodged high in the crook of his arm; I kept my eyes on the banks of the islands, resisting drowsiness with every fiber of my body. Only swarms of bees broke the silence of the hot glassy river.

I lurched awake to a scrape and a hiss and the giggles of children. It was after four o'clock. We were running aground in shallows amid a profusion of villages. Villagers were emerging from their huts and lining up on the banks to stare at us. Flustered, I shouted a friendly *"Mbote!"* but they did not respond. They stood still, their arms crossed, their eyes expressing nothing, neither welcome nor fear nor anger.

"Desi! Amisi! Wake up!"

They groggily opened their eyes and cleared their throats. Desi focused on the villagers and straightened up in alarm. He and I jumped out into the shin-deep water and dragged the pirogue off the shoal and back toward the channel, where we relaunched it and climbed aboard.

"Amisi, raise your gun."

Amisi hoisted his rifle and stood up, unlocking the safety. But we struck ground again and had to repeat the dragging procedure.

The banks by the villages were now lined with expressionless faces.

"These people are not good Christians," Desi said, paddling hard. "They are false Christians. These are people who can sing about God one day and rob the next."

A drumbeat sounded from one village, then from another. Despite the proliferation of villages, not a single pirogue was out on the water. *Why?* For an hour we continued, isolated by the stares, hoping to light upon a secluded spot to camp. But by five it seemed that there would be no seclusion, only eyes, drumbeats, and crowds coming forth to the bank from villages before we even reached them.

I asked Desi what he thought we should do.

"We should keep on. All night. We should not stop here."

With the mosquitoes and the loss of bearings night would bring, continuing in the dark might be even riskier than camping. I wanted to halt. But the drums were pounding, so we proceeded, eventually sliding into an uninhabited stretch.

Now the river behind us spread a pane of royal blue glass reflecting the diamond speckles of newborn stars, purpling at the edges where the forest met the sky; ahead, to the west, the fireball of the sun edged its way down into the water, filling the sky and river with molten lava light. We sailed into this widening lava reflection, scouring the banks for a sign of a suitable place to berth, finally descrying a solitary marshy islet surrounded by mangrove trees. Mangroves, we knew, meant swamp and bad air, but this spot had the advantage of facing uninhabited forest.

We veered toward its anvil-shaped head and poled the pirogue between two mangroves; the craft crashed and bounced against the root-entangled bank. Amisi and I hauled the pirogue into the brush, and we set up the tents behind the mangroves.

A stench of rot emanated from the mucky earth and the islet was buzzing with flies, crawling with beetles and biting black ants. Above the rising roar of mosquitoes Desi declared from his tent: "I am weak.

I want to travel all day and all night. We won't need to paddle. We will just float. We—"

Voices.

On the other side of the trees a pirogue was drifting downriver and positioning itself in front of our tents.

There was a shout in Lingala: "Are you the *mondeles*?"

Desi answered, "There's no *mondele* here!"

"What are you *mondeles* doing here?"

"We are not *mondeles*!"

"Tell us who you are!"

"We are merchants traveling to Mbandaka."

There was a pause, then a swish as the pirogue turned back upstream, and the receding sound of paddles cleaving the water.

Moonless and hollow and resounding with drumbeats, darkness engulfed the river. A chanting arose from somewhere, followed by a clapping of hands. All through the night we had to fend off suspicious queries, and none of us slept well. An hour or two before dawn the queries and the drumbeats ceased, and the silence, unbroken by even the peep of a tree frog, a silence filled with suspense, not tranquillity, put us on alert. Sore with fatigue, we decided to break camp before light, but on rising we discovered that a dense fog had settled over the river. Nevertheless, we loaded the pirogue and pulled out into the enveloping vapor, quickly losing our bearings and any perception of where the bank was, aware of only dark and fog and the shifting current.

"That campsite had bad air," Desi said as we drifted along, sightless. "It has made me sick."

I closed my eyes but couldn't sleep, disturbed by Desi's declaration of ill health, and his suggestion—impractical and foolish—that we travel all night. I had hoped he would have recovered in Lisala. But my own fatigue disordered my thoughts.

An hour later dawn was breaking. The burble and rush of water filtered into my drowsy purview; notions of brooks and streams mingled with fragments of faces, with vignettes from inchoate dreams. My eyes half opened, letting in a world of fog and pearly river, of warmth and encompassing wet, a world without lines or forms; there was only the sound of water, as of rapids, an ever-loudening splashing, as of water over rocks.

"Jeff!" Desi shouted.

Not thirty feet from us, directly downstream, a jutting black hulk materialized in the fog: the prow of a *pousseur* cutting a foaming V in the current. Amisi and I seized our paddles and threw all our weight into our strokes, Desi steered hard to port, we swung around and just evaded the steel monster. But the *pousseur*'s motion turned out to be an illusion: it was stranded on a sandbar, abandoned.

As we floated by, we stood up and peered inside, and Desi called out *mbote*. His voice echoed through the cabins, which, their doors hanging on hinges, their interiors stripped bare, looked to have been looted. Shattered glass lay all over the deck; trash covered the runways. Soon we slipped past the forsaken craft and returned to the world of pearly river and fog.

Desi stared at the fading shadow of the *pousseur*. "They must have lost the navigation route. The tribes around here looted them. The Ngombe are not good Christians, you see."

He paddled listlessly, then lay back in the stern. I thought about his words and grabbed the map. "Desi, if they lost the navigation route, what does that say about us?"

"We are near Bongela."

"But if they're lost, then so are—wait a second." Bongela was near Île Sumba: I remembered Paul's words about it being a robber village, about the treacherous *rivière* leading from Bongela behind Île Sumba. But the map showed them to be distant still. "Wait a second. What do you mean we're near Bongela? We can't be. We could not have covered that much territory in one day. Île Sumba and Bongela are a hundred and fifty kilometers away."

"We are either near Bongela or the Mille Quarante marker." He was now slumped in the stern, clearly indisposed. "I don't know why you talk of Île Simba. There's no such place as Île Simba."

"Île *Sum*ba, not *Sim*ba. Desi, we passed Île *Sum*ba on the way up, and the first mate on the barge warned me about it. It's right here on my map. And Bongela is at its head."

He put down his paddle. "There is no such place as Île *Sim*ba." He doubled over with pain, clutching his gut. "I'm feeling ill today. You're asking too many questions. I rely on Jesus. Please, have faith in Jesus. My stomach is aching."

It was no use. I put away the map. I found I barely had the strength to paddle myself, and I lacked the skill to steer. Amisi sat impassive as ever, staring at the water, his rifle on his knees. The heat hit and snuffed out our spirits, and I decided it would be better to join Desi and rest.

Around noon, Amisi and I ate a meal of smoked fish and rice; Desi declined, declaring, as he had before Lisala, that he needed monkey to recover his strength. I was beginning to wonder if he would be able to make it to Mbandaka.

But seeing the *pousseur* gave me an idea: if we made it to the navigation route (or if we were already on it), the Colonel's barge would have to pass us somewhere on its way downriver. If the need arose, we could deliver Desi to it, and I could hire a healthy replacement from among its passengers.

There were no more villages that day. The sight of the *pousseur* seemed to have made an impression on Desi as well: he asked me what I would do if the Colonel's barge were to pass.

"I think we should wait to see if we come across the barge before making plans. But for now, you must eat. You *must*."

He did not.

The current carried us along, spinning us slowly downriver; the forest rotated around us; cool damp air flowed over us. Now and then, objections to Desi's assertions about our whereabouts formed in my mind, but I didn't express them. For the first time in my life, I felt myself inclined to surrender to circumstance—not to fate, because I didn't believe in fate, but to circumstance, to happenings without sense or purpose, without significance or drama. I pondered

Stanley's descent of the Congo (or at least his account of it), the spirit of mission that imbued his orations to his crew. The descent was, he told them, "our work and no other! It is the voice of Fate! The One God has written that this year the river shall be known throughout its length! . . . Onward, I say; onward to death, if it is to be." In this wilderness nothing seemed more irrelevant than such high-flown words of mission and drama. All words seemed empty of meaning.

We drifted and drifted, until Desi felt well enough to paddle.

In the early part of the afternoon the sky blackened. Exhausted by forays this way and that, from one island to the next, in search of the navigation route, we erected our umbrellas and took to drifting close to shore. It began to drizzle, but there was no wind, so we kept on.

We were nearing the downriver end of an island. A thrumming distant whir evolved into the approaching chug of a motor. We perked up: it was a boat! Desi and I grabbed our oars and thrust them into the river. A hundred yards ahead, where one island ended and another began, in a stretch of river between the trees, suddenly appeared the rusty hull of a barge—the Colonel's barge!

We shouted and waved, we thrashed the river with our paddles. But the barge chugged resolutely on, passed behind the next island, and was gone, jealously dragging with it the echo of its engine, leaving us in aching solitude, drifting along the gloomy river, more alone than ever. Desi put down his oar, then sank to the bottom of the pirogue. Amisi raised an eyebrow.

"Well, at least we know where the navigation route is," I said. "Perhaps there will be another boat."

Desi looked at me, as if to say, "Not likely."

A boundless confetti of yellow butterflies was fluttering down around us. The river would give us no respite: they were set against a vista of thunderclouds churning in the east.

I took my paddle in hand and stood up. "Desi, we had better get ashore."

"That storm won't come this way," he answered, prostrate under his umbrella.

Like a supersonic missile of fire, lightning streaked from the iron vault of the sky and struck the forest; thunder exploded in deafening multiple claps. The wind hit and set the river aboil, and the gusts and rising waves nearly overturned us. Amisi grabbed his oar and did his best to help me pilot the pirogue toward the bank. The wind buffeted us into a wall of thorns and spiked ferns, and we became entangled in them; we had to relinquish one mooring spot then another, tearing our skin on the very bush we sought to approach.

Desi raised himself to steer us around the thorny thicket toward a sheltered break in a clearing. But as we drew near it, a crocodile, some twelve feet long, crashed out through the grass and launched himself torpedo-like into the churning river. Startled and frightened, nearly losing our balance, we back-paddled, skirting more thickets, and came to a second clearing. There a snag prevented us from landing; a particularly virulent blast of wind kicked up a wave that nearly pitched us overboard.

"We are in danger," Desi stated in a monotone.

Having seen the crocodile enter the water but having lost it from view, I felt totally exposed, vulnerable to ambush. Winds blew us past another clearing, and I, at the bow, had to jump into the shallows to drag the pirogue by the tow chain up to the bank, an ordeal during which I slipped in the clayey muck and banged my shin on a snag, all the while racing my eyes over the water in search of the croc.

With the rain washing over us in undulant silver sheets, we threw up our tarp amid giant spiked ferns sprouting from the forest floor, then crawled underneath to wait out the storm.

The moon hung a giant pale orange orb that night, the forest echoed with hoots from monkeys, with the tumultuous splashings of hippos in the shallows somewhere behind us. We had bivouacked early in a malodorous and desolate bight of palm and rubber vines. Biting ants, fat and black, infested our camp, scuttling over our legs, chomping away before we could scrape them off, and we had to seek refuge from them in our tents. We had passed no more villages that day. The banks were uninhabited and the absence of hostile locals set me at ease, but I grew certain that we were somewhere on the river we should not be. Desi insisted he knew the way, but I was beginning to see he did not, this far from his home.

"May God's will be done. I place my fate in the hands of *le bon Dieu*," Desi announced, and crawled into his mosquito net pale and weak. Amisi sulked. I called him over to my tent to talk. "Desi is sick," I said. "We have to decide what we will do if he cannot continue."

"We should just keep on. I'm a soldier and a Christian. If God wills me to die here, I die. I can do nothing about it."

"We will have to think of something."

"What?"

"I'm asking for your advice."

"I follow God's will. What God decides will be."

Whence this indifference? *Was* it indifference? I glared at him, I felt a sudden urge to strike him, to slap him out of this torpor. But, turning into my tent, I did nothing more than say *bonne nuit*.

"You must eat. You absolutely must."

"I will eat no more unless we can kill a monkey." Still pale and now more visibly weakened than ever, Desi stood trembling by his net at dawn, his eyes averted from mine. "I must have monkey, or, or . . ."

We had canned meat left, but the absence of fishermen meant it would be all we had for the next ten days to Mbandaka—sustaining, if monotonous, fare to be sure. But perhaps he was using this need for monkey as an excuse; he was sick and did not want to go on, or could not go on.

I did not know what to say. I felt I was to blame for having undertaken this trip, which now seemed like it could cost the life of this poor fellow, or leave him more debilitated than ever, which would ruin the lives of a dozen other people, given his position of breadwinner for an extended family. In all my preparations I had never imagined that it would be my guide whose health would fail, and not my own. But an isolating fear settled like a stone on my heart, isolating because, even in the company of others, we face death alone. If Desi gave up, Amisi and I would have a tough time making it to Mbandaka. This thought was too frightening to dwell on.

But I was overreacting. I grabbed my gear and tossed it into the pirogue. "We've got to move on, Desi. Let's get moving."

I looked to Amisi. His eyes registered no concern, only nonchalant comprehension. I finished loading the pirogue, Desi and Amisi got aboard, and we shoved off.

It was sunny but cool and fresh, a breezy day of luminous golden light, of soft golden light that saturated the forest and river without heating it, of comforting golden light that seemed to promise something good or to set the stage, conversely, for horrific evil: it was almost too idyllic to be true. The current came to our aid, flowing in a channel that cut across great silken-watered pools, dark pools spotted with mist. Just after noon, as we were drifting along the south bank, beneath a thicket low and dense, out of which protruded a second, jagged tier of broad-canopied trees, we spotted a monkey bounding away branch to branch. Desi livened up and steered us toward shore. Amisi unwrapped his gun, and the two of them stalked off into the forest.

After a while I got out, too. I walked in a ways and stood before the tangled creepers, the vines, the crisscrossing growths of ferns; I looked up at the dead palms, the soaring gum trees, at the maze of light and shadow, of green and green and bamboo yellow, here and there dappled with a vermilion blossom, a splash of violet petal. Save for the breeze rustling through the canopy, there was not a sound, and the silence boded desolation that accorded with what was turning out to be the barren reality of my hopes and plans, of the climax, the denouement that I had come to Africa to force upon my life. A denouement was taking place, to be sure—a stark and simple unraveling, as potentially lethal as it was mundane. Desi had taken on the job of guiding me to meet his obligations to his wife and child, his mother, his free-loading brothers, even his church. But it now was obvious that he had been ill since Kisangani, and I grew angry with myself for not recognizing it. Yet he would not resign or confess his condition: the specter of the Colonel (to whom he would ultimately answer for my safety) stood behind me, and no doubt he feared the consequences of failing him. Moreover, Desi was a man of his word, and rather than quit, he might simply die.

I began to understand Desi and Amisi's fatalism. If we perished in this wilderness, the forest would absorb us and continue silent and impassive, an eternal, if unfathomable, life force apart, endlessly renewing itself, indifferent to anything we feared, felt, or thought. For those on the Congo's waters, life was too filled with uncertainty, heat, disease, and hunger to permit resolution or defiance, to allow anything more than survival and gratitude for the scrawniest grubs, the smallest bananas. Fatalism was necessary here, as was surrender.

I walked back to the pirogue. It suddenly seemed clear that my expedition was not worth risking a life for, not Desi's, not Amisi's, not my own. If I could have called off the voyage at that moment, shot up a flare or radioed for help, I would have done so. But I had neither flare nor radio, and who would have come? There was no one to call. There was no turning back: the only way out was downstream.

Desi and Amisi returned, having had no luck with the hunt. We shoved off and let the current carry us.

The next day we moved on under clear skies. Around midday Desi plaintively asked me to take some photos of him with my Polaroid "for his wife," implying that they were to be remembrances of him. I agreed, and on an island we held a bizarre final photo session, with Desi donning his tracksuit and looking solemnly into my lens.

I thought of the sequel to my expedition. If Desi died and I lived, I would face the consequences: a grief-stricken family left without support; police and official inquiries; and guilt that I would carry with me for the rest of my life. But then the stone of fear pressed on my heart again: if he were to die, how would Amisi and I make it out? More than a hundred miles were left to Mbandaka, and we needed Desi's skill as a piroguist to cover them.

As we pushed away from the bank, I could not help but think about dying, about how there would be no closing ceremony to my life and no drama, just a cessation, as though it were a movie interrupted in the middle by the flare-up of a faulty projector bulb. Death seemed tangible and near; I felt distraught most of all because it might overtake me far from Tatyana, my parents, and my friends. I was afraid, but there was nothing to do except paddle and drift beneath the monster trees and vines.

That afternoon Desi's spirits lifted when he discovered two cans of pilchards (his favorite fish) hidden amid our provisions. He cooked and ate them with relish, and they somewhat revived his strength.

And now his strength would be needed. By four o'clock we had landed squarely in Ngombe heartland, passing village after village, unable to find a hidden spot to camp. He and Amisi took to raising their guns as a matter of course whenever we approached a village.

Darkness finally drove us ashore; we erected the tents as the mosquitoes descended. Soon pirogues were paddling up, invisible in the humid night, and baritone Lingala was booming in the blackness: "Is the *mondele* in there? What can the *mondele* give us!" Amisi would answer, "*Mbote!* Stay away. I have an FAL rifle and I'll shoot." It worked, but the hours dragged on, and none of us closed an eye.

The glow of the moon filled the sky and emanated from the water. I lay on my stomach, peering out of my tent's net door. Two pirogues bearing five people each materialized in the mists and moved toward us. I tried to warn Amisi, but I found my throat paralyzed; I couldn't speak or move a muscle. The piroguists pulled up to our camp and unsheathed huge machetes that glinted in the moonlight; I struggled to cry out but felt asphyxiated, immobile. As they stepped up to my tent I lunged into my net—and woke up. I had been dreaming.

On the river there were glints of silver—reflections of the moon— but no machetes or pirogues. Desi and Amisi had drifted off to sleep in their mosquito nets next to mine; the river lapped against the bank, flowing empty and silver far, far out into the channel.

Anybody Seen a Tiger Around Here?

by Tim Cahill

Tim Cahill (born 1943) spends his time dreaming up adventures that serve as excuses to meet odd or exotic characters and get into and out of trouble. His mission this time: Find a living specimen of the Caspian Tiger, a species last spotted (and promptly shot) 30 years ago in southeastern Turkey.

I was sitting in the Owl, a small bar in a small town in Montana, when I was lifted bodily from the stool—no small feat—and kissed exuberantly on each cheek. "Doctor C.!" Tommy the Turk said by way of greeting. He is a barrel-chested man, bald as a billiard ball, and he wore a blue-and-white woven wool cap, like a yarmulke. I assumed that he was back from one central-Asian war or another. People who know these disputes know Thomas Goltz. A war correspondent and author of certain distinction, Goltz is one of the few Americans who have met and interviewed the players in several shadowy and little-undetstood conflicts. He lectures frequently and once spent a day making the rounds briefing the spooks at the CIA. "I've got a quest for you, Doctor," Tommy said.

He showed me a clipping from the London *Sunday Express*. The lead sentence said that high in the mountains of Turkey "could lie a secret which will stun scientists: the return from the dead of a lost species." The article quoted Dr. Guven Eken of the Society for the Protection of

Nature: "The Caspian tiger is considered to be extinct, but in southeast Turkey local hunters claim to have seen tigers in the mountains."

We toasted Tommy's safe arrival back in Montana and discussed the idea of searching for the ghost tiger. As I recall, this involved a great many toasts. The next morning I woke up with some fuzzy recollection about an agreement to go to Turkey and search for the Caspian tiger with Tommy the Turk, a guy famous for covering wars. Was this a good idea? Would we get shot at? And what the hell did I know about tigers?

One week later, Tommy and I were in Istanbul, along with photographer Rob Howard, who is nicknamed—for reasons impervious to investigative reporting—the Duck. We were sitting at a cafe overlooking the Bosporus and talking with the aforementioned Dr. Eken. He was an Art Garfunkel—looking guy who confessed that he had never actually been to southeastern Turkey, didn't know the first thing about tigers, and didn't really actually have the names of any hunters who'd seen one. He'd only heard rumors.

So now we were tracking *rumors* of a ghost tiger. The less-than-helpful Dr. Eken sought to dissuade us. The southeastern part of the country was "sensitive," he said. "Security" could be a problem.

The problem, in a nutshell, involved the long-running Kurdish insurrection. Twenty million Kurds live in four separate countries, making these folks the world's largest ethnic group without a homeland. (The de facto statelet that has existed in northern Iraq ever since the United States made the area a no-fly zone doesn't really count.) The two dominant Iraqi Kurdish groups are largely sympathetic to Turkey and the United States. A third group, the Marxist-Leninist Kurdistan Workers Party, or PKK, which also operates in Turkey, advocates using whatever violent means are necessary to establish an independent Kurdish state. The PKK had been largely defanged by the arrest of its leader, Abdullah Ocalan, in February 1999, but pockets of resistance still exist, especially in the remote, mountainous, little-inhabited areas of southeastern Turkey. The day before, for instance, two insurrectionists had been killed by soldiers in a prolonged gun battle outside the town of Semdinli, near the border with Iraq.

It was Tommy's impression that things were winding down in the southeast and that we could talk our way through most military checkpoints. Eken insisted that we at least talk with the Society's big-mammal man in Ankara, Emry Can, a man who knew even more about tigers than he did, which seemed, on the face of it, to be pretty much a slam-dunk.

The rest of our brief stay in Istanbul involved sitting around in innumerable offices, smoking lots of cigarettes, while Tommy talked about tigers in exchange for press passes and letters of introduction. Foreign journalists assured us that we probably couldn't get to certain towns in the southeast. Mostly, we were given to understand that the authorities didn't want to see another story in the foreign media excoriating the Turks for oppressing the proud and noble Kurds. This story is written and broadcast so often it actually has a name: the "cuddly Kurd/terrible Turk" angle. The Turkish military and police strove to suppress such reports, and only weeks earlier American and British TV crews had been expelled from the area. Our quest, we explained to our friends in the press corps, was about cuddly, terrible tigers, and as such, a different matter entirely. They were dubious.

In the past week, in fact, I had done some research on the Caspian tiger. Its dossier was fascinating, but surprisingly thin. Historically, the animal once ranged from western China through the central-Asian "stans" to Iran, Iraq, Azerbaijan, and Turkey. It was this Caspian variety that gave the striped cats their name: Romans supposedly captured them on the banks of the Tigris, called them tigers, and took them back to the Colosseum for their circuses. This subspecies of *Pantera tigris*—one of eight to walk the earth over the past few millennia—looked a good deal like the Bengal tiger, with khaki fur and black bands on its back and legs. It was a big animal; only the endangered Siberian tiger is larger. Males measured up to nine feet from the nose to the tip of the tail and weighed in excess of five hundred pounds. In winter, it developed a distinctive bushy coat, which surely added to the various misgivings of travelers considering going mano a paw with one in the snow of a mountain pass. A carnivore status survey conducted in Iran from 1973 to 1976 failed to turn up any evidence of the creature. The last known Caspian tiger was shot in 1970 in the southeast-Turkish town of Uludere.

We took the night train down to the capital city of Ankara and talked with the big-mammal expert, Emry Can, who interrogated us fiercely— he thought we were hunters, looking to knock off the last tiger. Finally satisfied of our innocence, Can admitted that he himself had not been to the southeast, but was planning an expedition "next year, or perhaps the year after."

Anything we might find—tracks, confirmed sightings—would be of great significance, he said. Unfortunately, he had no idea where we might start our search.

And so, with no firm destination in mind, we flew to the major town in the southeast, Van, on the shores of Lake Van, the largest fresh-water lake in Turkey. There we met up with Saim Guclu, chief engineer of the National Forest, Eastern Anatolia Region, a big, jolly man in his early sixties with a white mustache. Saim would provide a driver and transportation: a small Nissan truck with an extended cab and a forestry-department decal. We would pay for gas and fork over $300 for each day we shot pictures in a national forest. In other words, Saim seemed to be what he claimed, a forestry official, albeit one with his hand out, not an intelligence officer assigned to keep an eye on us. "I am ashamed to admit that I have never been to Uludere, where the last tiger was shot," he said. "We have done no inventory of the animals in these places. Of course, our department has existed only since 1994. Your presence here is very helpful to me, you see."

Saim said he had pored over books and documents in the forestry department for information on the Caspian tiger and had found little there. It was dawning on me that it didn't take much to be an expert on this animal, and that I was getting to be right up there. "If we find evidence that the tiger exists," Saim said, "it will be a great thing, not only for Turkey but for all the world. Wildlife doesn't belong to any one country."

Unfortunately, not everyone shared Saim's enlightened view.

"How dare you!" Tommy was saying to the soldier at one of the many military checkpoints on the road to Uludere. We were in the forestry-service truck with Saim and his driver, and we'd been stopped at the summit of a pass. The soldier had just said. "Why don't you stay home? Why come here and stir up trouble?" By which we knew he meant, "We don't want to read any more cuddly Kurd/terrible Turk stories."

"How dare you speak to me in that tone of voice before you know what my mission is?" Something about this gave the soldier pause, and Tommy took advantage of the lull to trot out the passes and letters we'd smoked so many cigarettes to obtain. He explained about the tiger, and the conversation settled down into friendly banter and an invitation to tea. We soon found ourselves in the wooden guard shack, smoking more cigarettes and laughing about one thing or another. My name, for instance, was a matter of great hilarity. In Turkey, no one is named Tim, but many are called Timur, in honor of the fourteenth-century Mongol who conquered much of this part of the world. He was known for his cruelty; he is said to have ordered the deaths of seventeen million people between the Black Sea and Delhi. Historical mass murder was looked upon with a degree of respect. It was my last name that was the problem. Cahill is pronounced Djabeel in Turkish and means "ignorant." So Tommy and the soldiers sat around drinking tea, smoking cigarettes, passing around my passport, and laughing out loud at my name. Timur the Ignorant: It was like being called Attila the Dope.

We left the guard shack and plunged down a paved two-lane road onto flatter land and then drove parallel to the border with Iraq until we reached the turnoff to Uludere. The narrow road meandered up alongside a flowing green creek lined with white-bark poplars, and we passed an abandoned village of quaint stone houses, each with at least one wall leveled by artillery five. "We don't know who did this," Saim said, "the PKK or the military. Whoever it was, let Allah strike them blind."

And then we were in Uludere proper, passing ancient houses made of river rock and winding our way through streets crowded with tall, generally slender people with imposing hawklike faces: Kurds. We stepped out of the truck and were immediately surrounded by men, all of them answering our questions at full volume and at the same time. No one knew the man who had shot the tiger in 1970, but there had been a fellow who shot one in the sixties. He was dead. Forty years ago, the paved road we'd driven had been a mule trail. Uludere was now a big town. No one had heard anything about tigers for years.

An old man said there had been lots of tigers in the early sixties. He had heard them at night while he tended his sheep. They made a sound like the bray of donkey. Not the heehaw sound, but the ahhhh noise they make. Someone else said the animal was so heavy it took three men to carry a dead one, that its track looked like that of a domestic cat, but bigger, with claws as long as a man's index finger. The big cat, he said, seemed to seize the snow: When its paws flexed, the pads would leave little snowballs in the middle of the trail.

We had been talking with the men for about ten minutes when the subgovernor of the province arrived along with several policemen. This self-inflated little turd threatened to confiscate our film and detain us until he could ascertain the nature of our business in Uludere. Saim, the Duck, and I retreated to the truck behind a solid wall of Tommy-talk while our driver fired up the engine. A cop put his hand on Tommy's shoulder, but he shook it off, jumped into the truck, and said, "Go go, go!"

Back in Van, we were out of ideas. But it was a nice sunny day, and we drove to a dock about twenty-five miles outside of town and hired a boat to take us to the old Armenian church on Akdamar Island.

We'd heard rumors of a Loch Ness–type monster in the lake, and we asked the boatman about it. "There are no monsters," he said, "but there are some very large snakes." I assumed he meant eels. "I have never seen one. My father did: He said it was as big around as a fifty-five-gallon oil drum and as long as this boat." The boat appeared to be forty-five feet long. "But," Saim said, "you are describing a monster."

The island was rugged and rocky, and it rose out of the clear blue waters of Lake Van like a shattered sculpture. The domed church, built in the tenth century by the Armenian king Gagik Ardzouni, was surrounded by almond trees, the branches bare and gnarled in the winter sun. The lower walls were covered over in bas-relief. There were depictions of a naked man and woman in a garden, eating something that looked like an apple. There was a knight on horseback spearing something that looked very much like the Lake Van monster. Another sculpture showed a man being tossed from an open boat into the mouth of what could, once again, only have been the Lake Van monster.

More to the point, there were tigers all over the walls. Before the Armenians were eventually driven from the church by the Turks, they had painted animals around the upper dome: goats and wolves and tigers. Lots of tigers.

I sat in the sun, looking out across the lake at the shining, snow-clad mountains, and thought how, at least in historical times, there'd been tigers here. Also apparently present had been Saint George, and Adam and Eve, along with Jonah and the Lake Van monster.

That night, we walked through the maze of cobblestone alleyways off the main street of Van and finally found a shop where one of Tommy's boots could be resoled. The cobbler, Mustafa, talked as he worked. He had never seen any evidence of a tiger around Lake Van, and he hunted birds in the mountains quite often. Still, Mustafa said, if we liked, he could call the most avid hunter he knew and invite him down to the shop to talk. Halim was a man of fifty-six, a Jack Palance look-alike with long arms and hands the size of canned hams. He agreed that there were no tigers anywhere nearby and hadn't been for many years. He had heard rumors about tiger sightings to the east, however. We should talk to his hunting partner, a baker named Hamid Kaya. "Where does Hamid Kaya live?" Tommy asked.

"Semdinli," Halim said.

We drove southeast, passing from checkpoint to checkpoint and moving ever deeper into the mountains. The road took us over a pass in what could easily have been the Swiss Alps, with snow several feet deep. Far below, a narrow valley stretched out as far as the eye could see, and at its farthest extent, hard up against the mountains rising abruptly behind it, was the little town of Semdinli. Tiger town, terror town; take your pick.

We drove down the main street, an amalgam of two- and three-story buildings of the type that collapses during earthquakes. Small patches of sooty gray snow lay in the street. We parked next to the bakery and asked if Hamid Kaya, the bread maker, was there. Once again, we were surrounded by Kurds, a dozen or more of them, all wearing some variant of the tribal costume of baggy pants and a cummerbund.

Were we here to talk about the terror, they all wanted to know, and we said no, we were here to talk about tigers. We had read reports that there had been several recent sightings. Hunters, the paper said, had seen the animal in these mountains.

"Then they lie!" one man shouted. "No one hunts here." The dangers, men on all sides explained, were simply too great. The mountain trails were mined. A hunter could be mistaken for a terrorist and shot by the military, or he might be mistaken for a military commando and shot by the terrorists. Since the insurrection began in 1984, more than 30,000 people had been killed. "No one hunts here," a man repeated.

"*I* have been in the mountains." said a distinguished-looking older man wearing a wool sport coat over a pink sweater. Musa Iren, seventy-two, said he had seen a tiger in the mountains not far away, near Yaylapinar. That was eight years ago, and he had tracked it through the snow for two days.

"Do they make a sound?" Tommy asked.

"Like a donkey," Musa said. He made an *ahhhh* sort of sound.

"Describe the tracks."

"The tracks were like that of a cat, but as big as my hand, and the claws were as long as my index finger," Musa said. Tommy and I passed a significant look. "Anything else?"

"Yes," Musa said. "When the tiger walks, he seizes the snow and leaves small balls of packed snow in the middle of the crack."

"This is true," said another older man, named Cirkin, who said he shot a tiger, also near Yaylapinar, forty years ago. It required thirteen rounds from a shotgun to kill the animal, and three men to carry it.

"These animals are not extinct," Musa said. "I guarantee you they are up there. Not just one or two, but many."

There was some general scoffing about this, but another man came to Musa's aid. "Because no one hunts—it is sixteen years now—the animals are coming back. Even here, near town, we see more bears and wild goats and wolves and wild pigs. Why not tigers?"

There were now fifty or sixty men gathered about, all shouting out their opinions. "Listen to me," Musa said. "You know the village of Ormancik, on the border with Iraq? Four years ago, a man of that village, Haji Ak, killed a tiger. He brought me the skin, and I had it in my shop for two years. I could not sell it and gave it back to him."

I was wildly excited as I wrote placenames in my notebook: Yaylapinar, Ormancik, Ortaklar. It was at precisely that moment, of course, that we were arrested by the police.

Tommy the Turk—in a typical effort to seize control of the situation— refused to get in the police car. "We'll walk, thanks," he said, as if the officer were a pal who'd just offered him a ride. The crowd had melted away, and we trudged slowly behind the police car as it moved past a green army tank and down a steep hill toward the station.

Inside, the two-story cement bunker was a maze of corridors, with cops coming and going every which way, but down the longest hallway was a central office where a man in a stylish suit sat behind an imposing wooden desk. This had to be the chief, and Tommy bulled past the cop who had detained us, rapped once on the open door, and strode in. "Please tell me exactly what is going on here," he said in Turkish. "We need to know," the chief said in near-perfect English, "what you are doing in our town." As it happened, the chief was a sucker for Tommy-talk, and we left with his personal phone number in case there was any more trouble. He also called the military commanding officer of the province, Colonel Eshrem.

We were escorted to the army post that dominated the town, and then through a leather-padded wooden door studded with brass tacks, and then through a second padded door, like a kind of air lock. Certain military and police officers we'd met had regarded our mission as a highly laughable cover story for some nefarious activity or another. The colonel, however, not only believed us but thought the search for the Caspian tiger was a worthy goal. He was a man given to folksy aphorisms. "You search for the tiger," he said. "We say time spent searching for treasures lost is never time wasted."

Regrettably, the colonel could not allow us to travel any farther down the road to Yaylapinar and Ormancik. The two PKK insurgents lulled recently had been shot between Semdinli and Ormancik. That was just last week. The rebels were all over the area, and a military strike was planned against them within days.

Still, the colonel thought it would be a grand thing if tigers still existed in the midst of war. There was, he said, thinking aloud, a military exercise the next day. Several village guards, armed Kurds loyal to the government, would be meeting up with his soldiers and continuing on to Yaylapinar. "So, you could get to Yaylapinar with them," the colonel said. He didn't think the danger would be too great.

"And tonight," the colonel said, "you will please be my guests. Sleep here, in the barracks."

And so I spent a night in a Turkish military barracks, which, I know, sounds like a fantasy out of a John Rechy novel. (Actually, our private rooms were better than those in any hotel we'd seen.) But the next morning, we were finally on our way, searching for the tiger . . . with a military escort. We rode with a Captain Milbray in a Jeep Cherokee, between a truck full of uniformed soldiers and an armored personnel carrier, as the convoy made its way along the side of a ridiculously steep slope. Hundreds of feet below, a river churned over the floor of the gorge, and burned-out military vehicles littered the banks.

Captain Milbray didn't buy our tiger story, not even a little bit. "I've been out in these mountains for four years," he said. "I've seen bears and wild goats and wild pigs, but never a tiger. And none of my men has ever seen one."

"Have you ever looked for one?" I asked.

"No," the captain said. "Well, two days ago I shot one. But I ate it. Even the skin."

"What a good joke, Captain," Tommy said.

Presently, the road branched off to Yaylapinar. We stopped for a moment, and suddenly a dozen heavily armed Kurds appeared out of nowhere. They came pouring down the slopes at a dead run, swathed in baggy pants and turbans and cummerbunds, carrying knives, grenades, and automatic weapons. In the space of thirty seconds we were surrounded, and even though I knew they were with us, it was a little unsettling. This is how fast it can happen to you out here, I thought. And then the Kurds piled into a truck, and we were moving again.

The road dropped into the valley of the Peson River. There were patches of snow on green grass, and cows grazed in the fields. As we pulled into Yaylapinar, dozens of people converged on the Jeep. Someone put out white plastic lawn chairs, and Tommy and I sat down and interviewed a man named Zulfigar, who'd shot a tiger, a female, perhaps ten years ago. "The mark of this animal," Zulfigar said, "is that when it walks, it seizes the snow. The claws are as long as my first finger."

Other men were butting in now, talking about tigers in the old days. and even Captain Milbray seemed to catch the fever. "When you shot the tiger," he asked Zulfigar, "was it before or after your military service? Before or after your first child was born?" In this manner he ascertained that the tiger had been shot not ten years ago, but more like forty.

Still, Captain Milbray was no longer mocking us. "Why," he asked Zulfigar, "did you shoot the tiger?"

"In those days, he who shot a tiger was a hero."

"These are not those days," the captain said. "Today, he who shoots a tiger is my enemy. I will see that he goes to jail."

As quick as that, I threw an arm over the captain's shoulder, and we thanked each other in the manner of Alphonse and Gaston.

We went to another village, Ortaklar, then returned before dark to the army post at Semdinli, where the colonel was waiting to debrief us.

About that time, there was a knock on the padded door. A young officer stood at attention and reported that some village guards in Umurlu had seen a tiger. Word about our visit had apparently spread. "When was this?" the colonel asked.

"Five days ago."

"Ahh, I don't believe this," the colonel said. "I was there three days ago. They would have told me."

"Not," I suggested, "if they were out hunting when they should have been guarding the village."

"Just so," the colonel said. "Have the men come to Semdinli."

There were three of them. And yes, they'd been hunting wild goats instead of standing guard, which is why they hadn't said anything to the colonel.

It had happened about four miles north of the village, in a labyrinthine area called the Honeycomb Cliffs. The youngest of them, a thirty-year-old named Nuri Durmaz, had moved off to the west alone. "There was a little snow," he said, "not a lot. I was about halfway to the peak. There was an overhanging wall, like a cliff, and I saw something one hundred meters away. I couldn't see its head, but it was big. It would have taken two, maybe three men to carry it."

"What color was it?" Tommy asked.

"Like my pants," Nuri said. He was wearing khaki pants. "It had black stripes on the legs and resembled a large cat."

"Did you shoot it?' I asked.

"No. I was in a bad place. If I only wounded it, it could have torn me apart."

"What did you do?"

"I went to get my friends."

And here Nuri's friends chimed in with descriptions of the tracks: claws as long as a man's finger, the little ball of snow in the center of the print. It wasn't the only such creature up in the Honeycomb Cliffs, said one of the men. He'd seen the same tracks in about the same place almost exactly a year ago.

I brought out some pictures I'd copied for just this purpose. There was a drawing of the Anatolian panther, also thought to be extinct; a photo of a lynx, many of which still roam these mountains; and one of a Caspian tiger, taken decades ago in an Iranian zoo. Nuri discarded the panther and the lynx. "This one," he said, holding up the picture of the tiger.

"What do you think?" I asked Saim.

"I'd say 50 percent credibility."

The Duck and I both put it at a 70 percent sure thing. The colonel said, "I don't have an opinion to be expressed in a percentage, but I believe in nature. This is a wonderful thing for Turkey and the world. I will inform my lieutenant in charge of the area to monitor the situation. I will give him a camera and ask him to use his night-vision goggles whenever possible."

Nuri said, "The next time I see this animal, I will kill him for you."

"I don't think you should do that," the colonel said. This was expressed as an order. But then the colonel softened his voice. "If these men publish an article, and if peace is established, you will find that people with cameras will come here, and to your delight they will put much money in your pocket."

"This is true?"

"This is true."

"I can almost smell that tiger," Tommy was saying. We were now on our way to Iraq to try to enter the Honeycomb Cliffs from the southern side of the range.

The colonel had been kind enough to give us a glimpse of a classified map. Unfortunately, the cliffs were also ground zero in the war against the PKK, and there was no way he was letting us get anywhere near them. But Tommy and I had noticed that the cliffs stretched into northern Iraq. So we'd bidden goodbye to our military friends and started driving along the border with Iraq toward the town of Sirnak. Saim was in a state of high excitement. The colonel, he said, had told him that if he were ordered to do so, he, Colonel Eshrem, could use his resources, including helicopters and substantial manpower, to search for the tigers. If Saim, acting as a forestry-department official, were to write to the colonel's superiors, that order could come through in as little as three or four months.

"I asked him what was the best way to word such a request," Saim said, "and the colonel even dictated the letter for me." I gathered that forestry agents couldn't always count on enthusiastic cooperation from military officers.

At Sirnak, we parted in an orgy of embraces and kissed cheeks. Saim refused to accept any money, despite our agreement. He was a man of great honor and emotion, and he wouldn't take our lucre, "for the sake of the tiger." He said, "You have done a wonderful thing."

We hired a car and driver in Sirnak, then made a run for Ormancik and the border. Tommy was confident there would be no problem getting into the Kurdish-held territory: He had worked with several aid agencies, helping Kurdish refugees when Saddam Hussein rolled his tanks on his own people after the Gulf War. Tommy still had friends among the former refugees, and, in fact, the cap he wore, the one I had always thought of as a yarmulke, was a treasured gift from an Iraqi Kurdish general.

At the border, however, a Turkish official refused to stamp us out of the country. We spent two days there while Tommy worked the public phones, calling his friends in Ankara in an effort to, in his words, "find someone who'll squash this little prick for me."

For two days, I sat against a wall while Tommy stood at the phone, talking Tommy-talk as only Tommy can talk. "Look," he was saying to some English-speaking Turkish official in the capital, "we're not actually going into the mountains." (Not unless we could get into Iraq, he failed to say.) "We'll just be doing what we did in Turkey. We talk to the police and to the military and to the people in the villages. We raise people's consciousness, get them thinking about what it means if this animal still exists."

Day two at the border was now slipping into day three. "All we really want to do is make people aware of this magnificent creature," Tommy was saying.

Sitting there, listening to all this, it occurred to me that maybe that was enough. For now. Maybe, as the colonel and Saim had said, we actually had done something wonderful. People should be made aware. Because, in my almost-expert opinion, the tiger is out there.

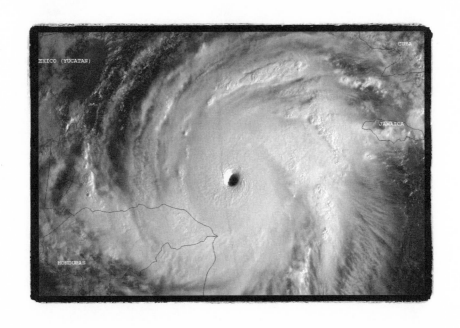

from The Ship and the Storm
by Jim Carrier

Guyan March, captain of the four-masted

schooner Fantome, *in October, 1998 dropped*

his cruise ship's 97 passengers in Belize and

took his ship and crew back to sea. He aimed

to dodge Tropical Storm Mitch—which grew

into the most destructive hurricane in Western

Hemisphere history. Jim Carrier (born 1944)

has done his best to learn what happened next.

C aptain Guyan March spotted the long spiny island of Roatán at about 5 a.m. on Tuesday, October 27. A short time later his boss, Michael D. Burke, called from his home in Miami.

"How was it?"

"A little lumpy."

Burke's memory of that conversation, colored by the cool British countenance of Guyan March, filtered out the crescendo of a storm's edge. The waves in the open sea at the time were "probably 20 foot," according to Kevin Brewer, the dive master at Anthony's Key Resort, who was up at dawn checking boats. "One gust blew me across the boat."

"There was a lot of stress," said Burke. "There had not been a lot of concern in the evening. But this is still blowing at 170 miles an hour. It's a huge weather system. He's boxed in a corner. I'm sure he got some sleep, but not a whole lot. Guyan never raised his voice. If anything, there was maybe a bit more hesitation, an edge, not exactly a comfortable tone."

When Annie Bleasdale called March on the bridge, he was more to the point.

"Beam me up, Scotty," March told her.

"He said conditions were pretty bad, Force 10, huge waves. The sails they had left up had been blown out and were now stowed. He still planned to shelter from the huge swell. He told me not to worry, that he loved me and would call in a couple of days."

"Force 10," in sea parlance, is a level on the Beaufort scale used by sailors to estimate wind speeds and sea conditions and their effects on ships. Force 10 conditions mean winds of 48 to 55 knots and waves of 20 to 40 feet, with overhanging crests. The sea takes on a white appearance as foam is blown in dense streaks. Visibility is reduced, though not drastically. On the Beaufort scale Force 10 is just two steps below a hurricane, which starts at 64 knots. At Force 10, ships begin to roll heavily, and control becomes tougher. Overnight, the *Fantome* had gone from the calm behind Belize's reef, 300 miles from the storm's eye, to storm conditions 140 miles from the eye. Based on Bowditch's calculations of an approaching storm, *Fantome's* barometer would have fallen 25 millibars.

At dawn, Mitch was again moving directly west at 7 knots. A Hurricane Hunter flight during the night had measured the eye pressure at 917 millibars, up considerably from the day before. But wind speeds were still as high as 164 knots. Mexico and Guatemala had raised hurricane warnings. The 4 a.m. forecast bent Mitch's track toward the Bay Islands by just a hair for twelve hours, "with a gradual slowing in forward speed and a bend toward the west-northwest then northwest thereafter." Plotted on a map, the forecast placed Mitch 60 miles due north of Guanaja by 1 p.m. that afternoon, 40 miles closer than predicted on Monday. Three days away it would be approaching Cozumel, Mexico.

Rounding Roatán's West Point, a spot he knew well, Captain March reported that big waves were "boiling" over the sandbar, curling around the island and following the south coast into Coxen Hole, the cruise ship port. His strategy, following standard Windjammer procedure in the eastern Caribbean, would be to stand off the island by one or two miles and steam back and forth, east and west, in the lee of the island. He would not anchor but would stay free to run or even move to the opposite side of the island when the storm passed to the west. Once he reached the south side of the island, behind its 200- to 600-foot-high ridgeline, seas dropped dramatically, to under 12 feet. March estimated the wind at 40 knots from the west-northwest and, according to Burke, put two staysails up again to steady her rolling. At 8:30 a.m. March sent an e-mail to Miami: "Good morning. We will require fuel this weekend because of our side trip we are on. Can we get 10,000 gallons on Friday or Saturday and then we'll top up the following weekend when we get the supplies. Please let the agent know which day so he can get pilots, etc. Capt. Guyan." The ship's tanks held 25,000 gallons of diesel fuel.

At 9 a.m. Hurricane Mitch began pounding the north coast of Guanaja. The sea began to rise, almost as if someone had flushed a plugged toilet. It was that fast: 1, 4, 6, 10 feet. Pushed from the eye wall of the storm like snow in front of a snowplow, the water climbed over Doug Solomon's dock on the northeast end of the island, setting boards adrift. It flooded the sand and flowers, surrounded the concrete block generator room, and began climbing the telephone poles on which his house was perched. A mile to the west, at Mangrove Bight, where scores of homes were built out over the water on pilings, the sea began churning underneath. Boats were tossed about, banging into each other, the docks, and the houses. As the waters reached floor level, people fled out on the rickety wooden walkways suspended between the shore and the maze of homes.

Harriet Ebanks' house was the first to go, at 9:45 a.m. Eyewitnesses said it looked as if a giant sea monster had just lifted it off its stilts. Heavy, wind-blown breakers, nearly 12 feet high, smashed her house as if with a fist, creating a scattered, floating woodpile. "Everything went under—the land stayed underwater," said Kerston Moore, a lobster diver. From the northernmost seawall of Mangrove Bight, townspeople on higher ground watched with horror as the sea popped, floated, and smashed houses one after another. Floating, they banged into each other like loose boats. Then they fell apart. Piles of shattered lumber—former houses—began washing ashore in a great splintered chaos. Panicked people ran pell-mell across the woodpiles, holding their babies, helping their mothers, stepping on nails, cutting their hands. Down the waterfront the surge and smashing came. The waves became waves of lumber, filling the space beneath Moore's house, surrounding the concrete block stilts. Every fifteen minutes or so a larger than usual wave would push the lumber higher. Hundreds of people ran to a church that lay at the center of the village, not 25 feet from the seawall. But lumber and water began wedging around the church, rocking it. "It's time to pray," someone cried. Just then the wind gave a shriek and someone howled, "It's time to run!" The church exploded soon after. People gathered in homes farther up the hill and huddled together in groups of twenty below granite cliffs and in canyons behind the village.

At the Bayman Bay Club, facing north from its cliffside perch, Don Pearly watched his 300-foot dock disappear. The sea rose and the water simply lifted the dock away from its moorings. "It didn't blow up. It just lifted, loosened, and floated off." Pearly and his guests were in a reinforced-concrete basement with a windowed front that looked out to the sea. He had screwed plywood over the windows, so light inside was minimal. They had mattresses and a bathroom. As gusts became stronger, they would speculate on what was going on outside: "There went such-and-such a cabin." The gusts got longer. "It would get scarier and scarier and longer lasting, until finally it was constant. Shortly after that, the noise disappeared from your mind. It was more like a feeling."

Pearly and his assistant manager, Chris Norris, struggled out to check on thirty-three employees and their families in an adjacent basement. It was 53 feet between shelters, but the trip back and forth was torture. "We'd fight to hold on to trees and beams under the cabins. The cabins were creaking and moving." Ten minutes later, coming back, it looked like a different route. New trees had fallen on the path. The noise was constant. The air was filled with salt water—"like a bucket, horizontally. You couldn't stand up. The hillside became a waterfall." Several cabins disappeared. Those that remained were badly damaged, with whole roofs missing.

At 10 a.m. Miles Lawrence reported that Mitch had moved only 10 miles in the previous six hours, and was 40 miles shy of where the last forecast said it would be. His fix, in fact, showed a 6-mile jog to the southeast from the previous fix. This "jog" involved two successive forecasters' best estimates of the storm's central point, a fix based on a jerky satellite loop with a stated margin of error of 23 miles. A 6-mile shift was "noise" statistically, particularly in a circle of hurricane-force winds 120 miles across. A re-enactment of the storm's track months later showed Mitch did not jog southeast but was making a slow left-hand turn to the south.

Based on his real-time analysis of the models, Lawrence wrote in his discussion: "The GFDL is almost stationary for 72 hours and the NOGAPS shows a slow, mostly northward drift." His official forecast was a "blend" of the models: a bit south of west (260 degrees) for a while, then a slow west to northwestward drift for 72 hours to near the Yucatán Peninsula. Lawrence warned in the discussion, "It would only take a 5-knot error in the forecast speed of motion for the hurricane to make landfall in 24 to 36 hours anywhere in the warning area from Honduras to the Yucatán."

Mitch's winds had declined by 10 knots to 145 knots, still a Category 5 storm. From space, the eye was a perfect hole inside a boiling white vortex. Drawn onto the satellite photo, the Bay Islands appeared as mites, insignificant, the eye itself as wide as Roatán's length.

Plotted on his chart, Mitch's reported 6-mile "jog" to the southeast shocked Michael D. Burke, who was hanging on every word and hoping for the best from the National Hurricane Center. Clutching at straws, the thought occurred to him that if the storm was going south-east, it was "going away. That's good. OK. We'll wait and see."

Aboard the *Fantome*, in the roiled wake of Roatán, March did not have the satellite photo, the weather fax, or the full array of "products" from the National Hurricane Center that were available in Miami. He was, in a very real sense, sailing blind—aided by men far away who could not hear the wind or feel the ship shudder, or sense the mounting fatigue of the helmsman at the wheel on the exposed bridge deck a few stairsteps and a couple of paces away. March himself was tired and stressed. Never very good at mathematics or at estimating time and distance, his keenness wore as he listened to the static-filled single sideband radio or talked on the satellite telephone and plotted Mitch's location on a chart table that heaved and pitched.

"Most of our discussion was about heavy weather preparation," said MDB, who, along with Paul Maskell, called the bridge periodically to check on ship conditions and boost morale. March confirmed that he had taken all possible heavy-weather precautions. Everything on deck had been removed and stored in cabins. The deck boxes had been drilled shut and duct-taped, as had the doors to the Admiralty suites on the main deck. Rope was strung across Decks A and B for safety lines. Watertight doors belowdecks were closed and dogged down, as were the lower bulkhead doors. Two empty fuel tanks had been flooded with seawater to lower the ship's center of gravity. Burke was worried about seawater splashing into the engine air intake, behind louvers near the entrance to the saloon. Water could damage or stop the diesels. March said he had put plywood over them and caulked the cracks with rags and rope. Burke also asked March to secure the heavy saloon doors with plywood. March said that one of the doors had been screwed down, but the other was left open. Burke interpreted that to mean that the crew was in the saloon and needed one door for possible escape. Open to the lobby, which ran with shipped water even in fresh winds, these doors were an obvious point of vulnerability. March reported that the ship was rolling somewhat but handling well, especially on the eastward tack with the wind on its port quarter.

As the morning passed, the ship's barometer dropped intermittently. Squalls washed over the deck. The wind was rising. Daylight was turning dark. It was clear that things were getting worse. When Annie Bleasdale called the bridge again, Guyan March "mentioned that MDB had said they could cut free the launches from the sides if they were rolling too heavily."

Burke, who had worried all morning about the ship being blown into the mainland of Honduras 25 miles away, asked March about other possible strategies, including tying up or anchoring at the cruise ship port at Coxen Hole. March said it was "very rough" at the entrance to the harbor. "Whitecaps were running perpendicular to the harbor. He said he couldn't get in."

"Why not anchor on the south side of Roatán?" Burke asked.

"It is too damn rough."

In his 1991 *Cruising Guide to the Northwest Caribbean*, a book written for small yachts, most of which draw 7 feet or less of water, author Nigel Calder described the southern shore of Roatán as "punctuated by a number of fjord-like inlets cutting back into the encircling hills, each one guarded by a shallow reef with a narrow opening and offering superlative protection." Calder sounded each of the inlets and found water at least 40 feet deep in Dixon Cove Bay, Brick Bay, French Harbor, Caribbean Bight, Bodden Bight, Port Royal, and Old Port Royal. In a second publication, *Honduras and Its Bay Islands—A Mariner's Guide*, another sailor-author, Rick Rhodes, cited Dixon Cove on the west and Port Royal on the east as "viable" options for a ship with the *Fantome's* 19-foot draft.

At the time of the *Fantome's* dawn landfall on Roatán, the west end was already roiling with seas. March did not report conditions for the other inlets to the east. They could have been navigable early in the morning, but he had never been in them, they were not marked with navigation aids, and no one had published GPS bearings to enter in bad weather. As time passed, as the winds picked up and waves refracted around Roatán, these narrow entrances—200 yards in most cases—were most likely covered with breakers, according to Calder. In those conditions there was no way to distinguish the deep water from the reefs. March could not eyeball the ship in as he did in fair weather. "In heavy, breaking seas they'd all be extremely intimidating," said Calder. "You'd basically be doing it on trust, knowing if you were wrong, you would lose the boat. Even Port Royal, with 80-foot depths, I'm not sure I'd take a 280-foot, 19-foot draft ship and put it in the hands of somebody else's cruising guide." Terry Evans, whose family runs Coco View resort and a boat chartering business on French Harbor, said it would have been "absolutely impossible to find a way in. I put my own sailboat on a reef coming in at night in just 3- or 4-foot seas."

At no point in the morning, according to Michael D. Burke, did he and Captain March discuss a scenario to anchor the ship and get the men off.

As it was, dozens of boats were rocking but otherwise snug in Roatán's harbors Tuesday morning. Numerous shrimp boats were tucked into French Harbor and Oak Ridge. Port Royal harbored several boats. In Jonesville Bight, sixty to seventy shrimp and lobster boats and a dozen yachts cowered. "I had Jack Daniels under my pillow," said one yachtie. Most were tuned to VHF or single sideband radio. "It was kinda fun," said another. "It was like a big party. When you're sitting here, you want to have somebody tell you what is going on—even if it's wrong. You turn to all the channels."

J.C. Garcia, who ran a dry dock used by shrimp boats, was at home in Oak Ridge watching CNN and boarding up his house, which faced Honduras. Sometime late that morning, he noticed a four-masted schooner heading east. "Why," he asked himself, "are they going that way?"

Twenty years before satellite photos were available to mariners, a typhoon overran a U.S. Navy convoy en route to the Philippines to support General MacArthur's invasion. The storm of December 17, 1944, came to be called "Halsey's Typhoon" after Admiral William "Bull" Halsey, the convoy's commander who ignored a precipitously dropping barometer. Three destroyers capsized and sank, several ships were seriously damaged, and 790 men were lost. "It was the greatest loss that we have taken in the Pacific without compensatory return since the First Battle of Savo," Admiral C.W. Nimitz, the navy's Pacific fleet chief, wrote two months later.

Nimitz concluded in a postmortem that there had been too much reliance on weather analysis from Fleet Weather Center in Pearl Harbor and a general failure by the commanders to give up the mission and refocus attention on saving their ships. In a letter that would be codified in navy policy, Nimitz wrote:

"A hundred years ago, a ship's survival depended almost solely on the competence of her master and on his constant alertness to every hint of change in the weather. . . . There was no radio. . . . There was no one to tell him that the time had now come to strike his light sails. His own barometer, the force and direction of the wind and the appearance of sea and sky were all that he had for information. Ceaseless vigilance in watching and interpreting signs, plus a philosophy of taking no risk in which there was little to gain and much to be lost, was what enabled him to survive. . . .

"In bad weather, as in most other situations, safety and fatal hazard are not separated by any sharp boundary line, but shade gradually from one into the other. There is no little red light which is going to flash on and inform commanding officers or higher commanders that from then on there is extreme danger from the weather. . . . Ships that keep on going as long as the severity of wind and sea has not yet come close to capsizing them or breaking them in two, may nevertheless become helpless to avoid these catastrophes later if things get worse. By then they may be unable to steer any heading but in the trough of the sea, or may have their steering control, lighting, communications and main propulsion disabled, or may be helpless to secure things on deck or to jettison topside weights. The time for taking all measures for a ship's safety is while still able to do so. Nothing is more dangerous than for a seaman to be grudging in taking precautions lest they turn out to have been unnecessary. Safety at sea for a thousand years has depended on exactly the opposite philosophy."

• • •

By noon on Tuesday, half the homes in Mangrove Bight on Guanaja had been reduced to woodpiles, awash in the surf. A mile to the northeast, lying in his dough with his wife and pets, Doug Solomon watched as leaves on trees and brush blew away. If he lifted his head above the ground, he estimated the wind at 35 knots. Sitting up, he encountered a rush of 80 knots. Twenty-five miles across the strait, on mainland Honduras, the power went out in La Ceiba, the banana port.

Aboard the *Fantome*, conditions had deteriorated to such an extent that a helmsman could no longer stand outside. He was sent below, and March and his mates in the deckhouse took over steering using a joystick, a round, 3-inch black ball that moved the rudders with hydraulic power. Engines were varied by hand in the engine room, with orders radioed down from the bridge. March reported that the staysails had blown out again.

"How is the rig standing up?" Paul Maskell asked March from Miami.

"Fine. It looks fine."

March sounded normal to Maskell, but the satellite phone shielded the rising noise of the storm, the groans of steel, unfamiliar vibrations, and unsettling lurches. Winds of 50 to 75 knots—roughly Category 1 force—were now sweeping over Roatán and through the *Fantome's* thicket of wires, wearing on the ears and nerves of those on board. The tops of waves 10 to 15 feet high were beginning to blow off and streak the sea white. The sky was turning a battleship gray. It was still possible to walk around the *Fantome*, but except for the mates in the deckhouse and the engineers below, most crewmen were believed to be jammed into the booths of the dining saloon. It was the most comfortable place on the ship—their bunks forward had become like bucking mechanical bulls, uninhabitable. In the saloon they could group together for moral support and they could get a sense of conditions outside through the quarterdeck windows. It was also the closest enclosed mustering spot to the lifeboats.

As he puzzled over the war room's computer models shortly after noon, Miles Lawrence was having twinges of doubt. For a full day Hurricane Mitch had defied the computers and official forecasts. It had not turned northwest. It was drifting southwest. Virtually all the models showed the hurricane curving slightly northwest and blasting across northern Belize and the southern Yucatán. Only the GFDL meandered, showing a little loop. But Mitch was moving so slowly that it occurred to Lawrence to fall back on an old-fashioned practice—if the storm's movements were slow and erratic, call it "stationary" until it showed its true track, or, if moving, extrapolate the current movement forward. With this on his mind, and Mitch clearly having a mind of its own, Lawrence sat down to write the 1 p.m. advisory.

"Mitch is moving slowly toward the west-southwest near 5 knots, and a slow west-southwest to westward motion is expected to continue for the next 24 hours." The winds had dropped to 134 knots, a Category 4 storm. Using shots from several satellites—GOES-8 had gone down at 2 a.m.—he centered the storm at 16.9° N, 85.4° W The center of Mitch was 30 miles from Guanaja and 60 miles from the *Fantome*.

"The goddamned storm is coming right at you!" Michael D. Burke blurted when he plotted it and called Captain March. Later he recalled, "Our hearts sank. It's hard to describe the feeling inside, a feeling of trepidation and fear, of the worst happening in front of your eyes." March, until now the picture of calm, uttered one line Burke remembered.

"It doesn't look good."

"It wasn't an easy conversation," Burke said later. "Obviously we were in trouble now. We had this huge, powerful storm bearing down, with few options."

The storm's edge, on the horizon the day before, was now on deck. Satellite photos clearly showed the terrible rush of air that was striking the hull, heeling it. March estimated the wind at 60 to 80 knots. Burke thought he was exaggerating. "He didn't have instruments. Past 60 it was a best guess."

"What are we going to do, Guyan? We can't stay in its path and hope for the best."

They talked over options that were rapidly falling away. They couldn't go south. It was 22 miles to the marshy mainland. With winds roaring from the west-northwest and waves of 20 to 40 feet in the open sea, they could not head west toward Guatemala and the port of Puerto Barrios. Northwest, back toward Belize, was out of the question. It was also too late to try a risky plunge through a boiling reef into one of Roatán's harbors. Nightfall was six hours away. In the storm, darkness would come sooner.

At 1:15 p.m., Captain March told Burke that on his last tack to the west, he had had difficulty getting the bow through the wind. The twin Caterpillar engines barely pushed the nose around. The high bow and tall masts were like sails. He could no longer point the bow north, to turn or stay near Roatán. Even if he had jibed the ship, worn the bow around in the other direction, away from the wind, he could not have swung the ship up into the wind, and would have wound up pointing southwest, away from Roatán and back toward the Honduran shore. The farther away from the island he got, the stronger the wind and the less control he would have. "So," said Burke, "he was committed to run to the east." Captain March and the *Fantome* had run out of options.

A lesser sailor might have panicked by now. A Category 4 hurricane was bearing down on him. The ship he'd been able to handle so well would no longer track and go west. The waves and wind around him were the worst he'd seen. But Guyan March was not given to panic. On the bridge of a ship he wore a look, born of ability, seasoned with success, of calm and assurance. "Never in his life did he lose control of a situation, certainly not at sea," said his brother Paul. "Calm and controlled was the way he managed and thought things through. He was very methodical and calculating."

So successful had March been as a young sailor that problems almost surprised him. Those who knew him saw this aspect occasionally—a passing, stunned look. "He would never actually express it verbally, mainly because there were people around who would pick up on it," said Jeremy Linn, his old sailing instructor. In 1986, while still in sailing school, March was motoring the 72-foot *Hoshi* into a lock in Scotland when the engine failed. He was doing 4 knots. If he had kept going and popped the gate, the ship would have dropped 30 feet. "A look of total horror appeared—only momentarily," said Linn. "He was very quick thinking. We both dove into the engine room and turned the key. The old diesel had been running too slow and stopped. I saw the same thing in handling sails when things weren't quite right. There would be a look of just complete horror. He would take a moment to think about it, and come up with the right solution ninety-nine times out of one hundred. He was calm and collected. He wouldn't shout or scream."

March also impressed his shipmates from the start of his Windjammer career. As a mate on the *Fantome* in the late 1980s, he took control of the bridge when the ship went aground in Antigua. When the captain seemed powerless, Guyan "was all business," said Sharon Patterson, the purser. He was "so self-assured and confident about all things pertaining to sailing that no one ever doubted his suggestions. He could weigh the large and the small, the crew, passengers, weather, ship, responsibility, business, fun, girlfriend, life, love, and laughter and keep them all orbiting in pretty much a well-balanced scheme. Like juggling a dozen balls at once. There were times when you could see rings under Guyan's eyes and knew he needed rest badly, but he never complained about it. I don't understand how he did it, but the man never showed a grouchy side."

Ed Snowdon, who served as mate under March aboard the *Yankee Clipper*, recalled, "I have never met a man, and I've been around a lot of circles, who had more of a sixth sense and innate ability to make the right decision and know the right thing to do. It was uncanny. He didn't have to stop and scratch his head. He was not at all daredevil. He was always making the most prudent decision. When I was sailing down a coastline, he might say, 'Ed, you're 2 miles off a lee shore. What happens if you lose an engine and a squall comes up? You're going to be set down. If you're another mile off, you're in better standing.' He taught me that kind of thing. He would always err on the safe side."

March had tasted rough weather. He'd crossed the English Channel in small boats with winds of 40 to 50 knots. "At home, in the dinghies, we would be the first ones out and the last ones in," said brother Paul. "In marginal, rough seas, everyone waited. If we started in, they knew it was time to head in. Everyone gauged it on us. It went to ability. If we thought it was marginal, it really was time to go in." At Windjammer, Guyan had seen waves sweep the top of the *Fantome* and felt its heeling in big waves. He'd known the edges of several hurricanes. March, like most sailors, had a fascination with sea storms and disasters and an encyclopedic knowledge of them, according to Patterson. "He told me about rogue waves: massive waves that appeared unexpectedly and took ships and crew by surprise. We talked at length about disasters at sea, ships that encountered storms and lost crew."

March must also have known that a career at sea sometimes requires periods outside the comfort zone. That's how sailors grow, through longer crossings and bigger waves. If they survive, the bold ones revel in newfound confidence. "Every time you go out there is a risk," Windjammer owner Mike Burke believed. "That's part of the beauty of it. When you've got a bone in your teeth? And you wonder. That element of danger. It's a good feeling—if it holds together." But the wise ones recognize that their survival sometimes has as much to do with good luck, or a guardian angel, as with their own ability. On Tuesday afternoon, October 27, Guyan March, full of pride and trim, was in the hands of the gods.

"I started to feel fear from him," said Michael D. Burke. "He wasn't too forthcoming with his acceptance that we needed to run to the east. I think he was afraid. Look at his circumstances. He is leaving a lee. He is heading out. It's going to get dark in a few hours, if it's not dark already. He's in hell. He's already facing pretty horrendous conditions. His circumstances will get worse, right at dark. There wasn't a whole lot to say."

Almost immediately, Roatán's protection disappeared. From the high point of a 700-foot peak, the one used to find Port Royal, the land sloped off rapidly into the sea to the northeast. Two low islands, Morat and Barbareta, stood offshore with no lee. Then came a 14-mile stretch of deep water before the ochre bluff of Guanaja, invisible beyond the dark squalls and veils of spume, rose abruptly from the depths. Running under bare poles, the *Fantome* was making 7 knots on a compass bearing of 90 degrees. As Roatán passed by the port beam, the wind on deck increased gradually, from a "garden variety" hurricane to something above 80 knots. Sea conditions worsened dramatically and rapidly. Within an hour, waves jumped from the 10- to 15-foot range to 20 to 40 feet. The waves generated by Mitch's outer winds were still piling in from the west northwest around Roatán's south side, more or less behind the ship. But in the open channel these waves encountered others refracting around both islands, as well as monster seas surging directly south through the channel from Mitch's eye wall, which was now just 30 miles to the north. The highest sustained winds in the eye wall were 133 knots. Gusts could have reached 198 knots. Mitch was right on the border between a Category 4 and Category 5 hurricane. The 282-foot steel *Fantome* plunged on, unprotected from the most powerful force on earth.

"Confused seas," the term used by March to describe the colliding wave trains, could not come close to describing the steep, irregular boiling that now surrounded the ship and its crew. The water leaped and sank, built mounds and cut cliffs. There was no rhyme or logic. According to wave theory, when 20-foot seas from one direction meet 15-foot seas from another, the coincident crests rear up an average of 25 feet, with periodic peaks of 37 feet and an occasional 50-foot giant. Around the *Fantome*, steep waves appeared from nowhere, then broke into cascading faces that crashed like breakers and hissed over a sea surface already white with wind-blown spume.

The rolling of the boat increased violently—30 to 45 degrees to port and then to starboard—March reported to Michael D. Burke. Waves struck the hull and poured water into the A-deck "lobby," forward of the dining saloon, and over the sidedecks between the bulwarks and the Admiralty suites. The top party deck was 20 feet above the water. B deck was a mere 12 feet. "He had gotten hit by a bow wave, a big wave, with lots of water on deck," said Burke. MDB was worried about broaching, a loss of control in which a ship heels wildly to windward, exposing its broad side to wind and sea. He questioned March about ways to prevent broaching, using a launch as a drogue trailed astern, or sails—jibs or staysails—tied to a mooring line as a sea anchor deployed over the bow. But the ship was rolling so much it would not have been safe for crewmen to be out rigging lines or wrestling a 3,000-pound boat over the ship's stern. Plus, March said he didn't think it was necessary. "The bow of the ship is broad and deep, so it is not squirrelly. So when it surfed, the ship would ride straight. It didn't turn off," said Burke.

At some point, Guyan March apparently left the deckhouse—when Burke telephoned, Brasso answered and said the skipper wasn't there— which would have required him to open the sliding hatch and struggle out onto the bridge. Grasping ropes and railing, or clipping a harness into one of the jacklines the crew had rigged, he would have pushed or perhaps crawled through wind and spray capable of etching a bloody tattoo on his face. The 20 feet across the exposed party deck to the closest stairway at the muster station would have seemed like traversing an earthquake. "He must have been blind as a bat," said Neil Carmichael, captain of the Windjammer ship *Polynesia.* "I don't think people appreciate what it's like when you start getting 50, 60, 70 knots and rains as torrential as that. I've been in 50 to 60 with a snorkel mask on. You can't see 10 feet." Having descended the forward stairs, March could have staggered aft along the port or starboard sidedeck between the Admiralty suites and bulwarks, crossed the "lobby," and pulled open the unsecured wooden door to the dining saloon in an interval between periodic deluges of solid seawater. Or, making his way forward 20 feet, he could have opened a watertight hatch and descended a ladder to Deck B, and from there reached both the engine room and the saloon. He might even have braved the length of the top deck and descended the duke's original stairway into the lobby.

Guyan March and Michael D. Burke never talked about where the men were, but Burke assumed that engineers Constantin Bucur and Pope Layne were in the engine room, perhaps with other engineers,

sealed off by waterproof hatches. They would have kept busy, moni-
toring engines and hydraulic pressure, watching the water level in the
bilge beneath them, thinking about sediment in the fuel. Routine work
would have been impossible as they grasped pipes and worried. Pope
Layne had been through Hurricane Marilyn in 1995 aboard Windjammer's *Flying Cloud,* the company's smallest ship, which was too
slow to outrun hurricanes and was tied to a mooring ball off Peter
Island in the British Virgin Islands when storms threatened. Pope and
other crew stayed aboard to run the engines against the force of the
wind. "He was scared to death. He said he had to crawl, literally crawl,
on deck," recalled Rhonda Epperson. "You couldn't hear anything. The
wind and rain were just so intense. The wooden covers to the benches
were flying off. He couldn't communicate over the radio because of the
noise. So people were sending messages back and forth by crawling on
the deck."

By Tuesday afternoon, the rest of the *Fantome*'s men were presumed to
be in the saloon. "That's where I'd be," Burke said later. That would have
put twenty to twenty-six men in a room that had once been filled with
rum and laughter and the twinkling brass lights of a cruise. Now
grunting, nauseous men, trussed into bulky life jackets, strained to stay
in their seats and hang on to the macramé-covered posts. The bur-
nished brass lamps, if not dismounted and stowed, would have
described crazy arcs, as would the gold chains on the crew's necks. The
men would have been suffering great fatigue. Their muscles had been
tense for twenty-four hours as they moved or hung on in the rolling
ship, fighting to stay in a bunk or not be tossed about. Their last good
sleep had been Saturday night, three days before. Ever since, they had
been in a flight-or-fight mode. They were scared. Several of the men
couldn't swim.

Deckhands and the more experienced crew, including bosun Cyrus
Phillips and bosun's mate Jerry King, probably would have walked
through escape routes in their minds. From where they were, they
would have to climb an exposed stairway and make a suicidal dash to
the topdeck muster station and life rafts. The hotel department heads,

chief steward Chrispin Saunders and chef Eon Maxwell, and their staffs most likely were petrified. Without normal duties to occupy them, their minds were free to roam, to their wives and kids, to plans for the future, to beautiful women, to random promises, prayers, and regrets. The scene outside the saloon's windows encouraged their worst fears.

Phillips, at forty the "old man" of the *Fantome*, Bequia-born and with twelve years with Windjammer, was the closest any of the West Indian crew came to being a sailor from birth. He "wanted to get money together and have his own boat for freighting through the islands," said his brother, Julian Peterson, who crewed on Wind-jammer's *Yankee Clipper*. "It was supposed to come time in 2005."

Jerry King, in his last call home, had told his sister how homesick he was. He hadn't been home since January. When the ship next docked in Trinidad, he told her, "I'm going to roll in all that mud."

Friday, three days away, was electrician Vernon Brusch's twenty-seventh birthday, and he had promised his mother he would be home to celebrate. In his last phone call from Omoa, Brusch had laughed and said that he would be the one bearing gifts. "Oh God, Mommy, my cabin is full." Piled on his bunk before the storm were a VCR, more CDs, and a plastic tricycle for Otaphia, his pretty child who liked to wear red and white beads in her hair. "He had no room on the bed to lie down," said Athelene Brusch, who set her mind to a birthday cake, a homecoming meal, "and those kinds of things."

Kevin Logie of Trinidad, who had followed his brother to Wind-jammer, was due to leave the *Fantome* in a week to become lead chef on another Windjammer ship. He still dreamed of saving money to open his own tailor shop. On his last trip through Miami, Logie had twenty minutes to spend with brother Neville. "He had footage on his camcorder of my three-month-old baby. I told him I would look at it another time. He was coming back to Miami with the camcorder, CDs, a TV, VCRs—everything was in that little cabin."

Jesús Hernandez, deckhand, the Honduran dock hire without a visa, was 25 miles from his estranged wife and two children, who were soon to be in the hurricane themselves. When he was ten months old in

1974, Hurricane Fifi barreled through the strait between the Honduran mainland and the Bay Islands and devastated the country. A small stream running through the village of San Marcos became a roaring torrent through Jesús' mother's house. "I couldn't hold all the children," she said later. "The river was taking Jesús away. But a neighbor came and grabbed him by the hand."

Alvin and Alan George, the Spice Brothers from Grenada, men taught to cook by their grandmother, were chefs at heart. Alvin, the neat one, had two kids at home. Alan, the good-looking brother, the life of the party, was saving his money to open a restaurant in Grenada. "I'll see you in November," he had said in his last phone call to their mother, Margaite. When she protested again about his life at sea, he had said offhandedly, "If I have to die at sea, I'll die there, instead of on land."

Francis Morain, deckhand and father of six in private school in Grenada, had turned thirty-seven on October 10. After enduring a $350-a-month job, he had the letter he'd worked for, the letter from Windjammer recommending a visa to the United States. He had told his wife, Elizabeth, to join him in Trinidad for Christmas shopping.

Carl "cool and deadly" James, engineer, was looking forward to Christmas, when he could take his sister's children downtown in New Amsterdam for ice cream.

Deonauth "Django" Ramsudh, refrigerator mechanic, had been an acolyte in the Lutheran church as a child. If he was to meet his Maker, at least he'd taken care of his three children with the $69,000 won at the casino.

Colin August, the launch driver, no doubt wished he'd taken some leave, like brother Chuckie, who was safe ashore.

Rhon Austin, deckhand, was experiencing his first tour at sea.

Maxwell Bhikham—Blinky, they called him—was a Muslim deckhand who never missed prayer time with Mohamed Farouk Roberts, another Muslim and first-year engineer. They were from Guyana, too.

Steadbert Burke and Vanil Fender were Jamaicans, a first-year carpenter and a cook. They had wives at home.

O'Ryan Hardware, the ladies' man, had followed his brother to

Windjammer and become an engineer. Brother Orville had reached his dream—enough money to marry and get off the boat.

Deodatt Jallim, another first-year carpenter, had followed his brother Harry to sea. He had called his wife from Belize and told her to expect him in two weeks.

Carlisle Mason, deckhand from St. Vincent, and Wilbert Morris, the quiet, muscled welder from Guyana who helped keep the ship together, huddled with the others. Anibal Olivas, the Nicaraguan dock hire, two weeks on the ship as steward, was there. Pedro Prince, the Honduran galley aide stuck without a visa, was thrown together by circumstance with Rohan Williams—Dr. Stone, they called him—another deckhand. Bobby Pierre from St. Lucia—so helpful and joyous as Chrispin's assistant steward and and such a good dancer—was there too. He looked remarkably like a smaller version of Horace Grant, the basketball star, and lately had been dating Chrispin's sister, Beverly McKenzie, who had gotten off the ship in Belize. Whatever these men were thinking was shoved aside with each bang and howl that brought the storm back like a question from Saint Peter. At some point, they became too seasick to care.

When a storm is violent enough, even experienced mariners will eventually begin to suffer from a type of motion sickness, not the nausea most think of, but an enveloping fatigue—the "feeling that we want to close our eyes whenever we get the chance," according to Carlos Comperatore of the Coast Guard's research branch. By itself, that might not be a problem. But when it combines with sleep loss, stress, and desynchronosis—the maladjustment of the body clock—endurance drops significantly. Even the most durable mariners begin to retreat into a personal shell, walled in and enervated by the motion of the ship, lack of sleep, the physical exertion of staying upright or in a bunk, and worry. It is the first sign of deteriorated performance that sooner or later overcomes any sailor. First, the man gets quiet. As conditions worsen, he becomes forgetful. It becomes tougher to do mental arithmetic. He is apathetic and slow to respond. He might forget to check critical information, or he might act when what is called for is no action.

When he reached his men, Guyan March would likely have told them the truth about their plight, about the loss of Roatan's lee and his hope for the run east. He would likely have reviewed safety matters, especially the use of life jackets and life rafts. His presence may have had a calming effect on the crew, who would have been praying and pushing back moments of panic. These would have been held back only by the rational thought that of all the Windjammer officers they knew, Guyan March, Brasso Frederick, and Onassis Reyes were the best. "He would have gone through every single scenario in his head," said crewman Julian Peterson, brother of bosun Cyrus Phillips. "If there was one person I would want to be with, it would have been March because of his control over himself and his ability to handle the vessel."

At some point, March rejoined Brasso and Onassis in the deckhouse. Knowing what they knew, the minds of these three men likely would have raced with all the things that could go wrong. How far would she roll before the ship no longer cared whether she came upright or kept going? At what angle of roll would water downflood, and from where? Would watertight doors hold? Would the square portlights on B deck shatter and flood? If the *Fantome* was laid over, would the large, rectangular saloon windows surrounding the crew stand up to wave crests? Could the ship's most vulnerable spot—their deckhouse—stay together? The highest, forwardmost, and flimsiest shelter on the ship—25 feet above the water on calm days—must have been hell, the rolling and pitching exaggerated, the noise debilitating. In one grunted exchange with Miami, March described a chair flying.

Their conversation limited to brief shouts, the officers, too, likely withdrew inside, to that private space forced open by the knowledge that they could die. When the weather was rough, Brasso liked to sleep below the saloon, in a C-deck cabin near the center of the keel, where motion was dampened. Now, in the worst possible place on the ship, he could well have imagined time at home in his big new house on Antigua. Built from scratch on his Windjammer earnings, it was probably worth $400,000. So big in body and spirit, a rock in the midst of crisis, even Brasso could have legitimately concluded that if the ship came to grief, it would be impossible to get anyone into a life raft.

Onassis, full of vigor and promise, could have flashed on the crewmen he knew who couldn't swim, his girlfriend Glenn and their Christmas plans, or the feeling of being trapped underwater that he had experienced when a launch had flipped and he'd been snared in the canvas top. It had scared the hell out of him, Parkinson said later. "It was a realization of the reality, a random fluke. He knew how dangerous it was." He must have considered the irony that failed love had put him there to replace a heartsick mate. Or maybe he recalled his last e-mail to his mother, sent Friday night for her birthday. "Remember that you finish a new year every time you begin a new day. So it's never too late to start something new. Like doing more exercises or writing a new diary, etc. . . . My time in these waters will end soon because I finish on December 26. . . . I'm very healthy. Running 30 miles a week (in the mud) and lifting weights. I have to buy some vitamins. Take care of yourself, Mama, and you will be hearing from me soon. Your son loves you. Onassis."

At 2:30 p.m., on Guanaja's southeast shore, veterinarian Alex Patterson watched his beach house slide into the ocean. He was 100 yards away in his sister's hillside house. "There was so much salt spray, I could only see the top of it." Shortly after, the house he was in began coming apart. "The roof started leaving. The walls started leaving. There were seven of us inside. Two of them were seventy-five years old." He helped them into the crawl space beneath the house. He and his wife, Monique, then fought their way 50 yards behind the house to the 2,000-gallon concrete cistern. The others stayed behind because they didn't think they could make it there. The cistern, 8 by 8 feet, had a square hole on top covered by a heavy concrete lid, 2 feet square. The shed over it, used to collect rainwater, had blown away. "The wind was blowing like crazy. The sand was coming out of the ground. It felt like it was sandblasting us, hitting us from the back. It would blow like crazy for twenty, thirty seconds, and you'd have a three- to five-second lull. You've got pieces of trees falling around you. I got there ahead of my wife. I waited behind the cistern to get out of the sandblast. I waited for the lull and then, here she came. She probably got blown down three times in 100 feet." They climbed into the cistern.

North, across the island, Black Rock, the size of a barn, and a cute cottage tucked in its lee were underwater. The storm surge, at least 20 feet high, poured into the raised home of Doug and Mary Solomon. By 3 p.m., all but 8 of the 150 homes in Mangrove Bight were gone. In his elevated home on land, Kerston Moore could feel the waves slapping against the plywood over his windows that faced the bay. Looking out through a crack, "it was like an airplane in fog. Like a white wall. It was too much for a person to witness."

At 3 p.m., the *Fantome* was midway between Roatán and Guanaja. The storm's center was 40 miles to the northeast, but the eye wall was less than 20 miles away. Winds and waves from the outer edge of the eye wall surged straight south at the ship through the channel. The wind speed rose to Category 2 level, 95 knots. Since the wind's force increases with the square of velocity, the effect on both the sea and the ship was torturous. March reported waves so high that 3 feet of solid "green water" poured repeatedly onto the ship's main deck. On the top, party deck, barrels of water arced over the bow and sides and surged around like surf on a rocky shore. "As the water sloshed, it would break up a lot of benches and tables," said Michael D. Burke. "It was not unexpected. They were made of one-by-threes. There was a lot of water on deck." The deckhouse, the nerve center of the ship containing all the electronics, was built of the same wood, bolted to an angle iron frame. The roof over the officers' heads was plywood reinforced with fiberglass mat.

March also reported water cascading into the whaleboats that hung 25 feet off the water on the top deck.

"Cut 'em off. Don't worry about it," Burke said.

It was a moot point. The deck of the *Fantome* had become a no-man's-land. Walking anywhere was impossible with the deck at a 45-degree tilt, steeper than a home stairway. As the ship's well deck rolled toward the water, Guyan, Brasso, and Onassis, trapped in their deckhouse, braced and fought to remain upright. In Miami, Michael D. Burke paced by the phone, biting his lip. "Shit," he kept saying. "Oh shit."

At 3:40 p.m., the *Fantome* cleared the channel between Roatán and Guanaja and was 7 miles south of the tip of Guanaja's West End. Burke asked March if he could get into the lee of the island, which lies northeast to southwest. The wind was blasting the ship on its port rear quarter.

"There's no way," March replied.

"What about turning, putting the wind on the beam and running northeast?"

"No way." Even if Captain March could have done that, exposing the full length of the ship's topsides, superstructure, and rig to the force of the hurricane was what he had been struggling to prevent.

Fantome plunged east.

Flying toward Mitch in NOAA's P-3 turboprop, researchers James Franklin and Michael Black were afraid that they had missed their hurricane party. As their boss had warned, Mitch appeared to be weakening. When they had taken off from Tampa just after noon, Mitch's eye was clouding over, and Miles Lawrence was reporting winds down to 135 knots, a borderline Category 4/5 storm. In keeping with their habit, Franklin and Black had stocked up on junk food. Black, who never got sick, usually carried a greasy burrito. Franklin, who always got sick, still tried to eat a lot to keep his stomach "busy." He'd gone to Subway for a sandwich and "really good chocolate chip cookies—good and buttery. I like Hershey's chocolate with almonds. Barbecue potato chips. Generally, nothing healthy. I've never thrown up. I get nausea and incredible headaches from the noise and vibration. The whole airplane is in a low-grade vibration from the turboprops."

The scientists still hoped to observe other details within the eye using Doppler radar and GPS dropsondes. Armed with a belly radar,

spearlike wind probes, and the "score" of two hundred hurricane pen-
etrations painted on its fuselage, the P-3 was a veteran. "It's a four-
engine turboprop. It can take a beating. We frequently overstress the
airplane past its design specifications," said pilot Phil Kenul. "You
don't do it intentionally. Sometimes the storm flies you."

Black-bearded and with the roundish, gentle look of a manatee,
Michael Black was typical of hurricane researchers. One side of his
brain loved the mystery of storms, while the other mourned their
havoc. He loved flying into hurricanes.

"I've been flying into storms for fourteen seasons. I always look forward to it. Sometimes it is extremely rough, though usually not. You
never know what you're going to get. The strength of the storm is not
equal to the roughness of the flight. We flew into Gilbert, the lowest
pressure on record—888 millibars—in 1988. The stronger ones are like
being on a roller coaster; the upward motion is so broad that the plane
will rise up and descend very smoothly, down into the downdraft. At
times you actually float. Briefcases have flown and hit me. We've had
computer paper fly around the cabin. We have a coffee urn, a commercial cylinder with a bungee cord around the top, and at times that
has come off and coffee grounds go all over the back. We have obvious
scientific objectives. Hurricanes, still, in a lot of ways, are mysterious.
There is a lot we don't understand. It is such a potentially beautiful
sight when you go into a strong storm, with a clear eye and mountains
of clouds. It is truly an awesome sight."

At 3:30 p.m., an hour from penetration, the storm showed up on the
nose radar.

"You can see the outer and inner rain bands and the eye wall—a
circle. It is phenomenal," said Kenul. On the plane's belly radar, the
colors were measured in "decibels," a measure of return echo from the
rain. "Black is innocuous. Green not much. Yellow, caution. Red basically means stop, you're going to get the shit kicked out of you. Magenta
is for extremely high decibels, plus turbulence. That we avoid like the
plague. Red and magenta are basically the 'holy shit' colors." As they
nosed toward Mitch, red and magenta stood out in its circle of doom.

• • •

Coming up to his 4 p.m. deadline for another forecast from the National Hurricane Center, Miles Lawrence surveyed the computer models with dispassionate dismay. The storm had been moving southwest for twelve hours, but none of the models showed the slightest interest in going along. Lawrence began to sketch out a track with a bit of southern motion, and then a landfall in Belize in 36 to 48 hours. He fixed the center of Hurricane Mitch at latitude 16.8° N, longitude 85.8° W and described its motion as west-southwest at 4 knots.

Mitch's center was now directly north of the ship, 32 miles away. With an eye radius of 10 miles, Mitch's eye wall was now over northern Guanaja. Winds were still near 134 knots with gusts 50 percent higher.

Doug Solomon, lying soaking wet beside his wife and cowering dogs and cats on Guanaja's northeast coast, tasted the eye wall's arrival. The rain mixed with salt water blown out of the ocean. "The worst thing was the sound. You have no comprehension. It was like having an express train blowing steam right next to you. What we could see were huge, high, wide mangrove trees self-destructing. They were 40 or 50 feet high. Gradually they wore down to stumps. Breaking off to nothing." As the sky darkened prematurely, Solomon watched his barometer drop to 960. "I knew we were in real trouble then. The wind speeds picked up. It felt like it was right above us."

In his little West End cabin with five employees, David Greatorex described the hurricane noise by inhaling and making the sound "Wvzzzsssss. And every ten or fifteen minutes, it would go Who Who WhoWhooooo. And the cabin would go Ssh Shhh Shsssh, shaking, then all of a sudden, Whoo whho whooowhoo and quit."

Greatorex tuned a portable radio to a station from La Ceiba, on the mainland. Someone was interviewing a weather station in Florida, with translation to Spanish.

"What about the Bay Islands?" the Honduran interviewer asked.

"The Bay Islands. Just a moment. Oh, you mean Isla de Bahía?"

"What should they be doing there?"

"Oh dear, everyone on those islands should evacuate immediately."

In Omoa, *Fantome*'s home port, the storm was now upon the little fishing village, with wild surf and winds of 50 to 60 knots. Waves were striking the wooden window pulled down over Carlos Arita's tiki bar.

At 4 p.m. the *Fantome* was approaching Mitch's longitude. Michael D. Burke thought that was good news.

"Soon," Burke assured Guyan. Soon, the ship would be east of the center. It would be in the "navigable quarter." Wind would be blowing the ship away.

Shortly after, Captain March reported that, in fact, the wind was clocking more westerly. It was coming over the stern. Burke was elated. Things were working out. Things couldn't get worse. "I asked Guyan to bear a bit south of east, to get as far away as possible." March toggled the ship's big rudder to 93 degrees.

But aboard the *Fantome*, the suffering only increased. The ship was surrounded by chaos. The sky overhead was turning a charcoal gray-black. The rain beating on the deckhouse was horizontal and as heavy as a fire hose. If he could have opened his copy of Bowditch, Captain Guyan would have seen the book's classic description of the view now outside his ship:

"As the center of the storm comes closer, the ever-stronger wind shrieks through the rigging and about the superstructure of the vessel. As the center approaches, rain falls in torrents. The wind fury increases. The seas become mountainous. The tops of huge waves are blown off to mingle with the rain and fill the air with water. Objects at a short distance are not visible."

In good times the *Fantome* creaked comfortably. Now she would have brayed. The hull, rising and falling, would have shuddered, slammed, and struck water as if it were stone. Rolling through a 90-degree arc, beefy masts waved like willows. Even well-stored items would have come loose. Cans on shelves, glass in the refrigerator, spilled milk, rum bottles, books, CDs, toys for kids and VCRs for their mothers would have mixed in a great, cacophonous salad. Standing water sloshed around. Doors, windows, and seams would have leaked water.

If they could see anything, March, Brasso, and Reyes in the deck-house and the men in the saloon would have watched the slate-gray, white, and turquoise mountains rise above them. Then, as if riding an elevator, they would have risen to look out on a frightful battlefield where wind and spume raged. Down again they would go, into a trough, the seas hissing around them before cascading seawater covered everything. "The radar, if working, would be giving a dubious picture," said Neil Carmichael, captain of the Windjammer ship *Polynesia*. "They're inside the bridge, with limited visibility, three or four small windows. The bridge wasn't set up to be used on the inside." Maneuvering to avoid the worst breaking seas would have been impossible, even if visibility had permitted it.

Michael D. Burke remembered the captain's description: "It was terrible, squalling, dark and dirty, yet it was not like he was about to die," said Burke later. "He was not out of control. We didn't have far to go. It was a race. If we could get to the east, with the winds southwest, we'd have the Honduran mainland to protect us from heavy seas. It was a matter of time before we and the storm got further apart. We never discussed getting into rafts or the lifeboats. We weren't of the opinion that all was lost."

In *Typhoon: The Other Enemy*, retired navy captain C. Raymond Calhoun sketched the domino effect of a hurricane (called a *typhoon* in the Pacific) on his destroyer, *Dewey*. Halsey's Typhoon, which struck the Third Fleet in the Pacific on December 18, 1944, was similar in strength to Hurricane Mitch. When the typhoon's center was 50 miles away, the aircraft carrier *Monterey* reported rolls so heavy that airplanes on its deck broke loose, caught fire, and rolled into the sea. Steering systems on light carriers failed. Two men went overboard on the *Independence*. The carrier *Cowpens* had a fire on deck. The *Langley* began rolling 35 degrees to both sides.

"At 0911 our voice radio went out. . . . electrical failures now became a recurring problem. Everything was being short-circuited by the driving rain and spray. Our helmsman was having to use from 20 to 25 degrees of right rudder to maintain a heading. At 0928 with the ship rolling 40 degrees to starboard the *Dewey* lost suction on the port main lubricating oil pump. We had to stop the port engine in order to prevent wiping the main bearings. . . . the *Dewey* was corkscrewing and writhing like a wounded animal. The inclinometer registered 55-56-57, then 60 degrees. I tried to recall the stability curves . . . my recollection was they had shown that the *Dewey* could recover from a roll of 70 degrees."

The wind "drove spray and spume with the force of a sand blaster. Capillary bleeding was etched on any face exposed directly to it." The doctor reported several men injured by falling, some with fractured ribs.

The navy ship was "tossed, shoved, beaten." Metal covers ripped away, despite heavy screw-down hasps. In two hours, despite "water-tight" hatches, a foot of water filled every living space. "The pounding and rolling grew worse. We were now going over consistently to 68 and 70 degrees. Each roll I would dispatch a silent prayer, 'Dear God, please make her come back.' Engineers reported that on each starboard roll, the blower intakes, on main deck, were submerged and 500 to 1,000 gallons of water gushed into the fire rooms. Water tenders grabbed fittings and hung like monkeys. Sometimes they fell into the starboard bulkhead, shoulder deep into sloshing water, striking machinery and pumps. During one roll, a starboard hatch sprang open. Seawater poured on switchboards. There were flashes, short circuits, fires. The power went out. Steering went out. The wheel required 6 to 8 men.

"Many times I found myself hanging by my hands, with feet completely clear of the deck, in such a position that if I released my hold, I would drop straight down, through the starboard pilot house window into the sea. Several times I looked down past my dangling feet and saw the angry sea through the open window, directly below them," Calhoun wrote. The men prayed aloud: "Don't let us down, now, dear Lord, bring it back, oh God, bring it back." Each time it did, they shouted, "Thanks, dear Lord."

Outside, guy wires on exhaust stacks slackened and snapped taut with each gust. One broke with a noise like a cannon. The stack collapsed. The steam line broke. A whistle and siren and roar went off. When a fireman burned his pants, he told Calhoun: "It didn't really matter, Cap'n, I'd probably have had to burn 'em anyway."

At 4:20 P.M., Glenn Parkinson called Windjammer's headquarters and learned that Onassis Reyes had relayed a message to her. "He loves you," said a voice in Miami.

"Tell him I love him, too," she answered. Later she said, "I don't know if he ever got the message. I went home and watched the storm on TV."

For moral support as much as anything, Michael D. Burke asked Captain March to stay on the phone, to keep the satellite line open. "Me and Captain Paul [Maskell], we were not doing a lot of talking. He's in a battle for his life."

Captain March reported waves of 30 to 35 feet, "right on the stern— except for confusion. He was saying the sea was terrible. Rough. He indicated it was getting worse. He was starting to lose the lee, which was all the more scary to me. I fully realized what he was going into over the next few hours."

"Don't worry about the lifeboats," Burke repeated to March. "Even if you lose a mast, don't worry. The debris on deck—it's not an issue. Get through it. We'll fix the ship later." He asked March if the water pouring on deck was falling off.

"It's discharging," March said.

The seas were terrible. "Confused," March yelled. The ship was making 7 knots. March reported a GPS fix of 16°15' N, 85°51' W, about 10 miles south-southeast of Guanaja.

"You could feel the grimace," Burke later recalled. "The ship was rolling heavily. And that's pretty scary in itself. He would have to hold on. You'd hear sounds of exertion. I heard him groan. I heard him say, 'That was a big one.'"

"Is it falling off? Is it shedding?"

"Yes, that's not a prob . . ."

At 4:30 p.m., the satellite telephone went dead.

Surviving Galeras

by Stanley Williams
and Fen Montaigne

Nine people died when Colombian volcano Galeras erupted on January 14, 1993. Volcanologist Stanley Williams (born 1952) almost died with them. Here he remembers that day, in an account written for Outside with journalist Fen Montaigne.

My colleagues came and went in the clouds. Banks of cumulus drifted across the peaks of the Andes, enveloping us in a cool fog that made it impossible to see anything but the gray rubble on which we stood. As morning gave way to afternoon, the clouds occasionally dispersed, offering a heartening glimpse of blue sky and revealing the barren, imposing landscape around us.

We were perched at 14,000 feet, on top of the Colombian volcano Galeras. It was January 14, 1993. At the center of the tableau was the volcano's cone and its steaming crater. Surrounding the cone on three sides were high walls of volcanic rock forming an amphitheater almost a mile and a half wide, a subtle palette of dun, gray, and beige. Occasionally I glimpsed in the west a forested, razorback ridge sloping toward the equatorial lowlands below the flank of an ancient volcano, one of many vestiges of earlier Galerases, in various stages of decay.

Around 1 p.m., four other geologists and I, part of our larger party of 13 scientists, stood on the crater's lip and gazed inside. Some 900 feet wide and 200 feet deep, the mouth of Galeras was a misshapen hole strewn with jagged boulders. Sulfuric gases shot from fumaroles, or vents, with a hiss, assaulting the nostrils with acrid odors and further obscuring the landscape in a swirl of vapors. The gas clouds often veiled Igor Menyailov, a Russian volcanologist sitting amid a jumble of rocks and thrusting a glass tube into a fumarole. The 55-year-old, who'd learned English by listening to black-market Elvis recordings, swiveled his head away from the vents as he talked with Colombian scientist Nestor García. Circling the rim of the crater, appearing and reappearing in the fog like a phantom, was English volcanologist Geoff Brown, accompanied by Colombian scientists Fernando Cuenca and Carlos Trujillo. Brown was taking the volcano's pulse with a highly sensitive device called a gravimeter. Like Igor, he was trying to determine if magma was on the move. We all used different methods, but our goal was the same—to forecast eruptions, to predict when Galeras might blow. We all wanted to save lives. Nine people would lose theirs that day.

This is what I remember. I know now what an elusive thing memory can be.

I had arrived in Pasto, Colombia, the week before to join an international team of more than 100 fellow scientists studying the Galeras volcano. Old friends and colleagues streamed in for our convention, a conference I would run with Pasto native Marta Calvache, the director of the Colombian government's geological observatory here and my close friend and prized graduate student. We had worked together in Pasto, and on Galeras, for years.

The city of Pasto (pop. 300,000) sits at 8,400 feet in a wide green bowl. Its central square is only five miles from the crater, and on a clear day residents can see steam rising from the squat, barren volcano, its apron stained green, brown, and gold by a patchwork of crops. The mountain's lower realms are thick with white-flowering coffee bushes, yellow-flowering guava trees, red and purple bougainvillieu. Galeras seems to be a generally benign presence; Pastusos are quick to point out that, despite being the most active Colombian volcano in recent centuries, Galeras had never killed anyone in recorded history.

But Galeras had grown more threatening. In 1988, after slumbering for 10 years, the volcano awoke with a series of minor earthquakes. In March 1989 it coughed up a cloud of ash that fell on Pasto. Two months later, an eruption sent a plume two miles high, sprinkling dust on the surrounding towns. Then, in August 1991, this activity rose sharply. By November a hardened lava dome was being squeezed up out of the volcano, eventually growing to a height of 150 feet. On July 16, 1992, the dome was blown to pieces, catapulting 12-foot boulders throughout the amphitheater and sending a column of ash 3.5 miles into the air.

By the time we arrived in Pasto six months later, Galeras seemed like the perfect specimen—active, but quieter than it had been in four years. Only a faint twitch of seismicity occasionally etched a tornillo, a screw-shaped signal, onto the black seismograph drums in the geological observatory. Sadly, my colleagues and I failed to appreciate the significance of these subtle signals.

On the morning of January 14, I led a convoy of a half-dozen jeeps west out of Pasto. Seventy-five scientists would be working around Galeras that day, but ours was the only group that would study the crater itself. The temperature was in the forties, and thick clouds drifted slowly across the mountaintops. About 3,000 feet from the summit we entered a national park, the mountainside thick with frailejon, a succulent with silvery-green leaves and vivid yellow flowers. Before entering the clouds, I caught a final glimpse of Pasto a few thousand feet below. Above the red tile roofs, wisps of smoke drifted from the chimneys.

The convoy parked at a small, stucco police station perched on the rim surrounding the volcano's amphitheater. I'd stood here many times: Standing at the police post, you gaze down at the active volcano, its crater lip 300 feet below. In the center of the amphitheater rises the present cone of Galeras, 1,500 feet in diameter, and in its center, 450 feet above the amphitheater floor, is the active crater. To get from the police post to the crater you descend the declivitous wall of the old volcano, with its layers of hardened lava at the top and scree at the bottom. Then you cross 150 feet of amphitheater floor before reaching the cone, whose scree slope rises at a 45-degree angle. An old wooden soccer goal sits in pieces at the base of the cone, placed there by soldiers who once played on what was undoubtedly the world's most dangerous soccer field.

The 16 of us—13 scientists, a two-man Colombian television crew, and our driver from the observatory, Carlos Estrada—moved to the lip of the scarp. Geoff Brown checked his gravimeter. Igor Menyailov peeked into his box of sampling tubes. José Arlés Zapata made the sign of the cross. Around 10 a.m. we began to descend the amphitheater wall, holding on to a thick, yellow nylon rope for the initial 100-foot drop. The clouds were still dense, and after a few dozen yards the rope disappeared into a gray void.

Our group consisted of four teams. Igor and Nestor García would sample gases in and around the crater. Geoff, accompanied by Colombians Fernando Cuenca and Carlos Trujillo, would check the gravity levels around the cone and the crater rim. Americans Mike Conway and Andy Macfarlane and Ecuadoran geochemist Luis LeMarie were going to insert temperature probes, known as thermocouples, into the fumaroles. Andy Adams from New Mexico's Los Alamos National Laboratory and Guatemalan Alfredo Roldán, along with Colombian Fabio García, would reconnoiter the volcano for later research on its magmatic fluids. I was overseeing the trip.

Our group spent about 90 minutes at the main fumarole, called Deformes, about 30 feet down the cone, as Igor meticulously collected gases in double-chambered bottles. Then he moved up to the lip of the crater and watched as Igor and Nestor descended the sheer sides of the volcano's mouth. Geoff's team circled the rim.

By 1 p.m. I was itching to get off the volcano. We'd been on Galeras for more than three hours. I like to wrap up work on Andean volcanoes by early afternoon, before heavy clouds roll in. The Colombian TV crew had left earlier, as had Fabio García and Carlos Estrada, and now Adams and Roldán started down the cone. At the top of my lungs I yelled to Igor that it was time to clear out.

"How are the samples," I hollered.

"Good," he yelled back. "Not *govno.*"

Govno is Russian for "shit." Igor had taught me the word, and he was smiling as he saw me catch the meaning. Squatting next to the fumarole, a cigarette dangling from his lips, Igor talked with Nestor and packed up his bottles. They shouted that they would rest a minute while Igor smoked, and then they would go.

José Arlés was standing next to me on the crater rim, checking in by radio with the observatory in Pasto. He was helping me organize the field trip, and I liked having him by my side. A 35-year-old with black hair that fell over his forehead, José Arlés had been on Galeras countless times, and I was reassured by his ritual of communicating with the observatory. Time and again, the staff there told him that the eight seismic stations around Galeras showed no hint of unusual activity.

José Arlés and I rounded up the others, three tourists, who had hiked up to see what we were doing, stood a few feet away. Suddenly, a rock tumbled off the inside wall of the crater. Then a second rock clattered down the crater mouth, and then a third, and soon a cascade of stones and boulders rained onto the door of the volcano. It was either an earthquake or an eruption.

"Hurry up! Get out!" I shouted in English and Spanish. I vaguely remember seeing Geoff Brown on the opposite rim and gesturing at him to flee. I remember looking down and seeing Igor and Nestor scrambling to get out of the crater. (My surviving colleagues contend I could not have seen such a thing, since, they say, I had already started down the cone.) After that I remember turning. I remember running madly downhill, the world reduced to jouncing boulders and scree. I had no idea where my colleagues were, saw nothing but the charcoal universe of the cone.

Then there was a hellish, ear-shattering *boom!* as the earth blew apart and Galeras disgorged its contents, ejecting tons of rock and ash. Instantly, a fusillade of red- and white-hot stones—some the size of tennis balls, some the size of large TV sets—sizzled through the air. Protecting my head with my backpack, I raced down the ragged gray flank of the cone.

I did not get far.

I have heard that time slows down in a disaster, that for some it even stands still. For me, nothing was further from the truth. Everything moved at warp speed. The crater was roaring, the volcano throbbing, the air crackling with shrapnel. My mind seemed to blow a fuse. After a few seconds, however, something instinctual took charge. I flew down the slope, my only impulse to put as much distance between me and the crater as possible.

Then the rock hit me. It was as if someone had taken a swing at my head with a baseball bat, rudely interrupting my progress. The projectile, probably no bigger than an orange, struck with such force that I was knocked a few feet sideways and crumpled. The blow landed just above my left ear; it caved in my skull, I later learned, driving several bone fragments into my brain. Stunned, I lay on the slope, my head ringing, the air still bellowing. Bomblets from the volcano, many more than a yard in diameter, shattered when they hit the earth, flinging out red-hot, hissing fragments.

I had made it no more than 20 yards from the crater's lip. Pulling myself to my feet, I looked to the side and noticed, just a few yards away, a vivid patch of yellow set against the lead-gray flank of the volcano. It was, I realized, the body of José Arlés Zapata. His head was bloody, his body contorted. His radio lay smashed beside him. Not far away, the three tourists were splayed across the field of scree. Bloodied and disfigured, they too were dead.

My backpack was now on fire. I managed to run a few more yards before a barrage of rocks cut me off at the legs, knocking me down once more. Rolling on my side, I looked down. A bone protruded from my lower left leg, poking through my torn. smoldering pants. Another projectile had nearly severed my right foot at the ankle; my boot dangled by a skein of tendons and flesh. I stared at my mangled legs and thought it odd that I didn't feel more pain.

There was no hope of supporting any weight on my right leg, so I tried to pull myself up on my left, which still had one bone intact. Wobbling, I rose to a crouch and teetered there. Bent in two, I lifted my eyes and saw a roiling, black plume of ash and debris ascending into the sky.

In seconds I fell on my face once more. This time I knew I was down for good. The eruption, only a few minutes old, was still going full bore. The ground shook as Galeras underwent what turned out to be the most powerful eruption in five years. The stench of sulfur filled the air as I dragged myself across the scree and hunkered behind a dark boulder.

Then, strangely, after ten or 15 minutes, it began to rain. Drizzle mingled with the ashes, coating my head with a gray paste. Rain penetrated the holes in my jacket and pants. Galeras's shaking finally eased, and the adrenaline quit coursing through my system. Exhausted, I put my head down on the craggy slope. Stay awake, I kept telling myself. Stay awake.

When Galeras blew, roughly 75 scientists, including our team, were on field trips around the volcano—on its flanks, in the river valleys running off the mountain, in nearby towns. Besides ours, Marta Calvache's group was closest to the crater itself—perhaps 500 to 800 yards from the top. Marta was born in Galeras's shadow, and she has spent most of her professional life studying it. Her mastery of the volcano would save my life.

As soon as the eruption died down and the projectiles stopped flying, Marta and our colleague Patty Mothes bolted toward their jeep and headed up the mountain. Ash drifted down on the windshield as they sped toward the summit. At the police post, they confronted a grim scene. Volcanic bombs had knocked holes in the roof and walls.

White-hot, angular rocks littered the ground. When Patty spat on one, it hissed back at her. The volcano still thrummed, howling like a strong wind.

Andy Adams and Mike Conway—both suffering minor burns and Conway with a broken hand—had made it to the top of the scarp. Luis LeMarie, both of his legs fractured and his clavicle broken, had been helped up the last few meters by Carlos Estrada. Now Marta and Patty, joined by several other rescuers, scrambled down the amphitheater wall. The group found Andy Macfarlane, who had collapsed with a minor skull fracture about 150 yards below, and hauled him up. Then, ignoring radio warnings of another possible eruption, Marta, Patty, and the others raced across the slopes of the still-chuffing volcano in search of more survivors. Somewhere on the lower halt of the cone they found José Arlés, his skull cracked open. Patty saw the bodies of two of the tourists, their brains spilled out on the ground. And a few yards away from José Arlés, Marta spotted me. Of the rest—of Igor Menyailov and Nestor García, of Geoff Brown, Carlos Trujillo, and Fernando Cuenca—there was no sign. They had essentially been vaporized.

Six years after the eruption on Galeras I stood again at the crater's rim, scarcely recognizing the blasted pit spread out before me. The ledge on which Igor and Nestor knelt and sampled gases had disappeared. The western rim, where Geoff, Fernando, and Carlos had stood, had been partially blown away. Portions of the southwestern lip had collapsed.

As I gazed into the crater, I was struck by how tiny, in a geological sense, the fatal eruption had been. It was a mere hiccup, a blast so small that geologists decades hence will find no sign of it. Yet the eruption killed nine men, injured five others, and continues to ripple through the lives of dozens more. It nearly killed me.

What had happened? Galeras was not quiet, as we had thought, but merely plugged. The crater floor had effectively been welded shut, trapping the rising gas pressure. Eventually it gave way.

In hindsight, my colleagues and I realized that Galeras had been sending out clues—the tornillos, the screw-shaped seismographic signals indicating the slow movement of magmatic gas and fluids. Bernard Chouet, a seismologist with the U.S. Geological Survey, had noticed small numbers of them before the July 1992 eruption and had written a report stating that the same thing could happen again. He sent it to *INGEOMINAS*, the Colombian geological survey. I never saw a copy, and Chouet's Colombian colleagues, who had noticed 17 tornillos in early January 1993, never warned that this was a threat.

Only after further eruptions in 1993 did we finally come to understand that small numbers of tornillos at Galeras—even as few as one or two per day—might presage an eruption. But based on all available evidence at the time, the consensus at the observatory was that Galeras was safe.

Colleagues assured me I had done nothing wrong, that there was no way to have foreseen the eruption. What I didn't know was that a few of them had been saying quite the opposite to others, contending that I had recklessly led my colleagues to their deaths. When I first heard these accusations, I was too stunned to react. Now I shake my head in wonder. How easy it is to apply the knowledge we have now to the events of 1993. But for me, Marta, and the other scientists in Pasto, there was no such 20/20 vision. We studied the best available data. We made what looked like a sound decision. And just when we were on the cone, Galeras behaved capriciously, as natural forces are wont to do. I was fooled, and for that I take responsibility. But I do not feel guilty about the deaths of my colleagues. There is no guilt. There was only an eruption.

from Teewinot
by Jack Turner

Jack Turner (born 1942), a philosopher and a brilliant essayist (read his book The Abstract Wild), *has lived in Grand Teton National Park for more than two decades, teaching mountaineering during the summers at Exum Mountain Guides. Here we find him with three clients at the base of the Grand Tetons' Exum Ridge.*

The Exum Ridge is one of the classic climbs of North America. This narrow ledge on Wall Street ends in a bottomless chimney just short of the actual ridge. Glenn Exum jumped across this slot in his leather football shoes on July 15, 1931. He was unroped on his way up the first ascent—and the first solo ascent—of the Exum Ridge. The route is not difficult in good conditions; bad conditions are another matter. All of the guides have done the ridge in bad conditions—despite good judgment and a clear view of approaching weather. Sometimes we climb because we have strong clients and simply want the adventure; sometimes we say we will take a look, then go on because we hate the idea of retreating; sometimes the unpredictability of mountain weather simply jinxes what we do.

In any case, when things get grim, it's because of ice. Climbing in the rain is not pleasant, but it is straightforward—in Wales, they climb in the rain every day. Snow is not too bad either, since it is usually a squall and the rock is cold, so nothing sticks. Ice is a different matter.

Rime ice forms when the mountain is shrouded in cloud or fog, the water droplets are colder than 32 degrees and the wind is blowing. Feathers of rime ice grow into the wind: The stronger the wind, the longer the feathers. Rime ice is greasy, lubricating everything it touches. Climbing on it is like climbing on lard. Rime is also very beautiful. Few sights in the mountains are more grand than a steep ridge of good granite rimed with a filigree of ice crystals gleaming against the sky. Climbing on rime is always dicey, even if you are with another experienced climber; climbing on rime ice with three people who have only two days of climbing experience is mental torture.

Then there is verglas. Verglas forms when water flows over a cold surface and freezes. It is nearly always a shiny blackness darker than anything around it, so it can be avoided, if you can see it. In the dark it's hard to see it. If there is a lot of it, you can use crampons. All things considered, verglas is nicer than rime.

Since the village of Moose averages only thirty frost-free days a year and the mountain is a mile and a half higher, I imagine there are only several weeks a year when the upper mountain doesn't freeze. So if we have rain or cloud cover when it's cold, we have ice.

Williams and I continue to wait at the alcove. It does not look good: clouds swirling everywhere, lenticular clouds over the peaks. Directly to the south of us the Middle Teton glows in the muted light of dawn. Clouds sail over the Saddle, then beneath us, making the exposure even more noticeable, about a thousand-foot sheer drop-off—like standing on the top of the Empire State Building and peeking over the edge. Lisa and Martin are fine. Jim is tense and scared. You can always tell when someone is scared. Fear is the mind killer. They lose the finer mental abilities first: a sense of beauty, a sense of proportion, and, especially, a sense of humor.

Like, say, fighter pilots, surgeons, and hit men, climbers have a prizewinning talent for dissociating from emotion, a quality that is useful in the mountains. It is considerably less useful in relationships. As we say, when the going gets rough, the weird turn pro. That is, we dissociate. Most clients are not so blessed. As I watch the clouds build, I exercise my talent. When Kanzler arrives, I walk down Wall Street to where he's roping up.

"What do you think about the weather?" I ask.

"Spooky."

"Anything more helpful, James?"

"Yeah, well . . ." What follows is a technical discourse with big words I don't understand. I'm impressed.

"How in the hell do you know all that by looking around?"

"No big deal. I did a complete weather analysis yesterday for Doug Chabot [another Exum guide] so he wouldn't get fried on the north face. I think it's going to be weird this morning, then clear, then come back tonight. The main storm is north of us."

"Really. Well, I'm glad I'm not on the north face."

I yell back to Williams and he starts the lead off Wall Street. When his clients have gone, I place a large cam unit in a crack, clip it, and smile at my clients. "Civility pro. So if I fall, I won't rip you all off the ledge into the great void. Remember Civics 101?" Silence.

"Come on. I told you last night that it would look grim, and it does look grim, but it is easy. Without the exposure you wouldn't even need a rope." Silence. No one ever believes me.

And in my heart I don't blame them. I don't like the lead off Wall Street, even though it is indeed easy, even though I have climbed it many times, in high wind and no wind, in the dark and on still, sunny mornings, in the dark with a headlamp, in the dark with no headlamp, when dry, when wet with rain, when greasy with rime, when laced with verglas. I have climbed down it in snow with no belay, with and without gloves, climbed it in technical climbing shoes, running shoes, hiking boots, heavy mountaineering boots. No matter. Despite all that, the lead off Wall Street is still eerie.

I sidle across the ledge, loudly whimpering and complaining. Just before I disappear around the corner, I stop, look back, and smile. Lisa is the only one smiling back. After forty feet I reach a white triangular flake. I stand up on it with both feet, then reach up to the ledge above for several moderate handholds. I do a little pas de deux, stepping in front of my right foot with my left to smear it onto a sloping foothold. Then I stretch way off to the right with my right foot until I reach a small black foothold. I shift my weight onto the right leg, pull, grab a chock stone in the chimney, switch feet, stem tip the chimney for several moves, and exit right behind a large boulder. The feeling is not so much one of difficulty as one of vulnerability. If you fell, it would be like falling down an elevator shaft. People rarely have trouble with the move; they do have trouble looking down.

Above are twelve leads to the summit. I bring Lisa over and check that she is set up to belay correctly. Most of the time we will be belaying with sitting-hip belays in good stances, with several people climbing, several belaying—a moving chain. In the mountains, the quality of a belay position must be weighed against the factor of speed, for in the mountains speed is safety.

The eastern sky is light, the shadows beneath us fainter. Suddenly the Middle Teton glows, severe and golden under the first rays of sunlight. With the sun up, the clouds begin to dissipate.

I climb the next lead, the Golden Staircase, up some of the most beautiful rock in the Teton Range, orange and yellow rock with cups and nubbins and chicken heads and a wavy, thin flake blasted by eons of blowing ice. It is still cold. My hat is over my ears, my hood up, my hands stiff: No gloves, though. I hate climbing in gloves and don them only as a last resort.

Far to the southwest the shadow of the Grand Teton separates from the earth's greater shadow into a purple sky, a lone shadow, dark and shaped like a tooth—the mountain's ghost, I think, its shade. As it approaches, it grows larger and diffuse until it is finally just another shadow among many.

We stop so Jim can take photographs. He points the camera here and there—*snap, snap.* Chris remarks that no camera can take it all in with anything approaching the appropriate scale, not even a panoramic camera. The best one can do, I say, is paste a series of pictures together, but then the sense of severe exposure is gone, not to mention the sky above, tinged with wisps of pink cirrus. The full expanse, the grandeur, cannot be represented, only experienced.

After another belay on easy rock, we coil the ropes and walk with the coils several hundred feet up and across the ridge to the Wind Tunnel, a slit in the ridge that sucks air off the big face above Wall Street and funnels it onto the eastern side of the mountain. We move slowly in the cold; the wind blasts, battering us. I am a bit grumpy over their confusion about walking with coils, something we start teaching in basic school. When they mutter defenses, I say, "Hey, when the going gets tough, the weird turn pro." This is sufficiently opaque to make everyone pay attention.

Above the Wind Tunnel, we enter a wide gully that goes straight up the mountain just to the east of the towers that are so prominent from the Lower Saddle. The mountain opens to us. The ridge above is sunlit; there is light instead of humbling darkness, a feeling of refuge instead of exposure. We climb five leads up the right side of the gully, easy leads with good belays. The sixth pitch, called the Double Cracks, takes us into the sun. We have traversed left out of the gully to the edge of the huge face above Wall Street, left the place of trolls and entered the place of elves. In the sun, climbing becomes friendly.

The next lead is the crux of the climb, the Friction Pitch. Since we are right at the edge of a ridge several thousand feet up in the air, there is a heightened sense of exposure. The lead goes up this airy face of cups and small nubbins to a series of platforms marvelously overhanging the void to the west. The climbers in the team can't see one another, and this makes things even more scary. The lead is long and hard to protect, since there are few cracks for nuts or cams. Most guides climb it without protection and anchor at the top. When I clip in, I always sigh with relief.

Looking down on a party climbing up to these platforms is the finest view on the Exum Ridge. The rock arches right over space, the climbers in bright Gore-Tex hues are in the sun on yellowish rock, while 2,500 feet below is the Middle Teton Glacier with its crevasses and bergschrunds.

If the wind is blowing hard—as it often is—the lead is a fine line between being careful on something one has climbed many times and sheer terror at the possibility of being blown off. One grips close to the rock in precisely the manner that we forbid beginners to do in basic class. Your body instinctively seeks a position with no air between you and the rock, because the wind is now more dangerous than gravity.

On one occasion the wind blew so hard on the Friction Pitch that I bit a nubbin of rock while I moved my right hand to the next hold. A young lady from Southern Methodist University was behind me on the rope that day. She was a fine athlete, but was inclined to comment on every difficulty. I belayed her up. About thirty feet beneath me, she froze. "I can't do this," she yelled.

I was silent.

"I can't do this!"

"Well," I yelled, "you have to do it, because we can't go down."

Eventually she would tire of being in that exposed position. The gusts would pound her. She would become desperate and try something, anything. I yanked on the rope.

Louder: "I can't do this."

"You must!"

"I do not. My daddy can come get me with a helicopter."

Spoken like a true southern lady, but false: no daddy, no helicopter.

I waited for her to accept the reality of her situation. There is a point at which one cannot turn back. As Rilke says in another context, this is the point that must be reached, the threshold where something real and important is at stake, the threshold that leads to magic. In climbing, the source of the magic is this: *You can't be bored and scared at the same time.* Even though you are standing on sloping holds over thousands of feet of air, eventually you will get bored and try something, *anything.* And then the magic: The mind lets go; the will leaps forward.

After a few more minutes she climbed up. The gusts were so grim, I didn't even tease her about the helicopter. We lay against the rock with our bodies bent away from the wind, entwined in an intimacy of necessity, the withering blasts humbling all sense of propriety. After she tied off to the anchor, I jerked on the rope attaching her to the next climber as hard as I could: no one could hear signals that day.

But today the wind is mild, the Friction Pitch is mellow, and everyone climbs rapidly. We stop to drink and snack and admire the airy spectacle. Like most clients these days, my gang is loaded down with high-tech goodies: PowerBars, Clif Bars, and various treats offering large amounts of protein. I refuse their offers. To bite into a PowerBar when it is cold is to chomp into a serious adhesive, like those that hold airplanes together. It affixes to your molars with alarming tenacity. Try to release its grip and you risk your crowns, your fillings, that funky old wisdom tooth. Tearing it off is like ripping a chunk out of Levi's with your teeth. Clif Bars are no better, but for different reasons: They are best left to heartier species of ungulates. And protein? By the time your body can use the protein, you will be back in your car; then, if you are smart, you will be powering Mexican beer, chips, and green salsa as you drive to the nearest pizza joint. I expound on these matters while I eat my Snickers bar—one of the great achievements of Western civilization.

We wander upward for several hundred yards, walking and scrambling in coils. We belay one lead up a smooth slab of rock named the Unsoeld Variation, then walk in coils again to a dark, wet chimney best climbed by jamming one's hands in cracks above one's head. Lisa and Martin do great; Jim is still a bit shaky. Now he's worrying about getting off the mountain, even though he still hasn't made it to the top. Chronic worriers love climbing mountains—so many things to worry about, most of them fatal.

Two more easy leads and we are on the summit ridge with glorious views all around. Then we scramble along in coils toward the summit, now only several hundred yards off to the northeast. The weather is clear, only puffy clouds on the horizon. We've been lucky.

Like everyone who works outdoors, climbers develop an exquisite sensitivity to weather, constantly guessing and predicting, shuffling variables, learning.

Fifteen years ago, I was less lucky on this ridge. A mean thunderhead approached us from the west that day; however, I could see sunlight beyond it, so I thought it was a narrow storm. But it was huge. An anvil-shaped mass probably 30,000 feet high stretched south for forty miles; the jet stream raked its cap, throwing shreds of false cirrus in its path. Lightning bounced around in it like pool balls.

The wind was from the west, but the cloud was moving north. I could not tell from the wind alone where the storm would go, because the mountains funnel and shift air currents and hence wind direction. I was a bit worried, but I guessed the storm would pass to the northwest. I was wrong. Suddenly the top of the mountain became charged with electricity and the rock buzzed like a million flies working a windowpane.

I cannot recall if we went to the summit or not; I think not. Somehow we scuttled off the ridge onto the descent route and managed to get down a section of slabs before the storm hit. We untied the wet ropes and coiled them; we put on all our clothes. I told everyone to crouch, feet together, allowing only one point of contact with the ropes or packs. We crouched on our exposed ledge at 13,500 feet and waited.

Normally we view clouds in two dimensions. This thunderstorm arrived as a layered three-dimensional mass six miles high. Seven thousand feet below us, bluish lines of squalls dumped rain across the valleys. The layer level with us was chaotic with disturbance, a maw of whirling vapors and faintly greenish light. Above us, mature cumulonimbus bulged like muscles; higher yet, ribbons of cirro-stratus disintegrated like spiraled nebula. The world became lurid, apocalyptic—the mise-en-scène of opera. Visibility dropped to fifty feet. My climbing gear hummed in tune with minute halos of fuzzy sparks covering every metal surface. The rock buzzed in varying frequencies, like alarms.

Just before the cloud cover closed over us, a lightning bolt hit a glacier and turned it green. The world dimmed, the wind grew fierce, and graupel stung our faces and hands so hard that we shoved our hands into our armpits and put our heads to our knees. One of the men in my party asked if there was anything else we could do—the last clutch for control.

"You might try prayer," I replied. "We all have to die sometime. This is as good a place as any." All climbing humor is black humor, the joke of no control, the levity of fate.

Instantly—how else?—a light appeared in the cloud, looking and sounding like a big sparkler at a Fourth of July celebration. A bolt of lightning hit the ridge 200 feet above us. Several of us bounced in the air and landed on our elbows and knees in the talus. We scrambled back into our positions, wordless with terror. I noticed I was twitching, whether from fear or electricity, I do not know. The air stank of sulfur.

We waited. The wind dropped, then resumed, blowing hard from the south. I remembered the forty-mile-long train of cumulus. Ground currents from lightning strikes on the ridge hit us four times in twenty-five minutes. It snowed four inches. Still we waited.

Moving would be worse: The shocks could knock us off while we were climbing; the cracks and chimneys below us were streaming with water, which provided a natural conductor for electricity; and being tied together with a wet rope in such conditions is plain stupid.

In Cascade Canyon, 7,000 feet below us, the storm was so severe it closed the Exum climbing schools for the day. For a while it stopped the boats from crossing Jenny Lake. Two climbing parties below us on the Exum Ridge suffered burns.

Finally the dull grayness of our cloud lightened and the edge of the storm arrived, ragged with billowing gauzy clouds. The sky changed so fast from sun to mist the effect was kaleidoscopic. Then we broke clear. The sky was pure lapis lazuli and filled with speeding columns of cumulus—facing them was like being blown through a temple in the sky.

Squalls filled the valleys to the west. To the south, another thunder-head moved slowly toward us. We climbed down toward the rappel anchor on the Owen Route that would put us on the Upper Saddle and off the top of the mountain. We tied into one wet rope, close together, and moved cautiously, belaying often. Where it was too steep to hold the snow, the wet rocks gleamed like quicksilver beneath the glare of the sun. The world seemed fresh, newly minted. The climbing was slick, scary. As always in such situations, I retreated into the climber's sanctuary—dissociation and method.

The black wall kept coming. It hit us as we reached the rappel point. More graupel, lightning, snow, blasts of wind. We turned away from it, bending into the stone wall as if, finally, in prayer. Again we waited. The second storm passed. I belayed the four men as they rappelled to the Upper Saddle. No one spoke. As Flannery O'Connor said, "Nothing produces silence like experience."

The fates had touched us lightly and withdrawn, leaving us with the freedom and glory of life. We were overjoyed but also too humbled to talk—it might anger the gods.

The summit of the Grand Teton is on the northeast corner of the summit block, amid shattered blocks of gneiss. We can see for 100 to 150 miles in every direction, each horizon rimmed by mountain ranges. To the east, the Absaroka, Gros Ventre, and Wind River; to the south, the Salt River, Snaky, and Caribou; to the west, the Big Hole and the Lost River; and to the north, the Centennial, Madison, Gallatin, and Beartooth. Directly north is the blur of a geyser somewhere near Old Faithful, fifty-two miles away, in Yellowstone.

Everyone is happy. Lisa, Jim, and Martin are happy because they have achieved their goal. I'm happy because it is only 8:15—they have climbed rapidly and well—and the sky is clear.

Williams leaves for the rappel just as we arrive. Kanzler arrives on top a few minutes later. Everyone is taking photographs—of all of us in all possible combinations. I crawl down to a little ledge east of the summit, wanting a few minutes alone. In the parking lot 7,000 feet below, the windshields of our cars sparkle like tiny mirrors. Beside me are a few tufts of grass, fescue. I slice and eat an apple; I munch on cashews; I enjoy the clarity and count shades of blue as the sky pales into the distant mountains.

Despite the breadth of view, I always feel the summit is a place of great simplicity; but at 13,770 feet above sea level, one's perspective changes. Like the view from an airplane, one sees things that are invisible at ground level; but unlike the keyhole view from an airplane window, this view is expansive and whole, without artificial boundaries. Nor is one sealed in a machine, watching the scenery pass like a tracking shot in a movie and enduring the cacophony of roaring engines. The view from the Grand Teton is panoramic and embedded in silence, both of which invite reflection.

Here all the senses are clear, heightened, and vitally alive, for to reach this summit one uses the body, and in the face of perceived danger the senses grow keen, increasing one's chances of survival. One feels exulted, flushed with joy; the word *exult* is from the Latin *exultare*, "to spring out," and we have sprung free of the quotidian.

Like the perspective of earth that spacecraft provide from outer space, the view from the summit enhances some forms and diminishes others. The most obvious change is in boundaries. Most of the man-made boundaries—for example, the lines demarcating states, countries, city limits, private property, national forests, game refuges, and water districts—are diminished, though they do not disappear. Natural boundaries—for example, the patterns of vegetation and topology that emerge due to water, wind, rock, soil, and temperature—are emphasized. In a way that is never true at ground level, here one *sees* watersheds and bioregions.

Since what we see influences what we think, those who spend time on summits often disagree with those whose vision reflects more limited perspectives. I do not believe it is an accident that many leaders of modern conservation and bioregional movements—John Muir, David Brower, Arne Naess, George Sessions, Gary Snyder—have been mountaineers.

From this vantage point, one can also discern how the land has been affected by man. The land immediately east of the Grand Teton—peaks, canyons, and much of the plain surrounding the Snake River—is protected by the park. West of the Grand Teton is the Jedediah Smith Wilderness, part of Targhee National Forest. Farther west is the Teton

Valley or Pierre's Hole, the place Jim Bridger thought was the finest valley in the American West. Ranching, farming, and logging have chopped it into squares; now it looks like someone took a knife to the face of a beautiful woman. East and south sit the communities of Moran, Moose, Kelly, Jackson, and Wilson, with their junctures of highways and dense human populations. From this bird's-eye view, the explanatory principle is simple: What was protected by a handful of nature's patrons and the federal government remains beautiful; what was not protected has been forever despoiled for the benefit of a few.

Rosy finches arrive and wander about my feet. They are black, with a gray crown and patches of dusty rose about the belly, rump, and wings. Rosy finches are a true mountain resident, loving steep cliffs and snowfields, though in the winter they descend into the valley, often in large flocks.

What do they eat? What are they doing up here? The air up here is by no means empty. As naturalist David Lukas asks us to contemplate: "Consider that the atmosphere over a single square mile of the earth's surface contains twenty-five million airborne insects. Consider that the fraction of organic detritus that falls out of orbit can become thick enough to plow. Consider that within a very tall, imaginary top hat, fifty to one hundred million microorganisms swirl above your head." The air is just another ecosystem, one that seems to favor spiders especially—flying spiders, spider legs, pieces of spiders. And there are indeed spiders on top of the Grand Teton.

I assume shrews are on the mountain, though I have seen one only once, and that was lower down—near the Upper Saddle. I assume it was a dwarf shrew, since they are the only shrew likely to be this high. Dwarf shrews are tiny, only three inches in length, and can weigh less than half an ounce. They are the smallest mammal in North America and they are rare. Between 1895 and 1960, only eighteen specimens were known from their entire range; as recently as 1989, only thirty-seven specimens had been trapped in the entire Greater Yellowstone ecosystem.

I look down the East Ridge for marmots, pikas, and pine martens.

I've seen their tracks here, and over the years I have spotted two between the Upper and Lower Saddles; there is nothing today but the beautiful cornice at the top of the ridge.

No one knows what lives up here in winter, but when Jack Tackle and Alex Lowe reached the summit after completing the first winter ascent of the north ridge, they found it covered with tracks and an animal they believe was a fisher was wandering off down the west face toward the rappel!

When I'm on top of the Grand Teton, I always look and listen for white pelicans, though I've seen them only twice during the thirty-odd years I've climbed this mountain, and both times I've heard them before seeing them. The sounds are faint, so faint that they are sometimes lost—a trace of clacking in the sky. It is even harder to see them. Tiny glints, like slivers of ice, are occasionally visible, them invisible, then visible again as the sheen of their feathers strikes just the right angle to the sun. With binoculars you can see them clearly: Usually they are soaring in a tight circle far above the summit. Since this summit is 13,770 feet high, and in good light a flock of white pelicans is easily visible at a mile, the pelicans were at least a mile above us, or higher than 19,000 feet. This seems high for any bird, but geese have been photographed at 29,000 feet, and I have watched flocks of Brahminy ducks from Siberia cross the ridge between Everest and Cho Oyu, which is 19,500 feet at its low point. So although 19,000 feet is impressive, and no one knows how high pelicans can or do fly, the more interesting question is this: What are they *doing* up there? Soaring. Clacking. Yes, but why? I don't think anybody knows.

I have also seen them from the summit of Symmetry Spire and from the long ridge on Rendezvous Mountain. But it is rare—in part, I think, because the conditions for hearing and seeing them are so rare. Perhaps they are often above us, but with the wind and clouds and the ever-present anxiety of climbing, we fail to notice them.

After half an hour on the summit, we leave. The weather holds for us and the descent is uneventful. We scramble several hundred feet down the Owen Route at the top of the west face, then belay three short leads in Sargent's Chimney before scrambling several more hundred feet down to the rappel.

The rappel off the Grand Teton is another spooky place. Technically, it is straightforward: The first half is on steep rock; the last half is in midair. The landing area is roomy, the distance only a hundred feet. However, the ledge approaching the rappel anchor is narrow and filled with rubble that funnels into overhanging cracks: Anything knocked off can hit people below. Further, you can't see the bottom of the rappel from the start, though it is obvious it will take you down to the safety of the Upper Saddle. Instinctively the eye wanders northwest to the icy chutes at the top of the Black Ice Couloir, a difficult climb that drops 3,000 feet into Valhalla Canyon. There is no sunlight on this side of the mountain yet, either; it's cold again, and the wind always blows here. Often a line of climbers are waiting to get off the mountain. The stress builds.

Today there is no line and Williams has left a rope hanging for me. I belay my group without a hitch. It is not always so. To face a storm here is always wild. We are on a ledge at the side of a notch near the summit of an isolated mountain. The notch accelerates the wind, the ledge is on the west-southwest side of the mountain, right in the path of storms.

I usually anchor, tie off the rappel rope, carefully lap it into several hanks, and throw it as hard as I can straight down the cliff. Sometimes during a windy storm this doesn't work. Even though the rope is soaked with water, it drifts downward slowly; then it stops and uncoils into the air like an enormous snake before the next gust blows it back up the cliff, sometimes thirty feet past me into the rocks above. Sometimes another guide rappels first to get the rope down; other times, we just lower clients to the ground. In any case, the bottom of the rappel is another one of those places on the mountain that always bring a sigh of relief.

When we are all down, I coil the rope and take them down to the Upper Saddle proper for a good look down the Black Ice Couloir. Some people just can't believe Mark Newcomb and Stephen Koch have gone down there on skis and a snowboard. There are days when I don't believe it, either.

Just above us to the west is the summit of the Enclosure. The first ascent party found a ring of upturned black rocks on the summit, an obviously artificial arrangement that has led to speculations that it is everything from an American Indian vision-quest site to an entrance for little purple people who live under the mountain and have, let us say, a mysterious relationship to the Essences and certain Christian saints. I am inclined to the former interpretation. Lisa and Jim want to see it, so we dump our packs and scramble several hundred feet to the summit. The view of the Grand is great: You can see the Exum Ridge from the side and look straight at the Owen Route, our descent route, the route taken by the first ascent party, and the most popular route on the mountain.

Lisa, Jim, and Martin sit in the ring of black stones while I take their picture. Then I tell them a story about the huge face that drops off to the north so sharply you don't even notice it's there until you wander a few feet in that direction. Then you have the urge to sit down. The north face of the Enclosure is a great shield of rock that is home to the hardest routes in the Teton Range, routes that are cold, lonely, and rarely climbed. I've been on the north side of the Enclosure only six times in all these years, and it has always been an adventure.

On August 6, 1969, George Lowe, Leigh Ortenburger, and I bush-whacked up Valhalla Canyon, following a supposed trail that Orten-burger found, then lost, then found again. He knew, in his Ortenburgerish way, of a small, obscure shelf on the east side of Val-halla, snug against the big northwest face of Mount Owen, where there was space for three people to sleep—I call it Ortenburger's Ledge. It is, I swear, the only flat place in Valhalla Canyon. I doubt if anyone but Ortenburger even dreamed, much less knew, of its existence. Many climbers have climbed in the Tetons for twenty years without even entering Valhalla, much less spending the night. And for good reason— the upper sections are dark and ominous. Some never see sunlight.

Two ice routes—the Black Ice Couloir and the Enclosure Couloir—had been climbed by a few parties, including Exum guides Al Read, Peter Lev, and Herb Swedlund, but the big buttress between them remained untouched. Again, for good reason. It looked more like a buttress in Yosemite than anything in the Tetons: It was smooth and broken only by a system of chimneys and cracks that were wet, icy, and the wrong size—what we call offwidths. An off-width is too big to jam any part of your body into and too small to use the technique known as chimneying—back on one side, feet on the other—the way kids scamper up doorjambs in the kitchen.

Leigh knew every major route left to climb in these mountains—he was, after all, the author of the climbing guide to the range. He knew the north face of the Enclosure was one of the best unclimbed routes. He also knew it was going to be over his head—thus he badgered me and George to accompany him. He had recruited us, but it was his vision, his will that led us to a bivouac on that ludicrous ledge, studying what was obviously a very serious piece of work. Leigh was, in his usual elfish manner, delighted to be there—he was delighted to be anywhere in the mountains. I squinted at the buttress and thought, What a mean-looking son of a bitch. We ate dinner and crashed. At least the weather looked good.

We left the next morning as soon as it was light enough to move, traversing up and right toward the junction of the Back Ice and Enclosure couloirs. For a while, we had scree and easy slab climbing, but eventually we hit sheets of ice. We stopped; out came the ice gear. At that point it was obvious we faced a generation gap.

George and I had 70cm Chouinard ice axes with hickory handles and drooped picks. Leigh carried something that might have been taken up the Matterhorn in 1865: It was long, the pick was straight, and it had a wrist loop, for God's sake. Yvon Chouinard, the patron saint of American ice climbing, had said, quoting a French maxim, "He who drops his ax deserves to die." I was prepared to die in the best French fashion—hence no wrist loop. Leigh and George wore hard hats; I was bare-headed. But then I had scars on my head; they didn't.

Our crampons were also different. George and I had rigid chromium-molybdenum Chouinard crampons with front points filed to razor sharpness. Leigh wore hinged, soft-metal Grivel crampons that were about as sharp as erasers. Worse, he had cut the stitching out of the back of his ancient boots to make room for his bone spurs. His pants were baggy—probably army surplus—and his checked shirt made him look like a Maine canoe guide. Climbing across the slabs of ice, he seemed a figure out of World War II. But could he cut steps! The ax moved effortlessly, the ice chips flew, and he progressed with the grace and the precision of a master craftsman. I did not know how to cut steps; given my equipment, I didn't need to, but I wish now I had learned from him.

In short, Leigh's spirit was marvelous, his technique superb, his equipment antique. Unfortunately, the route above us could not be climbed with antique equipment.

When the time came to cross the Black Ice Couloir proper, it was George's lead. I belayed; he led it with no protection, standing on his front points with one gloved hand on the 50-degree ice and the other hand on the top of his ax, the pick at waist level. I followed in the same fashion. Leigh cut steps. I teased him, and he teased me back. It had always been that way between us.

We continued up the Enclosure Couloir until we reached the base of the buttress. Leigh made short work of the first lead, which ended behind a pillar. I led the next pitch over an overhang, where I used two pitons for direct aid, and up into the main crack system. I climbed past a big chock stone into the wet and slightly icy off-width crack and arranged a hanging belay (standing in web stirrups) from several shallow, tied-off pitons on the left side of the crack. I was freaked out. The weather was collapsing, I didn't like my belay, the next lead looked grim, and everywhere I looked I saw white shafts dropping straight into Valhalla, not a propitious spot for those of the heroic persuasion. I was glad it was George's turn to lead.

The memory of George's lead that day still makes my heart sing. Off-widths are not fun under the best of circumstances, but there he was, in heavy, rigid boots and a down parka, climbing rapidly up a hard, icy, wet shaft at over 12,000 feet. He tried to get in protection but couldn't. Finally he was out 80 feet, with no protection. I was standing in slings, with the rope clipped to the highest piton and circling my waist—these were the days before climbing harnesses and belay devices. He thrashed a bit, he rested, breathing hard, and then he thrashed some more—thrashing being intrinsic to off-widths. He stemmed, he jammed his elbows, and he canted his boots sideways in the crack. The lead went on and on. Finally he was up.

My turn. I clipped my pack to a sling hanging from my waist and went at it. Same thing: thrash, thrash, rest, thrash, thrash, rest. During hard climbing, the world shrinks to touch, pressure, kinesthetics. The mind is not separate from these. Your body is doing so many things at the same time that separate intentions merge, and at the most difficult points, surrender to the body's memory, a body that is smarter than your mind. It was indeed a hard lead, but I managed to climb it without a fall. I was terribly pleased with myself.

There was not much time for self-congratulation, however. The next lead looked just as hard—another off-width. Since Leigh was still below, I took the rack from George and kept going. It was cold. The sky was black with sooty clouds that had been building since noon. We were going to get nailed.

I climbed a ways until I reached a nice ledge. There were more ledges above, but I couldn't see them. I decided to wait until everyone was up and we could attempt a meeting of minds. When they arrived, we didn't need a meeting: The weather had collapsed— high winds, graupel, the usual. As Leigh was pulling his rain parka out of his pack, we were hit by a fierce blast that knocked him down. The parka flew into the storm like a crazed bird. We huddled together. I had on a double-layered French down parka and a rubberized French cagoule that came down past my knees. My feet were thrust into my pack, boots on but unlaced—after reading how Herzog lost his boots on Annapurna, I never take off my boots on a climb. George was arrayed in similar fashion; Leigh was going primitive.

It started to rain hard, driving rain that did not stop. We told stories, nibbled at food, and waited.

In the last light I looked down into the dreary space of cold rock and steep ice and wondered again, Why am I here? What possible chain of events could lead to this absurd moment? Ortenburger—it was his fault. I sent forth my best blast of excoriating vituperation. Leigh smiled. He loved it.

The temperature dropped rapidly; the water on the rock turned to ice. Snow fell; the wind blew. It was a long night, but we managed to catnap in the midst of chaos.

Waking at dawn was like waking up inside a freezer. The world was white with snow, rime ice, and verglas. It was clear, the storm gone. When we could see, we put on crampons and began to rappel down the route. Alas, we soon discovered that ice had filled the cracks, making it hard to place pitons. Finally we reached a point where we simply couldn't place pitons. George had a large triangular nut slung with a single piece of 9mm rope. We clipped two carabiners into it and reversed the gates so the rappel ropes would pull cleanly—it was not a place to hang your ropes.

Nuts were still relatively new in 1969 and more traditional climbers didn't yet trust them. And rappelling off a single nut—or any single anchor—is not something one likes doing. In Climbing 101, you learn never to rappel off a single anchor. Nonetheless . . . what to do? Leigh let us know in no uncertain terms that he was *not* going to rappel off a single anchor, especially a single nut, more especially yet a single *British* nut. We teased and argued. Leigh couldn't imagine how George and I had made it to graduate school.

Finally George went; then I followed. The argument was that since I was a good deal bigger than Leigh, if the nut held me, it would hold him. It did. We pulled the ropes and rappelled again into the Black Ice Couloir.

Rock along the edge of a couloir is often fractured and loose. The spot we landed on was no exception. We placed four or five pitons and tied them all off with a web of nylon slings. We were all a bit freaked: Although the rappel was short—we doubled one rope—it was not going to be easy. We would have to rappel at a roughly 45-degree angle across steep ice to reach the only point of rock in the area. We didn't have the anchors for rappelling off ice, so we had to reach that rock. I belayed; George rappelled with a friction device constructed from carabiners. He held the rope in one hand, his ice ax in the other, and reversed the technique we used climbing up. It was dicey. If he fell, he would, despite my belay, pendulum across the couloir into a rock wall—an unpleasant prospect. Also, the sun was up, warming the summits above us and loosening chunks of ice and rock. Soon they were roaring down the couloir, whistling as they passed. I pondered my bias against hard hats while Leigh lectured me on the fragility of the human skull.

As always, George made it look easy. Soon he had a good anchor in the rock outcrop. Since Leigh's crampons were so dull, we decided to belay him from both sides. Also, Leigh was addicted—it is the only word—to rappelling without a friction device. Instead, he wrapped the rappel ropes between his legs, around his hip, across his chest, over his shoulder, and down his back—where he held on to it with one hand. This does indeed provide a lot of friction, but it is rather hard on the crotch. I reminded Leigh that the body rappel had led to the decline of the Austro-Hungarian Empire.

I was worried, because when one rappels at an angle in a body rappel, the force is not up into the body, but across the upper leg. This throws one off balance. Sure enough, right in the middle of the couloir, Leigh flipped upside down, coming completely out of his rappel ropes. His hard hat came off and bounced several thousand feet in long arcs down the Black Ice Couloir toward Valhalla. Hanging upside down and belayed from both sides, Leigh looked like a slam dancer doing a jig. His ice ax hung from his wrist loop, though, and I decided right then and there to forever abandon French maxims as a guide to life.

George and I were amused, Leigh less so. He cursed me in particular because we kept a list of one another's mistakes and foibles. George pulled, I let out rope, and Leigh finally reached the anchor.

I rappelled across the couloir belayed from below as occasional chunks of ice clattered down the face.

Once we were all on the rock outcrop, a cloud lifted from our minds. We were off, free. After another rappel and some scrambling, we reached Valhalla, the Hall of the Brave. But we were alive, we saw no Valkyries, and we did not dine with Odin.

We left a fortune's worth of gear on that route. Several weeks later, George went back with Exum guide Mike Lowe and completed it—not least to collect all the iron we had left. We had climbed the crux leads, but there was still lots of hard climbing to the summit.

When completed, the Lowe Route was the hardest route in the Tetons; thirty years later, it remains among the hardest. Exum guide Jim Donini and his friend Rick Black are the only team to have climbed it since then—twice. The second time, Donini led the whole route without direct aid—a remarkable achievement. To my knowledge, the Lowe Route has not been climbed since 1977.

Leigh was the great elder of our Teton climbing tribe. No one was respected more. At the time of our climb he was forty years old, much older than we were, a mathematician who worked all year at an office job. I guided all summer; I climbed frozen waterfalls and hard rock during the winter. George was a climbing ranger and among the most talented climbers of his generation. The apex of his long and brilliant career was the first ascent of the great Kangshung face on Everest. Because George led the hard leads, the most difficult section is known as the Lowe Buttress. But as we descended Valhalla and Cascade Canyons in that giddy summer long ago, Leigh walked us youngsters right into the ground. And of course he teased us about it. We loved him.

The descent from the Upper to the Lower Saddle is circuitous, but if you know the route, it's easy. Most of the time we scramble down a trail, but there are two steep, exposed cliffs where we rope up again.

Because Lisa is the strongest climber, I send her down first. I bring up the rear.

At 12,500 feet, in cracks and sheltered depressions, we find flowers again: yellow draba, purple saxifrage, the ubiquitous alpine smelowskia, and, lower down, smelly sky pilot. Martin wants to take pictures, so we stop, strip off extra clothes, and drink the last of our water. The morning cold is a distant memory; now it is so hot, I'm back to shorts and my Hawaiian shirt.

We cross the Black Dike and follow the trail down to the hut. It is noon, the sun absurdly hot. The wind is blowing; the clouds are coming back—Kanzler was right yet again. I wash dishes, eat lunch. I take my usual dose of ibuprofen—we call them "Rocky Mountain M&M's"—then grab a bag of garbage. Time to head home. Lisa, Jim, and Martin are caught between conflicting desires: to stay at the beautiful place they worked so hard to reach, to get the long trip down over with as fast as possible, or to lie in the sun and sleep. I know we have to leave; another group of guides and clients are on their way up, so we must go down. And the sooner the better.

Our packs are light now, but we've already been at it for nine hours, and it is still eight miles and 5,000 feet back to the parking lot. When we reach the fixed rope, we are out of the wind, hot, and suddenly tired. I keep everyone moving, losing altitude, decreasing the distance over which something can happen. Going down the talus when you are this tired you can easily sprain an ankle, and I've seen people do face plants on the trail from sheer exhaustion. Afternoon thunderstorms with lightning are coming and we are exposed on fields of talus—the usual guiding situation: Hurry, hurry, hurry.

We stop briefly at Teepe Creek to refill our water bottles, then descend the steep drops to the Petzoldt Caves and the Meadows. We rest on grass beside the stream, happy to be among a rainbow of colors again. I eat a Snickers, share another with Lisa and Jim—no use carrying food out of the mountains.

The first drops of rain arrive as we traverse out of Garnet Canyon, but I do not put on my parka. The big cold drops feel too good on sunburned skin. The stone breaks, returns. Our legs become wooden, our feet swollen. The wind blows so hard we are frightened. Once four clients and I had to run the last several hundred yards of trail and out into the parking lot while perhaps a hundred trees blew down in the forest around us. Good old Wyoming. As a young woman wrote as the last entry in her diary, "God Bless Wyoming and keep it wild."

Then it is over. We drive to the Exum office and say our goodbyes. Everyone is happy. In a day or two they will return home. In a week I will barely recall their names or the little charms and riddles of our climb. I will have climbed the Grand again, perhaps twice, with other people, in other conditions. Things change. Only the mountain abides.

from Where Did It All Go Right?
by Al Alvarez

Al Alvarez (born 1929) has written well about subjects that include poetry, suicide, oil drilling, poker and mountaineering. Along the way, he picked up an addiction to adrenaline, which he indulges in this excerpt from his recent memoir.

never managed to hitch a ride with NASA and I missed my chance to learn to fly at post-war Oxford by catching the climbing bug instead of joining the RAF-sponsored flying club. But, in the end, I did get to fly in the kind of aircraft which I had yearned for and studied and made models of when I was a schoolboy—delicate, nimble machines one generation on from the Sopwith Camels my uncle Teddy had flown in the Great War.

I flew in them, though only as a passenger, with Torquil Norman, who comes from a family of fliers and has been messing around in planes since he was a kid. His father, who held one of the first pilot's licences issued in Britain and died heroically in the Second World War, flew him to Switzerland in his three-seater Leopard Moth when Torquil was just one year old. His brother Desmond, who is equally obsessed with flying (and eventually designed and produced the highly successful Britten-Norman Islander), taught him the rudiments while Torquil was still a schoolboy at Eton. Torquil got his pilot's license at 18, the minimum legal age, flew Seafires and Sea Furies with the Fleet Air Arm during his National Service and, while he was at Cambridge, spent most weekends flying Meteor jet fighters with 601 Squadron, the RAF's wild bunch (since disbanded), who jazzed up their drab uniforms with scarlet jacket linings and scarlet socks and were renowned for their rowdy parties and outrageous behaviour. He has been flying ever since whenever he could get time away from his work as founder and chairman of the board of Bluebird Toys, which was, until he retired, Britain's most successful toy manufacturer.

The planes Torquil flies are more like the planes I used to make out of balsa-wood and rice paper in my childhood than the cramped, impersonal metal tubes flown by commercial airlines. Torquil has a unique collection of ancient De Havillands, all of them 50 or 60 years old, and their only metal parts are the engines and the bearers that hold the engines in place. Everything else is a miracle of old-fashioned craftsmanship: wings, fuselages and tailplanes made of wood and covered with Irish linen, cabins kitted out like Rolls-Royces with Connolly leather, polished wood and cloth head-linings. But the machines are sturdy and reliable and, skydiving apart, flying in them is as close as you can get to a bird's three-dimensional freedom and a bird's-eye view of the earth.

In a commercial jet you know you are airborne only if you are lucky enough to be sitting by a window. Even then, all you can see from 35,000 feet is a flat carpet of clouds far below or, in clear weather, a small-scale map of the country. Torquil's planes can only climb to a few thousand feet and flying at that altitude is like being on an invisible seam between the earth and the sky. All the details below are intensely sharp: the harvest neatly stocked in the fields, a man walking his dog, a child waving from his back garden, the bright-blue swimming pool of a country house and, off in the distance, the office blocks of a town. Maybe this is what builders of luxury cars mean by 'grand touring': effortless progress across a road map, without dust or sweat or hassle, in a hand-built machine so beautifully crafted that it is itself a source of pleasure.

It is also a source of adventure, as flying itself used to be before it became just another form of boring mass transportation. Twice I have flown with Torquil from Tuscany to England in a single day—first in his Leopard Moth, then in his twin-engined Dragonfly. Neither plane could climb high enough to go over the Alps, so we went through them, threading the mountain passes, level with the seamed faces and well below the summit ridges. It was as though we had the whole range to ourselves—a private, inward experience, despite the steady roar of the engine. Moving across those bowls of rock in the little Leopard Moth, a couple of thousand feet above the valley floors, I was aware of the fragility of the aged machine and also of its sturdiness, the sureness with which it balanced on the air, the steady beat of its engine, the ingenuity and adventurousness of flight.

In the luxurious Dragonfly the flight from Arezzo to Rendcomb, in Gloucestershire, was stately and uneventful, but it was different in the Leopard Moth. We thought the leg through the Alps would be the hard part of the trip; in fact, it was merely the appetizer. The sky darkened steadily as we flew north over France. By the time we passed Amiens we had dropped from 3000 to 1000 feet, just below the clouds, and the rain was lashing down. Torquil sat up front with a map on his lap and one hand on the joy stick. He peered out at the shrouded landscape below, then back at the map, moving from side to side, tick-tock, like a metronome, and muttering to Air Traffic Control at Lydd Airport in Kent. The weather there was dreadful, he said: heavy rain and wind gusting to 30 knots. 'But we'll give it a try. If we can't make it, we'll go back to Le Touquet.'

By the time we crossed the French coast and moved out into the Channel, our altitude had dropped to 800 feet, the visibility was worse and the little plane seemed not to be making much headway against the wind. Because of the sheeting rain, there was nothing to be seen ahead through the windscreen. Torquil's metronome beat rose as he peered from side to side. From where I sat, behind him, the view was like Beckett's *Endgame*, 'Light black. From pole to pole': grey air, grey sea and great white horses rolling back towards France. So I watched the altimeter: 800 feet, 550, 400, 300, on down until the white horses seemed almost close enough to touch. Just off to our left, a huge container ship loomed out of the murk, the top of its superstructure level with our undercarriage.

After half an hour of blind man's buff there was still no sign of the English coast. Torquil shouted, 'I don't know exactly where we are' and put the plane into a wide, banking right-hand curve, until we seemed to be going in the same direction as the white horses. It's back to Le Touquet, I thought, and felt irrationally disappointed, as though the whole point of the journey had been missed: two old buffers with a secret agenda, Italy to England in one day, in a plane not much younger than we were. I knew that wasn't really the point, of course. The point was the pleasure in flying this immaculate old machine. But the bad weather had raised the ante, turning a pleasant trip into an adventure, and it seemed unfair to be beaten now, so close to home.

Five minutes later we were over land: a wide beach, tussocky dunes, pylons. England or France? I wondered. Then suddenly, Bingo! There, through the veils of rain, was the great bulk of Dungeness power station.

We landed gingerly and crabwise in the howling wind. As we taxied to a halt, the Lydd flight controller said, 'Welcome to terra firma.' 'Pleased to be here,' Torquil replied. The Leopard Moth was trembling like a whippet in the gale.

For the Customs officer, we were comic relief on a quiet day. He laughed when he saw us and went on laughing while he checked our bags. 'Had some fun, did you?'

'Piece of cake,' said Torquil, on his dignity.

'Where've you come from today?'

'Italy.'

The Customs officer's smile faded. 'Bugger me,' he said.

Later, on the train to London, Torquil said, 'Actually, I was a little doubtful when they said the wind was gusting to 30 knots.'

'Why?'

'Our stall speed is 42 knots.' He paused, then added reassuringly, 'Not that that was the real problem, of course.'

'Oh?'

'The real problem was the army firing-range at Dungeness. It was active. They had the red flags out. But the control tower told them to stop.' Another pause. 'All part of the fun,' he said.

The rat had a great meal that day, but it was as nothing compared to my first flight in Torquil's Tiger Moth. It's a trim little biplane with two open cockpits, one behind the other, a deep blue fuselage, white wings and tailplane, and struts of polished wood—every detail bright and clean and perfect. It was light enough for the two of us to manoeuvre it easily out of its hangar—we lifted it by its tail strut and pushed—and the engine started sweetly at the first swing of its propeller. We strapped ourselves in, Torquil behind, I in front. The seat harness was a four-point contraption made of three-inch khaki webbing. At the start it felt uncomfortable to be held so rigidly in place; later, when we were upside down, I was glad of it. We taxied out on to the runway, Torquil revved the engine to a pleasant roar, the plane moved forward, the tail lifted, and in less than 100 yards we were airborne. The instruments on the dashboard were minimal: an air-speed indicator, a rev counter, an altimeter, a turn-and-bank indicator, an oil-pressure gauge and a compass—ageing black dials with yellowish needles and figures. The joystick in my hands and the rudder-control pedals were linked to those in the rear cockpit, so I could follow what Torquil was doing to control the plane. My head was out in the air, the wind was in my face, the sun shone peacefully.

In an open cockpit in an English summer, you don't have to stop to smell the flowers; they come to you. At 300 feet on a warm day, great clouds of perfume envelop you as you go: mayflower from the hedges that bound each little field, wafts of pine scent from the intermittent patches of plantation. Torquil pulled back gently on the joystick. At 3000 feet we flew suddenly into cloud. One moment the clouds were above us, looking as solid as rock; the next we were moving through them at 90 miles an hour—great, softly streaming masses, as beautiful as the hair of one of Blackman's girls. Then, just as suddenly, we were out of them again in the sunlight.

The intercom was an old-fashioned air tube plugged into the head-phones of my borrowed leather flying helmet. Torquil's voice came in above the noise of the engine: 'Feel like some aerobatics? Nothing fancy.'

I nodded vigorously.

'Loop,' said the cheerful voice in my ear.

Torquil dipped the nose, then pulled back hard on the joystick. My mouth dropped open with the g force, and my stomach dropped with it. The sun, which had been obscured by the upper wing, came into view. Then the pressure on my stomach eased and we were moving downward fast. There was a blur of blue and green and yellow, which cleared slowly. I looked up and saw the fields, with their bales of hay in tidy rows, right in front of my face. I'm upside down, I thought. That's strange. I don't feel upside down. Then, still slowly, the sky was back where it should be and the horizon was steady.

'OK?'

'Terrific.'

'Right ho, then. Let's try a spin.'

Again the plane dipped and climbed, my mouth dropped open, my stomach lurched. At the top of the curve—this time I was ready for it and could see the earth clearly above my head where the sky should have been—the engine stopped and the plane seemed to hang motion-less. There was a violent movement of the rudder pedals, and suddenly we were falling in silence like a sycamore leaf, round and round, the landscape and sky spinning fast, until the plane steadied, the engine burst into life again and the world reassembled itself.

There was a third manoeuvre, a barrel roll, during which, I learned later, the aeroplane spirals like a corkscrew. I couldn't make that out at the time, because my stomach was rolling faster than the barrel and my mouth had dropped open so wide I thought it would unhinge itself. All I saw was a spinning vortex of sky and ground.

'Sorry about that,' Torquil said over the intercom. 'Bit untidy.'

The loop, the spin and the barrel roll are formal procedures—three of a large repertoire of aerobatic manoeuvres—with set rules and criteria for performance. You get it right or you do it shoddily or, worse still, you foul up. But essentially they are all variations on a single theme: play. And what distinguishes this particular style of play from earthbound equivalents is that it is in three dimensions. When Torquil put the Tiger Moth into a steeply banked turn it felt as if the plane had poised one wingtip on an invisible pinnacle then pirouetted around it. It was dancing in three dimensions, playing in space, and the effect it produced was one of total freedom.

It was freedom from gravity in every sense: from the earth's heavy pull and from the responsibilities of everyday life. Torquil calls it dancing on a cloud. As for me, my heart was pounding and the blood was coursing sweetly through my veins. I recognized my old friend and bad habit, the adrenalin rush, but this was purer than anything I had ever experienced on a rock face or a diving board or at the poker table. It wasn't just adrenalin, it was happiness. It was as if I'd got my childhood back in the way childhood is supposed to be—without the tantrums and confusion. I was a 60-something grandfather, with a gammy ankle and a walking stick, absurdly dressed up like the Red Baron in a leather flying helmet and goggles. But I was also back where I started on the high board at the Finchley Road swimming pool. Free as a bird.

from A Voyage for Madmen
by Peter Nichols

Donald Crowhurst hoped that the 1967/1968 Golden Globe round-the-world yacht race would change his life, and he was willing to cheat to win it. His bizarre scheme: Hide out in the Atlantic—sending home false progress reports—then rejoin the race in time to beat the leaders to the finish line. Writer and sailor Peter Nichols (born 1950) reports on how Crowhurst's voyage ended.

I f no accident or mishap disabled *Teignmouth Electron* before reaching England, Crowhurst would be the winner of the *Sunday Times'* £5,000 cash prize. He would join Robin Knox-Johnston, Nigel Tetley, Sir Francis Chichester, and the other *Sunday Times* judges and experts for the Golden Globe celebratory dinner aboard the tall ship *Cutty Sark*, where they would swap stories about their trials in the Southern Ocean and confirm their standing in the small company of men that has been called the Cape Horn breed. Of these, Knox-Johnston, Tetley, and Crowhurst would be placed among the rarest of the elite, the solo Cape Horners.

It was the sort of glory Crowhurst had always yearned for. The notoriety and speed of his voyage would turn his company Electron Utilisation into a solid success. Book and merchandising deals would be forthcoming. The brilliance and superiority of Donald Crowhurst would be acknowledged by the world.

Also, Captain Craig Rich of the London Institute of Navigation, Sir Francis Chichester, and others would examine his logbook and navigation records.

In fact, Chichester was already drafting a letter to Robert Riddell, the *Sunday Times* race secretary, asking for details of Crowhurst's messages and position statements, particularly his last message before leaving the South Atlantic and entering the Southern Ocean near the Cape of Good Hope and his next message about nearing the Horn ("Digger Ramrez"). "We need to know why the silence from the Cape to the Horn (from an electronics engineer too). . . . Why did he never give exact positions? It also appeared that he had an extraordinary increase of speed on entering the S. Ocean; I think he claimed 13,000 miles in 10 weeks, or something, which seems most peculiar considering his slow speed for the previous long passage to the Cape, and the succeeding 8,000 miles (Horn-home)." *Claimed*. Chichester had put the numbers and his own sea sense together and the conclusion was, to him, inescapable.

Crowhurst already felt the weight of scrutiny that awaited him. It was one thing to make up a story in the lonely, solipsistic space of *Teignmouth Electron*'s cramped cabin and feed it to the ecstatically credulous, geographically ignorant Rodney Hallworth, who passed it on to an equally gullible and wanton press. It was quite another to lay the lie before a committee of sea dogs and savants who had really done what he had only guessed at and pretended. Crowhurst knew this; he was a highly intelligent man. But he had chosen not to dwell on it. Now, only a few weeks away from stepping ashore into a klieg light of illumination and surrendering his logbooks, the fullest ramifications of his deception swept over him.

Crowhurst began to coast. He delayed, he zig-zagged, he let the wind blow the boat where it would. In the preceding weeks, since breaking radio silence, he had sailed faster and more steadily than almost any other period of his voyage, even clocking a genuine 200-mile-plus run in the 24 hours between noon of May 4 and May 5. But from May 23—the day he learned of Tetley's sinking—onward, his progress up the Atlantic became erratic. He passed out of the steady southeast trade winds and entered the light and fluky winds either side of the equator. *Teignmouth Electron* ghosted through the water while Crowhurst, naked and streaming sweat, sat in the messy overheated cabin amid the detritus of his grand plan—wires snaking to nowhere, radios, boxes of spare parts, and a contradictory set of logbooks—trying to see his way home and clear.

Early in June, his Marconi transmitter failed. Suddenly his new-found voice, which he had been exercising since ending his self-imposed radio silence, the precious link to the world outside the claustrophobic cabin, beyond the empty horizon, was taken from him. For Crowhurst, the breakdown of his core electronic device was unhingeing. For the next two weeks *Teignmouth Electron* drifted slowly north, largely untended, while he devoted all his efforts to fixing the transmitter. He spent 16 hours a day sitting in the boiling cabin, surrounded by the cannibalized innards of radios and open tins of food, while he soldered and tinkered with wires and transistors, ate when he remembered to, lost in his work, fascinated, challenged, sustained by the one realm he truly understood.

The sea—the watery blue reality beyond the cabin, the discipline of seamanship, the purpose of his adventure—receded.

In the cooler, dark, early hours of June 22, Crowhurst fixed his radio and finally made Morse contact with Portishead Radio. He immediately sent cables to his wife Clare and to Rodney Hallworth.

Then, as the sun rose, the cabin temperature increased, and so did the heat coming from the repaired radio. For much of the rest of that day, Crowhurst sat hunched beside it, exchanging cables with Hallworth, who was already working on deals and syndication rights, and with Donald Kerr of the BBC, who wanted to arrange a rendezvous for boats and helicopters to meet Crowhurst offshore. The welcome, the clamor, the end of the voyage, the end of the game, loomed.

On Tuesday, June 24, Donald Crowhurst turned away from it all. He turned away from the world and plunged deep into himself.

At the top of a clean page of his logbook—following weeks of

comment-free mathematical workings of his celestial sights—he wrote
a title: "Philosophy."

He began by discussing Einstein, whose book, *Relativity: The Special
and General Theory,* was one of the few he had brought along on his
voyage to read. Einstein had written the book to explain his theory to
a general audience; in its day it was as well-known and as widely
unread as Stephen Hawking's later explanation of the universe, *A Brief
History of Time.* But for Crowhurst, reading it over and over in the isolation chamber of *Teignmouth Electron's* lonely cabin, Einstein's statements took on the truth and gravity of holy writ.

One paragraph made a profound impact on him:

> That light requires the same time to traverse the path A to
> M as for the path B to M is in reality neither a supposition
> nor a hypothesis about the physical nature of light, but a
> *stipulation* which I can make of my own free will in order to
> arrive at a definition of simultaneity.

Einstein was only stating, or appropriating, a definition of the word
"simultaneity" for the purpose of his argument. But to Crowhurst this
Einsteinian exercise of free will appeared to be a godlike control of
physics, of the universe. "You can't do that!" wrote Crowhurst, imagining a dialogue between himself and Einstein. "Nevertheless I have
just *done* it," answered Albert. Crowhurst did not doubt Einstein's
authority to take such control. He took it as an example of the power
of a superior mind. This led him deep into a maze of tortured logic.

He was soon writing this:

> I introduce this idea $\sqrt{-1}$ because [it] leads directly to the
> dark tunnel of the space-time continuum, and once tech-
> nology emerges from this tunnel the "world" will "end" (I
> believe about the year 2000, as often prophesied) in the sense
> that we will have access to the means of "extraphysical" exis-
> tence, making the need for physical existence superfluous.

· · ·

As he wrote, Crowhurst was listening to the radio. Beside his philo-sophical writing, he now made annotations of what he was hearing: "1430 gmt, 24th, Radio Volna Europa. 1435: Hysterical laughter."

He continued writing. Through the day, into the night, all through the next day.

At 1700 on June 25, when he had been writing for about thirty hours, a Norwegian cargo ship, *Cuyahoga*, passed close by *Teignmouth Electron*. Crowhurst appeared on deck and waved cheerfully as the ship steamed by. The *Cuyahoga*'s captain wrote in his logbook that the man on the trimaran had a beard, wore khaki shorts, and appeared to be in good shape. Crowhurst had spent the day writing a history of the past 2,000 years, with a further look back to the time of cavemen, illustrating the way exceptional men have, through the shock of their genius, changed society through the ages. At some point in this his-tory, he put down his pencil, climbed up on deck, and waved at the *Cuyahoga*.

Over the next week, for 8 days from Tuesday, June 24, to midday Tuesday, July 1, Crowhurst wrote 25,000 words in his logbook (equiv-alent to almost a third of this book), stopping only to eat or nap as need overtook him. His hand flew across the pages, bearing down hard, the urgency of what he had to say outstripping the need to sharpen his pencil. His neat engineer's handwriting now grew large and irregular, the strokes thick with emphasis. The pages became dense with notes crawling around the margins, circled and crammed between distant paragraphs, as insight upon insight struck him and deepened his revelations. He wrote in a white heat of possession.

Stuff like this:

> The arrival of each parasite brings about an increase in the tempo of the Drama, causing first-order differentials in its own lifetime within the host, and second-order differentials within the host to the host, etc, etc . . .

And yet, and yet—*if* creative abstraction is to act as a vehicle for the new entity, and to leave its hitherto stable state <u>it lies within the power of creative abstraction to produce the phenomenon!!!!!!!!!!!!!! We can bring it about by creative abstraction!</u>

Now we must be very careful about getting the answer right. We are at the point where our powers of abstraction are powerful enough to do tremendous damage. . . . Like nuclear chain reactions in the matter system, our whole system of creative abstraction can be brought to the point of "take off." . . . By writing these words I do signal for the process to begin. . . .

Mathematicians and engineers used to the techniques of system analysis will skim through my complete work in less than an hour. At the end of that time problems that have beset humanity for thousands of years will have been solved for them.

Despair and the moral burden of deception had lifted and been replaced by the exhilaration of seeing a great truth. "I feel like somebody who's been given a tremendous opportunity to impart a message—some profound observation that will save the world," he'd confided to his tape recorder months before. It was something he had always wanted, believing himself cleverer than the normal run of men, and ready for a chance to prove it. Now that message had been delivered to him in the peculiarly receptive vessel that he had made for himself, and he was in a fever to write it down and pass it on to the world.

Was it another fake? A pose? A few pages of such writing could be made up by anyone with an ear for the the ravings of psychotic breakdown. Novelists and screenwriters do it all the time, sometimes convincingly. Nothing, however, but a genuinely deranged mind could spend 150 consecutive hours producing 25,000 words of such passionately insane verbiage.

There was, however, a consistent theme to Crowhurst's psychosis: that in the end, by an act of will, a person of superintelligence—a great mathematician—could alter, and deliver himself from, the bonds and rules and obligations of the physical world.

Crowhurst went from a functioning, if cheating, competitor, a sender of rational cables, to the total abandonment of navigation and boathandling, and deep into scribbling madness, in the space of a few days. But it had been long in coming, since his earliest days at sea when he had faced the "bloody awful decision." From that point on, when he made the most rational and sane appraisal of his impossible situation, he had seen no way to go forward, yet no way to retreat. It was, at its root, a moral dilemma, and there his reason had foundered. Crowhurst had the cleverness, possibly, but not the conscience to carry off his hoax.

When Crowhurst looked up a week later, he had no idea what time it was. Nor even what day. His Hamilton chronometer and both of his (prequartz) wristwatches had run down and stopped. His last navigational entry had been on June 23.

He went up on deck. It was daylight, but he saw the moon—full—just above the horizon. He went below and opened his nautical almanac, which contained tables giving the phase of the moon and times, of its rise and set in Greenwich mean time. He concluded that it must now be June 30. He worked out the time to be 0410 GMT. He added an hour to make this British standard time to conform with the times of BBC broadcasts. It was 0510, then, on June 30. He wrote the time and date in his logbook, with the note that he was starting the clocks again.

Then he realized he must be mistaken: if it was 5 in the morning English time, it would still be dark where he was, 40 degrees of longitude west of Greenwich, in the middle of the Atlantic Ocean. He had made the stupidest mistake.

He wrote in his logbook:

June 30 5 10 MAX POSS ERROR

After studying the nautical almanac again, he decided it must now be July 1. And as close as he could gauge, it was 10 in the morning, British standard time. As a navigator, for whom time, accurate to the second, is of religious importance—the navigator's life literally depends upon it—he had slipped up badly. Now he watched every second, for time was ticking to a countdown.

He wrote:

EXACT POS   July 1 10 03

It was a position in time. He had no need of a geographic position. He was past all that.

The minutes and seconds ticked by. Twenty minutes later, he wrote:

10 23 40   Cannot see any "purpose" in game.

10 29   No game man can devise is harmless.
          The truth is that there can only be one
          chess master. . . .

          there can only be one perfect beauty that is the
          great beauty of truth. No man may do more
          than all that he is capable of doing. The perfect
          way is the way of reconciliation
          Once there is a possibility of reconciliation there
          may not a need for making errors. Now is
          revealed the true nature and purpose and power
          of the game my offence I am I am what I am and
          I see the nature of my offence

I will only resign this game if you will agree that
the next occasion that this game is played it will
be played according to the rules that are devised
by my great god who has revealed at last to his
son not only the exact nature of the reason for
games but has also revealed the truth of the way
of the ending of the next game that

It is finished—
It is finished
IT IS THE MERCY

Against a great truth, the petty rules and structure of his voyage now
seemed to Donald Crowhurst, as they had to Bernard Moitessier, irrelevant. Now that the truth had been revealed to him, and he had written
it down for the world to find, his voyage was over. Finished.

The minutes and seconds had got away from him. He recorded them
again:

11 15 00   It is the end of my
                 my game the truth
                 has been revealed and it will
                 be done as my family require me
                 to do it

11 17 00   It is the time for your
                 move to begin

                 I have no need to prolong
                 the game

                 It has been a good game that
                 must be ended at the
                 I will play this game when

I choose I will resign the
game

11 20 40   There is
no reason for harmful

He had reached the bottom of the logbook page. There was no more room to write, and time was ticking along.

Time might, if he didn't watch it, even get away from him. So he unscrewed his round brass chronometer from the bulkhead and took it with him.

from The Shadow of the Sun
by Ryszard Kapuściński

Polish journalist Ryszard Kapuściński (born 1932) has spent his career traveling in and reporting from developing countries. His recent book about his travels in Africa is a moving portrait of the continent, a place of great beauty and unimaginable suffering.

I n the darkness, I suddenly spotted two glaring lights. They were far away and moved about violently, as if they were the eyes of a wild animal thrashing about in its cage. I was sitting on a stone at the edge of the Ouadane oasis, in the Sahara, northeast of Nouakchott, the Mauritanian capital. For an entire week now I had been trying to leave this place—to no avail. It is difficult to get to Ouadane, but even more difficult to depart. No marked or paved road leads to it, and there is no scheduled transport. Every few days—sometimes weeks—a truck will pass, and if the driver agrees to take you with him, you go; if not, you simply stay, waiting who knows how long for the next opportunity.

The Mauritanians who were sitting beside me stirred. The night chill had set in, a chill that descends abruptly and, after the burning hell of the sun-filled days, can be almost piercingly painful. It is a cold from which no sheepskin or quilt can adequately protect you. And these people had nothing but old, frayed blankets, in which they sat tightly wrapped, motionless, like statues.

A black pipe poked out from the ground nearby, a rusty and salt-encrusted compressor-pump mechanism at its tip. This was the region's sole gas station, and passing vehicles always stopped here. There is no other attraction in the oasis. Ordinarily, days pass uneventfully and unchangeably, resembling in this the monotony of the desert climate: the same sun always shines, hot and solitary, in the same empty, cloudless sky.

At the sight of the still-distant headlights, the Mauritanians began talking among themselves. I didn't understand a word of their language. It's quite possible they were saying: "At last! It's finally coming! We have lived to see it!"

It was recompense for the long days spent waiting, gazing patiently at the inert, unvarying horizon, on which no moving object, no living thing that might rouse you from the numbness of hopeless anticipation, had appeared in a long time. The arrival of a truck—cars are too fragile for this terrain—didn't fundamentally alter the lives of the people. The vehicle usually stopped for a moment and then quickly drove on. Yet even this brief sojourn was vital and important to them: it injected variety into their lives, provided a subject for later conversation, and, above all, was both material proof of the existence of another world and a bracing confirmation that that world, since it had sent them a mechanical envoy, must know that they existed.

Perhaps they were also engaged in a routine debate: will I—or won't it—get here? For traveling in these corners of the Sahara is a risky adventure, an unending lottery, perpetual uncertainty. Along these roadless expanses full of crevices, depressions, sinkholes, protruding boulders, sand dunes and rocky mounds, loose stones and fields of slippery gravel, a vehicle advances at a snail's pace—several kilometers an hour. Each wheel has its own drive, and each one, meter by meter, turning here, stopping there, going up, down, or around, searches for something to grip. Most of the time, these persistent efforts and exertions, which are accompanied by the roar of the straining and overheated engine and by the bone-bruising lunges of the swaying platform, finally result in the truck's moving forward.

But the Mauritanians also knew that sometimes a truck could get hopelessly stuck just a step away from the oasis, on its very threshold. This can happen when a storm moves mountains of sand onto the track. In such an event, either the truck's occupants manage to dig out the road, or the driver finds a detour—or he simply turns around and goes back where he came from. Another storm will eventually move the dunes farther and clear the way.

This time, however, the electric lights were drawing nearer and nearer. At a certain moment, their glow started to pick out the crowns of date palms that had been hidden under the cover of darkness, and the shabby walls of mud huts, and the goats and cows asleep by the side of the road, until, finally, trailing clouds of dust behind it, an enormous Berliet truck drew to a halt in front of us, with a clang and thud of metal. Berliets are French-made trucks adapted for roadless desert terrain. They have large wheels with wide tires, and grilles mounted atop their hoods. Because of their great size and the prominent shape of the grille, from a distance they resemble the fronts of old steam engines.

The driver—a dark-skinned, barefoot Mauritanian in an ankle-length indigo djellabah—climbed down from the cab using a ladder. He was, like the majority of his countrymen, tall and powerfully built. People and animals with substantial body weight endure tropical heat better, which is why the inhabitants of the Sahara usually have a magnificently statuesque appearance. The law of natural selection is also at work here: in these extremely harsh desert conditions, only the strongest survive to maturity.

The Mauritanians from the oasis immediately surrounded the driver. A cacophony of greetings, questions, and well-wishings erupted. This went on and on. Everybody was shouting and gesticulating, as if haggling in a noisy marketplace. After a while they began to point at me. I was a pitiful sight—dirty, unshaven, and, above all, wasted by the nightmarish heat of the Saharan summer. An experienced Frenchman had warned me earlier: it will feel as if someone were sticking a knife into you. Into your back, into your head. At noon, the rays of the sun beat down with the force of a knife.

The driver looked at me and at first said nothing. Then he motioned toward the truck with his hand and called out to me: *Yalla!* (Let's go! We're off!)" I climbed into the cab and slammed the door shut. We set off immediately.

I had no sense of where we were going. Sand flashed by in the glow of the headlights, shimmering with different shades, laced with strips of gravel and shards of rock. The wheels reared up on granite ledges or sank down into hollows and stony fissures. In the deep, black night one could see only two spots of light—two bright, clearly outlined orbs sliding over the surface of the desert. Nothing else was visible.

Before long, I began to suspect that we were driving blind, on a shortcut to somewhere, because there were no demarcation points, no signs, posts, or any other traces of a roadway. I tried to question the driver. I gestured at the darkness around us and asked: "Nouakchott?"

He looked at me and laughed. "Nouakchott?" He repeated this dreamily, as if it were the Hanging Gardens of Semiramis that I was asking him about—so beautiful but, for us lowly ones, too high to reach. I concluded from this that we were not headed in the direction I desired, but I did not know how to ask him where, in that case, we were going. I desperately wanted to establish some contact with him, to get to know him even a little. "Ryszard," I said, pointing at myself. Then I pointed at him. He understood. "Salim," he said, and laughed again. Silence fell. We must have come upon a smooth stretch of desert, for the Berliet began to roll along more gently and quickly (exactly how fast, I don't know, since all the instruments were broken). We drove on for a time without speaking, until finally I fell asleep.

A sudden silence awoke me. The engine had stopped, the truck stood still. Salim was pressing on the gas pedal and turning the key in the ignition. The battery was working—the starter too—but the engine emitted no sound. It was morning, and already light outside. He began searching around the cab for the lever that opens the hood. This struck me as at once odd and suspicious: a driver who doesn't know how to open the hood? Eventually, he figured out that the latches that need to be released were on the outside. He then stood on a fender and began to inspect the engine, but he peered at its intricate construction as if he were seeing it for the first time. He would touch something, try to move something, but his gestures were those of an amateur. Every now and then he would climb into the cab and turn the key in the ignition, but the engine remained dead silent. He located the toolbox, but there wasn't much in it. He pulled out a hammer, several wrenches, and screwdrivers. Then he started to take the engine apart.

I stepped down from the cab. All around us, as far as the eye could see, was desert. Sand, with dark stones scattered about. Nearby, a large black oval rock. (In the hours following noon, after being warmed by the sun, it would radiate heat like a steel-mill oven.) A moonscape, delineated by a level horizon line: the earth ends, and then there's nothing but sky and more sky. No hills. No sand dunes. Not a single leaf. And, of course, no water. Water! It's what instantly comes to mind under such circumstances. In the desert, the first thing man sees when he opens his eyes in the morning is the face of his enemy—the flaming visage of the sun. The sight elicits in him a reflexive gesture of self-preservation: he reaches for water. Drink! Drink! Only by doing so can he ever so slightly improve his odds in the desert's eternal struggle—the desperate duel with the sun.

I resolved to look around for water, for I had none with me. I found nothing in the cab. But I did discover some: attached with ropes to the bed of the truck, near the rear, underneath, were four goatskins, two on the left side and two on the right. The hides had been rather poorly cured, then sewn together in such a way that they retained the animal's shape. One of the goat's legs served as a drinking spout.

I sighed with relief, but only momentarily. I began to calculate. Without water, you can survive in the desert for twenty-four hours; with great difficulty, forty-eight or so. The math is simple. Under these conditions, you secrete in one day approximately ten liters of sweat, and to survive you must drink a similar amount of water. Deprived of it, you will immediately start to feel thirsty. Genuine, prolonged thirst in a hot and dry climate is an exhausting, ravaging sensation, harder to control than hunger. After a few hours of it you become lethargic and limp, weak and disoriented. Instead of speaking, you babble, ever less cogently. That same evening, or the next day, you get a high fever and quickly die.

If Salim doesn't share his water with me, I thought, I will die today. Even if he does, we will have only enough left for one more day— which means we will both die tomorrow, the day after at the latest.

Trying to stop these thoughts, I decided to observe him closely. Covered with grease and sweating, Salim was still taking the engine apart, unscrewing screws and removing cables, but with no rhyme or reason, like a child furiously destroying a toy that won't work. On the fenders, on the bumper, lay countless springs, valves, compression rings, and wires; some had already fallen to the ground. I left him and went around to the other side of the truck, where there was still some shade. I sat down on the ground and leaned my back against the wheel.

Salim.

I knew nothing about the man who held my life in his hands. Or, at least, who held it for this one day. I thought, if Salim chases me away from the truck and the water—after all, he had a hammer in his hand and probably a knife in his pocket, and, on top of that, enjoyed a significant physical advantage—if he orders me to leave and march off into the desert, I won't last even until nightfall. And it seemed to me that was precisely what he might choose to do. He would thereby extend his life, after all—or, if help arrives in time, he might even save it.

Clearly Salim was not a professional driver, or at any rate, not a driver of a Berliet truck. He also didn't know the area well. (On the other hand, can one really know the desert, where successive storms and tempests constantly alter the landscape, moving mountains of sand to ever different sites and transposing features of the landscape with impunity?) It is common practice in these parts for someone with even a small financial windfall to immediately hire another with less money to carry out his tasks for him. Maybe the rightful driver of this truck had hired Salim to take it in his stead to one of the oases. And hereabouts no one will ever admit to not knowing or not being capable of something. If you approach a taxi driver in a city, show him an address, and ask him if he knows where it is, he will say yes without a second's hesitation. And it is only later, when you are driving all over the city, round and round, that you fully realize he has no idea where to go.

The sun was climbing higher and higher. The desert, that motionless, petrified ocean, absorbed its rays, grew hotter, and began to burn. The hour was approaching when everything would become a hell—the earth, the sky, us. The Yoruba are said to believe that if a man's shadow abandons him, he will die. All the shadows were beginning to shrink, dwindle, fade. The dread afternoon hours were almost upon us, the time of day when people and objects have no shade, exist and yet do not exist, reduced to a glowing, incandescent whiteness.

I thought that this moment had arrived, but suddenly I noticed before me an utterly different sight. The lifeless, still horizon—so crushed by the heat that it seemed nothing could ever issue forth from it—all at once sprang to life and became green. As far as the eye could see stood tall, magnificent palm trees, entire groves of them along the horizon, growing thickly, without interruption. I also saw lakes—yes, enormous blue lakes, with animated, undulating surfaces. Gorgeous shrubs also grew there, with wide-spreading branches of a fresh, intense, succulent, deep green. All this shimmered continuously, sparkled, pulsated, as if it were wreathed in a light mist, soft-edged and elusive. And everywhere—here, around us, and there, on the horizon—a profound, absolute silence reigned: the wind did not blow, and the palm groves had no birds.

"Salim!" I called. "Salim!"

A head emerged from under the hood. He looked at me.

"Salim!" I repeated once more, and pointed.

Salim glanced where I had shown him, unimpressed. In my dirty, sweaty face he must have read wonder, bewilderment, and rapture—but also something else besides, which clearly alarmed him, for he walked up to the side of the truck, untied one of the goatskins, took a few sips, and wordlessly handed me the rest. I grabbed the rough leather sack and began to drink. Suddenly dizzy, I leaned my shoulder against the truck bed so as not to fall. I drank and drank, sucking fiercely on the goat's leg and still staring at the horizon. But as I felt my thirst subsiding, and the madness within me dying down, the green vista began to vanish. Its colors faded and paled, its contours shrank and blurred. By the time I had emptied the goatskin, the horizon was once again flat, empty, and lifeless. The water, disgusting Saharan water—warm, dirty, thick with sand and sludge—extended my life but took away my vision of paradise. The crucial thing, though, was the fact that Salim himself had given me the water to drink. I stopped being afraid of him. I felt I was safe—at least, until the moment when we would be down to our last sip.

We spent the second half of the day lying underneath the truck, in its faint, bleached shade. In this world circled all about with flaming horizons, Salim and I were the only life. I inspected the ground within my arm's reach, the nearest stones, searching for some living thing, anything that might twitch, move, slither. I remembered that somewhere on the Sahara there lives a small beetle which the Tuareg call Ngubi. When it is very hot, according to legend, Ngubi is tormented by thirst, desperate to drink. Unfortunately, there is no water anywhere, and only burning sand all around. So the small beetle chooses an incline—this can be a sloping fold of sand—and with determination begins to climb to its summit. It is an enormous effort, a Sisyphean task, because the hot and loose sand constantly gives way, carrying the beetle down with it, right back to where he began his toils. Which is why, before too long, the beetle starts to sweat. A drop of moisture collects at the end of his abdomen and swells. Then Ngubi stops climbing, curls up, and plunges his mouth into that very bead.

    He drinks.

• • •

Salim has several biscuits in a paper bag. We drink the second goatskin of water. Two remain. I consider writing something. (It occurs to me that this is often done at such moments.) But I don't have the strength. I'm not really in pain. It's just that everything is becoming empty. And within this emptiness another one is growing.

Then, in the darkness, two glaring lights. They are far away and move about violently. Then the sound of a motor draws near, and I see the truck, hear voices in a language I do not understand. "Salim!" I say. Several dark faces, resembling his, lean over me.

a c k n o w l e d g m e n t s

Many people made this anthology.

At Thunder's Mouth Press and Avalon Publishing Group:
Neil Ortenberg and Susan Reich offered guidance and support. Dan O'Connor and Ghadah Alrawi were also helpful. Maria Fernandez oversaw production with scrupulous care and attention, with help from Paul Paddock and Simon Sullivan. Tracy Armstead worked hard to find photographs. Sue Canavan designed the book and Patti Ratchford and David Riedy designed its cover.

At Shawneric.com:
Shawneric Hachey deftly handled permissions and found cover photographs.

At The Writing Company:
Nate Hardcastle and Nat May helped find the selections for this book. Taylor Smith, Mark Klimek, March Truedsson and John Bishop took up slack on other projects.

Among friends and family:
Will Balliett made it fun. Jennifer Willis gave me good advice. Harper Willis and Abner Willis made me smile.

Finally, I am grateful to the writers whose work appears in this book.

b i b l i o g r a p h y

The selections used in this anthology were taken from the editions listed below. In some cases, other editions may be easier to find. Hard-to-find or out-of-print titles often are available through inter-library loan services or through Internet booksellers.

Alvarez, Al. *Where Did It All Go Right?* New York: HarperCollins, 1999.

Bradley, James and Ron Powers. *Flags of Our Fathers*. New York: Bantam, 2000.

Cahill, Tim. "Anybody Seen a Tiger Around Here?" Originally appeared in *Men's Journal*, June 2001.

Carrier, Jim. *The Ship and the Storm*. New York: McGraw-Hill/International Marine, 2000.

Child, Greg. "Fear of Falling". Originally appeared in *Outside*, March 2001.

Clynes, Tom. "Dangerous Medicine". Originally appeared in *National Geographic Adventure*, May/June 2001.

Duane, Daniel. "The Climber Comes Down to Earth". Originally appeared in *Outside*, May 2001.

Kamler, Kenneth. *Doctor On Everest*. New York: Lyons Press, 2000.

Kapúscínski, Ryszard. *The Shadow of the Sun*. New York: Alfred A. Knopf, 2001.

Nichols, Peter. *A Voyage for Madmen*. New York: HarperCollins, 2001.

Oufkir, Malika and Michele Fitoussi. *Stolen Lives*. Paris, France: Editions Grasset & Fasquelle, 1999.

Picket, Lynn Snowden. *Looking for a Fight*. New York: Dial Press, 2000.

Quammen, David. "Megatransect Part II". Originally appeared in *National Geographic*, March 2001.

Tayler, Jeffrey. *Facing the Congo*. St. Paul, MN: Ruminator Books, 2000.

Tidwell, Mike. *In the Mountains of Heaven*. New York: Lyons Press, 2000.

Turner, Jack. *Teewinot*. New York: St. Martin's Press, 2000.

Williams, Stanley and Fen Montaigne. "Surviving Galeras". Appeared in *Outside*, April 2001.

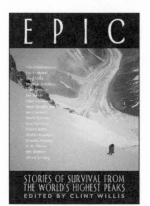

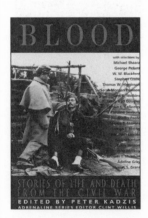
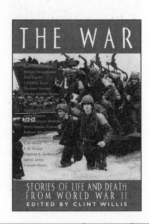

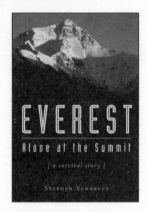

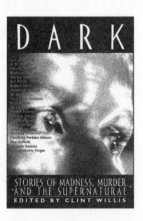